TOTAL QUALITY

A TEXTBOOK OF STRATEGIC

QUALITY LEADERSHIP AND PLANNING

K.D. Lam

Frank D. Watson

Stephen R. Schmidt

Air Academy Press
Colorado Springs, CO

OTHER TEXTS BY AIR ACADEMY PRESS

Understanding Industrial Designed Experiments, 3rd Edition (1991) by S.R. Schmidt and R.G. Launsby. ISBN 0-9622176-2-X
The primary motivation for this book was to provide material that would bridge the gap produced by texts too mathematical and those that attain simplicity by omitting important concepts. This is an applications oriented text which blends the competing Taguchi, Shainin, and classical approaches to designed experiments. Included are over 200 pages of actual industrial case studies plus software.

Basic Statistics: Tools for Continuous Improvement, 3rd Edition (1993) by M.J. Kiemele and S.R. Schmidt. ISBN 1-880156-01-6
The primary motivation for this book is to educate the readers (managers, engineers, researchers, analysts, practitioners, and statisticians) in the application of statistical tools to achieve continuous improvement in how they do business. It is designed for those taking a first course in statistics, as well as those who may have already taken a statistics course but need a refresher. The book uses applied examples to illustrate the use of statistical tools for continuous process improvement. It is easily read (calculus not needed) and there are no proofs. A statistical applications package, as well as other software, is included with the text.

Surviving the '90s and Winning! (1990) by B.D. Wellmon. ISBN 0-9622176-3-8
This book has been written specifically for everyone who has to work for a living–from the worker on the floor to the CEO or owner of the company. Whether your company has 91 people or 91,000; whether your business is manufacturing, service, or government; whether your customer base is local or global; this handbook should not only be read but used as a primer on your quest to survive the 1990's. This management survival handbook is designed as a practical reference guide and implementation tool for anyone in the business world. There are no theorems or claims of instant answers to all of your problems. There are no slogans or hidden secrets to be found. There are just three basic steps to be followed to guide you down the long and confusing path to improved quality. This book will help you master a system which is unique to your situation and which will contribute to your survival.

Total Quality Management: A Resource Guide (1990) by K.D. Lam.
This resource guide is designed to save you time and money. In it you will find hundreds of references to help you improve your TQM capabilities. In a hand-some looseleaf binder, this well organized, comprehensive reference guide is designed for both TQM experts and novices. Those new to TQM will benefit from a chapter on "Getting Started," steps to take to start the TQM journey. It includes your role in the TQM process, your customers, key first steps, important tools and techniques you need to learn, and potential pitfalls to avoid.

***   WIN A **FREE** BOOK   ***

HELP US WITH SOME PROCESS IMPROVEMENT!

This book has been printed in very limited quantities to give a selected sample of our customers an opportunity to tell us what they like and don't like about it.

Please complete this questionnaire and **mail** to:

> K.D. LAM
> EXCELNET
> 2110 Oak Hills Drive
> Colorado Springs, CO 80919
>
> or **FAX** to (719) 531–0778.

Your name will be entered into a drawing for a copy of one of the following books:
  Understanding Industrial Design of Experiments
  Basic Statistics: Tools for Continuous Improvement
  Total Quality Management: A Resource Guide

1. Best target audience for this text (check all that apply):
      _____community colleges
      _____Department of Defense
      _____universities
      _____manufacturing companies
      _____service companies
      _____small businesses

2.   Check the chapters you read and please rate those on the following scale:
                        5 = outstanding
                        4 = excellent, needs fine tuning only
                        3 = average quality, needs more work
                        2 = below average, hard to understand
                        1 = poor, delete or completely re-do

      Chapter 1:   Did you read _____   rating _____
      Adden. 1:   Did you read _____   rating _____
      Adden. 2:   Did you read _____   rating _____
      Chapter 2:   Did you read _____   rating _____
      Adden. 1:   Did you read _____   rating _____
      Adden. 2:   Did you read _____   rating _____
      Chapter 3:   Did you read _____   rating _____
      Chapter 4:   Did you read _____   rating _____
      Chapter 5:   Did you read _____   rating _____
      Chapter 6:   Did you read _____   rating _____

Chapter 7:   Did you read _____ rating _____
Chapter 8:   Did you read _____ rating _____
Chapter 9:   Did you read _____ rating _____
Chapter 10: Did you read _____ rating _____
Chapter 11: Did you read _____ rating _____
Chapter 12: Did you read _____ rating _____
Glossary: Did you use _____ rating _____

3. Please indicate your preferred format for this text:
    _____ current format (wire bound soft cover)
    _____ hard bound
    _____ soft cover perfect bound
    _____ don't care

4. What is your opinion about the price?
    _____ about right
    _____ too high
    _____ should charge more

5. How do you like the cover of the book?
    _____ great
    _____ so–so
    _____ change it

6. Please give us any specific comments you have on the text and indicate below whether you would be available by phone to give more detailed comments about the book.

Name _____

Address _____

Yes! Call me for more comments: Phone _____

Thanks very much!!!!!

TOTAL QUALITY

TOTAL QUALITY

A Textbook of Strategic
Quality Leadership and Planning

ISBN 0-9622176-9-7

The authors recognize that perfection is unattainable without continuous improvement. Therefore, we solicit comments as to how to improve this text. To relay your comments or to obtain further information, contact:

AIR ACADEMY PRESS
1155 Kelly Johnson Blvd., Suite 105
Colorado Springs, CO 80920
(719) 531-0777
(719) 531-0778 FAX

ACKNOWLEDGEMENT

Total quality requires strong cooperative partnerships with suppliers who are committed to excellence. We had many "quality" suppliers to whom we would like to give special thanks:

Cover: Tom Bulloch of Bulloch & Haggart/Sindt, Inc., Colorado Springs

Typing: Ronda Churchill, Judy Schmidt, and Rosemarie Koch

Editing: David B. Porter, Vicki Prudhomme, Mark Kiemele, and Lt Col John Mitchel

Intellectual Genius/Painful Criticism:
Michael Cleary, Jay Gould, Rick Weintraub, Jeanne Brown, Pete Malpass, Joe Maio, Ted Bloomer, Bob Colyar, and many students who gave us their comments.

Chapter 1   Author: K.D. Lam
            Addendum 1 – William Lareau
            Addendum 2 – Lt Col John Mitchel
            Addendum 3 – Frank Watson

Chapter 2   Author: K.D. Lam
            Addendum 1 – Lt Col Michael Prowse
            Addendum 2 – Tasso Christie

Chapter 3   Author: K.D. Lam

Chapter 4   Author: Major Steve Green

Chapter 5   Author: K.D. Lam

Chapter 6   Author: K.D. Lam

Chapter 7   Author: K.D. Lam

Chapter 8   Author: Barbara Bicknell

Chapter 9   Author: Steve Schmidt, Mark Kiemele, and Bob Launsby

Chapter 10 Author: Steve Schmidt and Lt Col Sue Hermanson

Chapter 11 Author: David B. Porter

Chapter 12 Author: Frank Watson

TABLE OF CONTENTS

TABLE OF CONTENTS

PART II: IMPLEMENTATION

PART III: SPECIAL APPLICATIONS

TABLE OF CONTENTS

PREFACE

Let's face it, TQM is not new. That is, the components and concepts of TQM are not, by themselves, new. They are based on fundamentals—management and business fundamentals. These basic principles are often ignored, assumed, or overlooked in favor of exotic new structures or schemes. Fundamentals are not exciting—they don't draw one to embrace them as though they are necessary. The key is in superior and innovative application of the basics. TQM uses fundamental concepts to organize a structured and disciplined approach to managing in today's evolving world. TQM, as a disciplined philosophy, is new, but the components and concepts are basic fundamentals integrated into a usable format.

This book will focus primarily on the substance of TQM rather than the form. The form is usually created individually in each unique business setting. We desire that you learn the essence of TQM and how to generate a competitive advantage using a TQM approach to business. While there is no magic formula or single best way, there are specific tools, techniques, and methodologies directed from a set of principles and a philosophy embodied in the term "TQM". Awareness of the TQM concepts and approaches presented in this book will help managers develop their own perspectives and enhance and expand their ability to effect substantive TQM transformations.

We have written this book for an audience of introductory students who are attempting to grasp the principles and philosophy of TQM. Some of what we have written may create the impression that managers are currently doing an inadequate job, or have poor skills. This is not the case. The success we enjoy as a nation is a direct reflection of the capabilities of the managers and individuals in our organizations—corporate and government. However, the business environment is changing, and we must adapt to these changes or face further decline, as Chapter 1 will discuss. Our intent is to encourage individuals through self-assessment and analysis, to: 1) find those things that are working well for him or her and make them work better, 2) find those things that can be made to work better and use them, and 3) find and use things that aren't being accomplished that could be.

All this should be done within a framework to produce an integrated "whole" that reflects a philosophy resting upon a set of underlying values. It is a "state of mind" or an attitude towards people that starts with a basic assumption of each individual's value. We each express this attitude in our own way through our mannerisms and behavior. But the essence of TQM's implementation is our basic underlying feeling of our own self-worth and how we value ourselves, which is then expressed in how we treat those who work for us and with us.

Chapter 1

WHY TOTAL QUALITY?

INTRODUCTION

People approach learning about total quality from many different perspectives:

1. **"Why do we need to change?"**

    Some individuals simply do not see a need to change things. They may be well-off in their current situation, or are just very accepting of the way things are. They simply don't see the need to transform organizations to anything different (total quality or anything else). They are used to things the way they are.

2. **"We need to change the way we run organizations, but why is total quality the answer?"**

    Recognizing the need for change, some individuals are skeptical about total quality being "the answer." They have significant doubts about the success of the Japanese being related to total quality, and believe it to be more related to the Japanese "culture" or "work ethic." They are also skeptical about the successes of American companies, suggesting no one has really "proven" their improvement is "caused" by transformation to total quality.

    They may have been through many management "programs" and fads. They want to know how total quality will be different than any of the others, (e.g., MBO, zero defects, quality circles, etc.). They demand "Show me."

3. **"Why not total quality?"**

    Many people are so convinced of the need for change they are ready to try just about anything. They have watched companies and whole industries go out of business. They are watching friends and neighbors lose their jobs. They look around and see many people unhappy with their world of work and the way they are treated at work.

WHERE DID TOTAL QUALITY BEGIN?

Many people connect the beginnings of total quality with the Japanese. However, many are unaware that the total quality message was brought to the Japanese by Americans. At the end of World War II, Japan was considered a nation of "cheap copies." They consulted with Dr. W. Edwards Deming who suggested a cultural shift was required.

Instead of accepting a small percentage of poor quality products or services (such as is suggested by Mil Std 105 and AQL's (acceptable quality levels) of 5%), Deming suggested companies should look up-stream to discover the causes of the defects. Resolving quality problems through prevention, rather than inspection, detection and repair, would result in increased profits and decreased cycle time.

Total quality is a cultural shift. It answers the question "Why total quality?" with an assertion that close enough is no longer good enough to achieve success in the marketplace. It is a philosophy that requires changing some very ingrained ways of doing business. No longer can mediocre outputs be accepted—from ourselves, our processes, and our suppliers. No longer can we accept unintelligible feedback from our customers. No longer can decision making rely on intuitive opinions, rather than measurement and statistical inference. No longer can we consider management the keeper of the brains, and the workers the keeper of the brawn. Some organizations don't wake up to this realization until their backs are against the wall and they are in real trouble. It is much more difficult to recover from an eight count, than it is to change before you hit the mat.

On a global, conceptual level, change is needed to:

- Reduce waste in our organizations

- Improve our economic health

- Stem the tide of increasing costs

- Cope with the rapid rate of technological change

- Increase our global competitiveness

- Reduce the adversarial relationship:

  — between managers and employees

  — between organizational functions

  — between unions and management

— between suppliers and customers

— between government and industry

• Improve the quality of education

• Improve the value of government

Is total quality the means to achieve these changes? There may not be any "one" answer. However, the philosophy and concepts of total quality hold great promise as a foundation upon which organizations can architect continuous improvement. Total quality brings to organizations:

• A philosophy that speaks to the people. You don't need to have a PhD in organizational development or statistics to understand it. It is not characterized by constructs and verbiage to which only a small percentage of the population can relate.

• A philosophy which is not so canned or cook-book oriented that it robs people of the opportunity to be creative.

• A philosophy which is intuitive and very logical.

Although it brings these positive things to organizations, it may also take away from organizations. A philosophy of total quality may diminish the levels, titles, rank and perks managers have accrued over the years. Many managers have been spending a great deal of time managing their position and their bosses, not the work. Currying favor with the levels above has been a popular way to get promoted. "Up is from where cometh the goodies," and up is where many managers have been focusing. Much of what we have done in the name of management has robbed workers of dignity, and has robbed companies of the opportunity to achieve excellence.

Total quality is not, as you will read in many different chapters in this text, a magic wand. Neither is it a short term solution to all organizations' ills. It is a long term commitment to satisfying customers, to treating employees like they have hearts and minds, to using systematic, data-based methods to continuously improve, and to continuous learning.

BENEFITS OF MANAGING USING TOTAL QUALITY

What payback can a long term commitment to total quality have for an organization (GAO, 1991)?

- Recoup 10% to 40% in hidden waste

    — Reduce scrap, rework and repair

    — Eliminate waste in service and white collar areas

- Decrease product/service cycle time

    — Eliminate non-value added activities

    — Decrease time to field current/new products

- Increase market share

    — Decreased costs/cycle time = more customers

    — Increased quality = more customers

- Increase the capability of our human resources

    — Reduce attrition, turnover, and absenteeism

The remainder of Chapter 1 includes three addenda, each bringing a slightly different perspective to the "why total quality" question.

REFERENCES

"U.S. Companies Improve Performance through Quality Efforts," GAO, National Security and International Affairs Division, May, 1991.

ADDENDUM 1

A TALE OF TWO DINOSAURS[1]

Once there were two dinosaurs. They were twin brothers. One was named Gigantus Traditionalus. He was a giant, lumbering dinosaur: fat, well-fed and used to the very best that dinosaur life could offer. Traditionalus was a very cautious dinosaur. He never ventured far from his birthplace, he never explored the cliffs surrounding his valley, and he never walked too far out into the deep water of the swamps. He was careful to eat only small mammals and dinosaurs known to be safe. And, each day, he always ate a bit of vegetation for regularity.

His twin was named Gigantus Innovatus, also a big, lumbering well-fed dinosaur used to the very best as well. More curious than his brother, Innovatus always experimented by eating strange plants and prey and traveled to distant water holes and explored the nearby cliffs and swamps. Both were content and expected to live out their days in tranquility.

Their peaceful existence was shattered by "The Disaster." Some dinosaurs said it was caused by a giant rock falling from the sky. Others said it was caused by a giant fire mountain beyond their valley. Nobody knew for sure. (How could they know?) The environment changed rapidly. The tender, tasty tropical vegetation quickly evolved into tougher plants that were not easily digested by the dinosaurs. The small, plant-eating dinosaurs, a significant part of the larger dinosaur's food supply, began to disappear.

As the small dinosaurs died off, small mammals, once very few in number, began to multiply. The small mammals were very fast and able to rapidly climb tall trees to escape predators. Thus, while the large dinosaurs enjoyed the taste of small mammals, they were not able to catch them very often. Deprived of easy-to-catch prey, the large meat-eating dinosaurs began to lose weight and weaken.

There were countless suggestions about how the crisis should be handled. Many of the dinosaurs felt that if everyone ignored the situation, the problems would go away. Other dinosaurs felt that complaining about the situation was the answer. Their conversations contained phrases such as "burdensome government regulations," "unfair practices by Pacific Rim dinosaurs," and "low prey requirements by foreign dinosaurs." But even as such talk went on, things continued to get worse. All of the dinosaurs were affected and none could deny that the situation was bleak.

Many dinosaurs spoke about the possibility of evolving into a dinosaur that could survive the new changes. A popular notion was that changing skin color or fang length

---

[1]This addendum was written by William Lareau. Originally published in *Quality Digest*, January 1991, Vol.11, No.1, pp. 71-85. Reprinted with permission of *Quality Digest*.

would suffice. Some dinosaurs theorized how minor changes would so significantly impact survivability. Others formed groups to talk endlessly about causes of the crises, rather than working on potential solutions.

Later, a great deal of the talk began to focus on what advantages being smaller might bring to the larger dinosaurs. Upon hearing this, a great many of the smaller meat-eating dinosaurs became consultants to the larger dinosaurs. After all, they reasoned, no one knows as much about being small as they did.

Being a consultant was a big advantage because larger dinosaurs would not generally eat their consultants. Better yet, the consultant dinosaurs were able to get a share of the larger dinosaurs' prey as a fee. The consultants quickly discovered that it was much easier to get paid to give advice than it was to hunt. And, much to their pleasant surprise, the advice was sought. So many small dinosaurs became consultants that someone coined the phrase, "If it's a small dinosaur more than 10 miles from home, it must be a consultant."

Soon, many of the big dinosaurs grew tired of the continuous talk about smallness. Since most took pride in their large size, they felt uneasy when focusing on smallness. They sought advice about alternative, less-threatening strategies. The consultant dinosaurs feared they would lose their clients and possibly become prey if they continued to limit their advice to the one thing they knew. In no time at all, each consultant dinosaur was telling its clients exactly what they wanted to hear.

So some dinosaurs were told to change their color, others to grow smaller tails, many to become warm-blooded, some to learn to swim, and most to make friends with large, overseas dinosaurs. A few unfortunate dinosaurs fell into a consulting frenzy, rapidly switching from one consultant to another and embracing one short-sighted evolutionary change after another. Thus, the ancestors of the duckbill platypus and the camel were created. Of course, the more typical result of such a haphazard approach to evolutionary change was a quick death at the hands of a predator.

After listening to many consultants and the talk of his friends, Gigantus Traditionalus decided to respond to the crisis by doing what a large faction of dinosaurs called "rightsizing." The rightsizers theorized that various parts of the dinosaur should shrink disproportionately, depending upon their contributions to, and needs for, survival in the new environment. For example, since the new prey animals were much faster, the rightsizing theory was that dinosaur legs would have to be faster too; they should have less bone and more muscle.

The problem was that the heavy, speed reducing weight of a large dinosaur's legs was necessary to support its huge body. If rightsizing were to create a more competitive dinosaur, a great deal of body weight would have to be eliminated. This didn't sit well with many of the large dinosaurs. "We have suffered enough," some said. Others complained, "How can anyone suggest that we get smaller after we've already lost 10 percent of our weight? Our size is what makes us powerful. We can't sacrifice that."

As a result of this reasoning, many of the dinosaurs claimed they were already rightsized by the crisis. Gigantus Innovatus noticed that the dinosaurs who attempted additional rightsizing most often simply scaled down proportionally. Thus, rightsizing as a strategy turned out to be nothing but the consequence of slow starvation, rather than a planned, carefully orchestrated survival strategy. Yet, because of its fancy name, rightsizing remained a popular topic among the dinosaurs. Gigantus Innovatus realized that effective rightsizing required an accurate vision of the characteristics needed in order to survive in the new environment.

Gigantus Traditionalus did not possess such a vision (few dinosaurs did; how could they know?) but decided that the accepted form of rightsizing was the best alternative. He could not refute the argument that a smaller belly required less food. Following the advice of a consultant dinosaur he found a place to hide and began to make himself smaller.

At first, he made an attempt to disproportionately reshape his body, to rightsize the best way he could imagine with his limited imagination. He attempted to keep his legs longer to run fast and shrink his massive chest and tail to be lighter. But his body departments (it is not widely known, but dinosaurs customarily referred to their body parts as "departments") screamed out in protest. "How come the legs get to be longer if I have to shrink?" cried the chest. "Without me, your booming cry would not be heard throughout the jungle." The massive, heavy tail department complained, "In a fight, I am your foremost weapon. How could we survive if this department has to cut back in size?"

Every body part pressed self-serving arguments while contending that it was interested solely in the welfare of the entire dinosaur body. In the end, not being a strong enough leader to resist their pressure and whining, Traditionalus ordered all body parts to shrink equally–the so-called "peanut butter" approach to rightsizing in which percentage reductions are imposed equally on all departments across the board.

Over the next few months, Gigantus Traditionalus rightsized himself from 100,000 pound Gigantus to a 1,000 pound Gigantus. While there were some differences of scale, his new body was essentially a mirror image of the old; each part faithfully represented in miniature. When the process was over, Traditionalus stumbled out of his hiding place and immediately began to hunt, for he had run up very high consulting fees prior to the change process.

At first, it was difficult to hunt with the new body. He had to learn the habits of his new prey and adapt his tactics to his new size: no longer could he crash through trees and blindly charge through deep brush. At the same time, there were advantages: he could find and root out small game that he never noticed from his former perspective high above the ground. And, as the consultants promised, he could get by with only 1/100th of his former food intake.

But there were subtle, disturbing problems that not many newly rightsized dinosaurs noticed. They were still always hungry and scrambling for prey. To Gigantus Innovatus, who continued to watch and listen carefully, it seemed as if the rightsized dinosaurs spent just as much time hunting as he did. And another problem that few of the rightsized dinosaurs dared speak about: in their smaller state, they were easy prey for many of the larger dinosaurs. Every week, a rightsized dinosaur or two would disappear from the after-hunting get-togethers at the water hole, having been "merged" with the digestive system of a larger dinosaur.

The presence of rightsized dinosaurs brought a new threat: foreign competition from other valleys. The very largest, meanest dinosaurs, Megamonsterus Congolmeratus Traditionalus, began to migrate to the valley of the Gigantus dinosaurs when they discovered that the Gigantuses' valley was populated with easy-to-catch rightsized prey. The Conglomeratuses were soon joined by the large but somewhat slower Megamonsterus Aerospacus Defensaursus and the extremely fierce and fast Behemouthus Commercialus Productus. Soon the valley of the Gigantus species was a charnel house, as increasingly hungry, desperate predators fought over a rapidly vanishing supply of prey.

One month to the day after emerging from his transformation, Gigantus Traditionalus met the perils of rightsizing. He was feeding on the remains of a small rotting mammal carcass when he heard the roar of a Behemouthus Commercialus Productus. He looked up and saw the 80-ton Commercialus burst from the edge of the jungle and thunder into the field at him. At full size, Gigantus Traditionalus would have had the option of either running or fighting. As a rightsized Gigantus, fleeing was the only option.

It was no contest. Making his rightsized legs blur, Gigantus Traditionalus was still not fast enough; his legs were limited by their design constraints. Even though both the dinosaur's body weight and legs were 99 percent smaller than before, the relative diameter of his leg bones was disproportionately more than was necessary to support his greatly reduced weight. His rightsized legs looked perfectly proportioned, but they were much heavier and thicker than they should have been for maximum speed.

Also unchanged was his Traditionalus mitochondria, the energy-generating machines within his cells. They could not provide enough energy to allow him to run fast enough, long enough. Before Traditionalus was even halfway to the trees, his rightsized legs slowed and began to cramp up. The Commercialus caught him easily and squashed him with a giant foot. Those portions of the Traditionalus not torn asunder and wolfed down by the Commercialus were picked clean within hours by jungle scavengers (mostly Arbitratus Raideratus Leechus and Junkus Bondus Milkenus).

His brother, Gigantus Innovatus, witnessed this gruesome tragedy from a distant ridge. He was sad (although he had resisted a few incestuous, carnivorous thoughts since his brother's rightsizing). Right up to the moment of his brother's merging with the Commercialus, Innovatus was toying with thoughts of rightsizing because he could not conceive of any other viable approach. His brother's fate only served to reinforce his views that it was an impoverished survival strategy. He resolved to continue to listen and learn in search of an alternative survival tactic.

It was not easy to be patient in the face of rightsizing and the constant danger from the opportunistic intruders from the other valleys. On those rare occasions when he met other dinosaurs for a drink at the water hole after hunting (something few of them had time for anymore), some of them made fun of him and teased him because he was not "making any progress" in rightsizing, recoloring himself or modifying his fang length. Even those dinosaurs who were doing little or nothing quickly became experts at waxing poetic about all the incredible changes that would soon be evident. Most, of course, were doing nothing but talking, but they talked well.

Many body departments of Gigantus Innovatus felt bad when they perceived they were behind the power curve in pursuing the latest transformation crazes. Several of them, notably the fangs and the legs, attempted to initiate changes on their own. The fangs wanted to grow longer, and the legs wanted more muscle. Innovatus, being a good leader, quickly pulled them into line. He told all his body departments that each was interrelated to the entire organism and that they would all change in a single, consistent manner that would be best for the entire body. He told them that there would be no changes until he and the heads of the various departments developed a comprehensive vision about where they should go as a team. They didn't like it, and they grumbled; but they did what they were told.

Several weeks later, Innovatus was scavenging for some tidbits in the swamp mud when a large insect flew by his eye. He idly snapped at it. It swerved and flew up and away, out of danger. That's such a great defense mechanism, he thought, as he began to poke his head back into the mud. He froze. Fly. Fly! What if I could fly, he thought with an electric jolt. No way, he yelled to himself in near hysteria, dinosaurs do not fly. What a ridiculous thought! But what if? He couldn't stay away from the idea. In order to fly, he would have to be very, very small. That would mean lower prey requirements. Best of all, if he could fly, he could soar above the jungle, safe from starving predators! Should he try it? Could it work?

He thought about it constantly for the next few weeks. The change would be extremely painful. It was much more than any rightsizing he had ever seen. His departments would have to grow wing bones, muscles and skin where none existed. His massive legs, tail and hips would have to go. He would even have to change at the cellular level, so he could generate enough energy to sustain flight. It gave him headaches just thinking about the complexity of the change.

If it worked, he wouldn't even be a dinosaur anymore, at least not like any that had existed before. He knew it would be dangerous. Something could happen during the metamorphosis, and there could be complications, perhaps the growth of a lethally burdensome extra wing or leg. There were few guidelines, other than what he could intuit from dead flying insects that he had examined. But the danger and risk weren't issues to be considered if you thought about the big picture, he told himself. With the supply of available prey decreasing every day and the arrival of more and more desperate Commercialus and Defensaurus dinosaurs in the valley it was clear that Gigantus dinosaurs were going out of business. He saw that the rapidly deteriorating situation required radical changes in survival tactics. If you didn't make such changes, he reasoned, you'd either get it fast like his brother, or you'd get it slowly, like those (including himself) starving to death. The end result was the same: oblivion.

The few consultants to whom he could bring himself to talk to advised doing something less risky. They tried to convince him to rightsize, to play it safe. The consultants argued that they were right because so many dinosaurs were paying big prey for their advice. But not a single consultant could provide him with information about becoming a flying dinosaur. In fact, he noticed that the number of consultants seemed to be decreasing even faster than the Gigantuses. Innovatus concluded that the survival experts were less adept at survival than many of their clients. This realization finalized his decision: he decided to become a flying dinosaur.

He found a small cave and stocked it with what little prey he could find. He took one last look at the world as a large dinosaur and then jammed himself deep into the cave and began the change. It was horribly painful. Every department of his body screamed in protest and tried to convince him that it had unique requirements and should not be required to change. Each department argued (behind the others' backs) about how much better things would be for the entire body if it were allowed to stay the same, or get bigger, while the other departments got smaller.

When the individual pleas for exemptions failed, the departments tried to talk him into forgetting this "crazy plan about flying" and to settle for "accepted, proven rightsizing." A less self-assured and more conservative dinosaur might have buckled under the pressure, but Innovatus held firm. He had a vision of the future and he would not waver. He endured the same agony himself (the brain had many changes to make) even as he endured the whining and complaining of his many departments. As must any bold visionary, he stood alone against the crowd.

Curled deep within the cave, every fiber of his being changed, from the way his bones were shaped (he made them hollow to decrease weight and dissipate heat) to the texture of his skin (smoother and much thinner). He radically modified his cellular metabolism: the mitochondria were improved and multiplied 100-fold, and the primary metabolic engine was switched from fats to carbohydrates.

He was even forced to modify his digestive system. As a Gigantus, he would gorge on prey when it was available and then digest it for up to two weeks. He often thought of this strategy as "living off inventory." In order to assure a continual flow of energy between gorgings, his digestion, or food throughput, was designed to work very slowly.

As a flying dinosaur, he would not be able to carry as much inventory. He would have to eat constantly a little at a time. Of course, that would mean that his digestive department would have to quickly convert food to energy and eliminate waste in order to reduce the weight to be carried. He thought of this new approach as just-in-time eating. As expected, the stomach and intestines screamed in protest at this radical new concept. "We'll never be able to work that fast!" they cried. "What if you don't find food every day?

We'll all starve and run out of energy!" they whined. Not having had a vision of alternative digestive approaches, how could they know? But Innovatus was great leader; he taught them and coached them, and they eventually began to understand a little.

Finally, after months of agony and protest, the change was over. He weighed only 500 pounds, 1/200th of his original weight. But more than that, he was nothing like a Gigantus anymore. He painfully pulled himself up on tender, skinny legs and stumbled from the cave into the sunlight. The new body was strange! It felt, walked, moved, even smelled different. Before, he had made the ground tremble with each step; now he moved lightly and made little noise. He carefully walked to a small puddle and looked down at his reflection for the first time.

He was shocked and terrified! Never had he seen anything like it! He was something that never walked the earth before. His mouth, once wide and massive, had become a narrow, savage wedge of razors—all the better for grasping small prey. His eyes, once large and round and four feet apart, designed for short-range vision, were now yellow slits only five inches apart, designed to spot game from great distances. His massive tail had become a thin, flat rudder. His back legs, once as thick as large tree trunks, were now long, muscular and bony, each ending with four skinny, razor-sharp claws. And his front legs? Gone?

He panicked for a moment, thinking that he made a terrible mistake. Where were his front legs? Then he remembered: the wings. In his anxiety, he had been holding them tight to his side. Even folded, he noticed, the tips were high above his head, with little razor-sharp claws at the joints. If they did not work he was doomed, for he was now too small and frail to contend with his former dinosaur colleagues, both for and as prey.

He closed his eyes and slowly unfurled his wings. They felt light, yet they crackled with power. He held them out wide and fought to keep his balance as a small breeze pushed against them. They moved easily. Slowly, he opened his eyes and looked at his reflection. They were magnificent! He was magnificent! The wings stretched to either side in perfect, awe-inspiring symmetry. He held them wide and screamed with joy. He flapped them vigorously and screeched his hunting cry. It had worked! He proclaimed himself Atmospherus Innovatus Terrorus, scourge of the skies. With a deep sigh of relief and vindication, he carefully folded his wings, drank deeply from the puddle, and returned to the cave to rest.

The first few days were difficult. Walking on two legs was not easy, and any attempt to use his wings for balance usually resulted in his being blown over by a breeze. This prompted his less enlightened body departments to cry out in "I told you so." But he knew he was right. He hadn't counted on the loneliness, though. When he went to visit the old water hole, nobody recognized him, and they laughed at his talk of flying because they could not imagine it. Several of his old friends even made half-hearted attempts to catch him for food. The only thing that saved him was their fear of eating anything strange or new. He never tried to visit the water hole again.

He was afraid to try to fly. He did not know how, and he was afraid to hurt himself, for comprehensive medical coverage had been one of the first things to go when the environment became hostile. For the next week or so, he hunted small game on the ground and avoided bigger dinosaurs by hiding in the rocks above the canyon.

His reluctance to fly was overcome by necessity only two weeks to the day after he had completed his transformation. He was standing on the edge of a small cliff, flexing his wings in the sun and enjoying a light lunch of small reptile when a Megamonsterus Aerospaceus Defensaururs charged from the jungle behind him. He was trapped. He could not outrun the Megamonsterus, he could not get around it and hide in the jungle. It was fly now or never. He tossed the reptile carcass over the cliff (no sense leaving it for the Megamonsterus, he reasoned), spread his wings and jumped into the air.

He fell toward the jungle below. He flapped his wings a little, then a lot, but nothing happened except that he started to spin. All that suffering for nothing, he moaned to himself. Just when he thought he was doomed, he subconsciously trimmed his wings and tail, slowed his flapping, caught an updraft and was flying!

"I fly!" he exulted, "I am the first flying dinosaur!" How could I have known what to do, he wondered. He concluded that function must be forced by form: he was a lean mean flyin' machine, an Atmospherus Innovatus Terrorus, scourge of the skies. So he had simply "known" how to fly; his new form had instinctively forced the proper behaviors into his awareness. He soared high above the jungle, pausing only to relieve himself onto the puzzled face of the Megamonsterus Aerospaceus Defensaurus who was standing at the edge of the cliff and staring into the sky with fear and awe.

There were benefits to flying he had not even imagined. The air above the highest jungle trees was thick with dense masses of flying insects that no land-bound dinosaur could see. He could simply swoop among them with an open mouth for a tasty, high-protein, high-fiber snack whenever he wished. And he could see just how small his former valley was. He could raid the Megamonsterus nests and feast on their eggs without any danger of being caught. He fed voraciously, and his strength grew as his weight topped out at 545 pounds. Small compared to his former self, he admitted, but big enough for his new role. Size meant nothing; efficiency and performance meant everything.

After some months, he located an attractive female Gigantus Innovatus and guided her through the transformation. She was successful, and they began to raise a family. Life was good. The suffering had been worth it.

Every now and then, while hunting or flying on the weekends with his new family, he would think about his brother and all of the others who had died. His brother was killed because, until Innovatus had succeeded, nobody had known how to transform a Traditionalus into an Atmospherus. He could accept that sorrow as the cruel work of fate. But he had difficulty understanding why he was having so little success convincing other Traditionaluses to make the change. He shared (from a safe distance, of course) his technique with every Traditionalus he had seen, but he had not been able to convince more than a handful to try the transformation. Most would listen and nod but take no action. They have ear holes, Innovatus said to himself, but still they do not hear.

After much reflection, he concluded that the other dinosaurs' resistance to change was driven by fear of the unknown and self-delusion about their own prospects for survival. Even with his successful transformation as visible proof, most Traditionaluses could not bring themselves to believe in a new vision of what they could be. And, he reasoned, part of the problem was the inability of many dinosaurs to overcome the protests of a chorus of resistant, sub-optimizing, short-sighted body departments. He could appreciate the anxiety and stress that led dinosaurs to take no action when action was required. But he still could not understand how so many could be so blind to the dimensions of the crisis that faced them if they did nothing. A decision not to change guaranteed oblivion: he hadn't spotted a Traditionalus in over a year. Sad, he thought, but that's the nature of competition and change. The new world would go to those who could change with it; all others would be killed off.

He wondered what other evolutionary changes might be possible. What improvements in flight physiology could be made? He was sure there were many. He had done all that was required to adjust successfully to his current environment. But he knew that the changes he had made would not be enough to assure the survival of his descendants. It would be up to future generations to pursue continuous improvements in all of their systems in response to the changing environment.

"I've done my part," he told himself, "by passing on the Innovatus urge to change." He did not know whether that genetic willingness to try new things would be sufficient to assure the survival of his future progeny. He could not know (how could he know?) that, tens of millions of years in the future, his greatly modified chromosomes would be in every single member of the ultimate, flying, reptile derivatives: eagles and hawks.

But one thing he did know: taking the first bold step into the unknown is the hardest part in dealing with threatening times of change. No doubt about that, he thought, but the first step is also the most rewarding. He smiled around the tasty mammal squirming in his mouth, did a loop-de-loop and continued his flight home to his executive nest high above the canyons, where his happy family eagerly awaited the return of the bread-winner and leader, Atmospherus Innovatus Terrorus, scourge of the skies!

ADDENDUM 2

AN AIR FORCE OFFICER'S PERSPECTIVE ON TQM[2]

Many view Total Quality Management as "just another program" or a short term fad that will fade away, like "Zero Defects", "Management By Objectives" or other initiatives that hang around for a while until their advocates retire or transfer. TQM is different. First, its advocates are growing in number. The tables have turned—now the TQMers are patiently lighting the fires wherever they can, and waiting for the nay-sayers to either get on the train, step aside or stop fighting for archaic, "single (or limited) interest" bureaucracies that waste our valuable national resources. Second, TQM is for the long term. Anyone with a basic understanding of TQM will tell you there's no "quick fix" or "instant pudding" intended. Finally, there's strong support for TQM at the top of both the private and government sector, and those leaders wisely see that TQM or "continuous process improvement" may be our last chance. But there's much work to be done, it will take time and we may encounter resistance along the way, as two surveys discussed later, seem to indicate. Apparently those that do resist, fail to see that TQM's three pillars (*trust, communication and teamwork*), have a significant relationship to productivity, competitiveness, standard of living and, ultimately, economic survival. This writing is an attempt to illustrate that relationship does indeed exist and to add impetus to the TQM movement.

Although Total Quality Management can probably be traced at least as far back as Dr. Walter Shewhart's work at Bell Labs in the early '20s, the DoD wide initiative really didn't begin until recently (McGovern, 1990). If one were to try to pinpoint a date, it would probably be October 5, 1987, when DoD's second Under Secretary of Defense for Acquisition, Robert Costello, sent a memo to the services and the Defense Logistics Agency (DLA). That memo, also aimed at the private sector doing business with the DoD, called for "continuous incremental improvement" of quality and productivity within the Pentagon. It's important to note that Dr. Costello did not propose drastic, immediate reform, as previous unsuccessful initiatives had suggested. However, if you've been tracking the TQM initiative since October, 1987 and this publishing, it would be hard to argue against the notion that the TQM approach has met expectations.

Even though we shouldn't declare TQM a failure, there ought to be grave concerns on its progress, as many believe implementing TQM is our best and last chance to retain our nation's leadership of the world's economy, which most would argue, is critical to maintaining our standard of living, and perhaps more important, the security of our democratic society. In The Rise and Fall of the Great Powers, Paul Kennedy writes:

> "The triumph of any one Great Power in this period (after 1500), or the collapse of another, has usually been the consequence of lengthy fighting by its armed forces (See NOTE); but it has also been the consequence of the

---

[2]This addendum was written by Lt Col John Mitchel.

more or less efficient utilization of the states' productive economic resources in wartime, and further in the background, of the way in which that state's economy had been rising or falling, *relative* to the other leading nations, in the decades preceding the actual conflict. For that reason, how a Great Power's position steadily alters in peacetime is as important...as how it fights in wartime (Kennedy, 1987)."

NOTE: The collapse of the Soviet Union offers one obvious exception.

To most, the security of the United States is probably not a large concern as we approach the end of the century, especially in light of the collapse of the Soviet Bloc and the U.S. led coalition victory in the Middle East, but there are some very disturbing long term trends related to our economic future that could affect our security as well. One of them is declining *real* wages. At the end of World War II, in inflation-adjusted 1982 dollars, the average weekly wage of workers in the private sector rose from $196 in 1947 to $315 in 1973. Some of those years were recessionary, some expansionary, but over time, the result was an increase in real wages and standard of living. Then something happened. Wages stopped keeping up with or outpacing inflation. In inflation-adjusted 1982 dollars, from 1973 to 1990, the average weekly wage in the U.S., fell back to $258 (Mead, 1991). Some may ask, "How can that be?—I feel like my standard of living has increased, not decreased as your numbers indicate."

Well, perhaps we have increased our standard of living, but at what cost? We're working harder—longer hours and more two-income families. We've downsized the American dream—smaller families, smaller homes; and waiting until later in life to have both. And finally, we're accumulating massive debt that will eventually come due. Now, if any concerned reader notices anything in effect or on the horizon, other than TQM, that can reverse the negative trend in productivity, let us know. If not, then let's get on with it! Thus, the first answer to the question, "Why TQM?":

Because time is running out.

A second answer to the same question is,

Because nothing else has worked.

As indicated earlier, there have been numerous unsuccessful initiatives to improve the efficiency of the acquisition process in the Department of Defense. Not to suggest that reform efforts have been going on for a mere twenty years or so, but a 1988 RAND study outlines attempts at acquisition reform between 1970 and 1987 (Horgan, 1988). This chronology begins with The Blue Ribbon Defense Panel (1970), includes two iterations of Packard initiatives/recommendations, the establishment of DoD Directives (5000.xx series) and OMB Circular A-109, the Grace Commission and other studies, and ends with the study that created the Defense Advisory Board (DAB). In fact, we could go back to the 19th century Dockery Commission (1893), and identify an early forerunner to subsequent reform bodies—that's nearly 100 years of attempts at reform, and still the overwhelming consensus is that the acquisition process needs drastic improvement. The private sector has been somewhat more successful, but what about that large portion of the commercial sector that provides goods and services to the government? Often their "good faith" efforts to increase efficiency are frustrated by government bureaucracy, excessive oversight, over-regulation, agency parochialism, ineffective personnel management or a myriad of other obstacles.

Another concern surfaces in the wake of the Persian Gulf War. It seems to be very fashionable to point to our success in the Persian Gulf War with an:

"If it ain't broke, don't fix it."

perspective. Many are content to stick with the status quo since that preserves their particular position of influence. Well, just because we won the war in 42 days doesn't mean the government procurement system "ain't broke". Due to our superior leadership we were clearly effective in the employment of our forces and weapons, but *effectiveness* is only half the productivity equation. Perhaps an even more important aspect of productivity is the *efficient* use of resources (labor, capital, material and management skill) that comprise and complement our forces and the equipment they operate. The defense "build-up" beginning in 1978 and continuing through the eighties totaled nearly two trillion dollars (on procurement alone, not operations and maintenance). Even though defense procurement will decline significantly in the future, we're still looking at an immense acquisition budget. Because of its size, any positive changes or improvements in the process will have potentially large savings. Credible experts estimate that we could be from ten to forty percent more efficient in spending our DoD procurement dollars. Assuming mid-range, or 25 per cent inefficiency, would translate to a savings of nearly 500 billion dollars (from 1978 until the present) on defense procurement alone. Stated another way, we could have purchased more than five major weapons systems on the scope of the Advanced Tactical Fighter (projected cost–$95B), with the money we (presumably) WASTED since 1978! Inefficiency stems from many sources, ranging from poor management to obsolete production methods to unstable funding to over-regulation to poor requirements definition. The point to be made here is Total Quality Management provides a framework to continuously improve all processes, improvement that is still needed despite our recent success in the Middle East and the demise of the Warsaw Pact.

A final answer to the "Why TQM?" question is:

Because it makes sense.

I'm amazed at the number of managers that look at the decreasing budget and say "Here it comes again—they're telling us we're going to have to do more, with less". That may be a hasty assumption. To explain, let's compare the impact on buying power of six per cent inflation versus a six per cent reduction in any given budget. Taken separately, there exists an argument that the impact of each may not be that much different. After all, both situations cause a reduction in *real* dollars that buy goods and services. To take that argument one step further, let's look at historic methods that have been successful in lessening the impact of inflation, and if our assumption that a positive correlation exists between inflation and budgets "headed south", is correct, it follows that remedies to inflation may also have a positive impact on declining budgets (in terms of buying power.) One of the most potent "inflation fighters" that comes to mind is increasing productivity. Advances in productivity come in many forms, but can be reduced to the two common denominators mentioned earlier; increased effectiveness of a product or service, and/or increased efficiency from equal or reduced input. If TQM is successful, it will virtually guarantee some measure of increased productivity year after year after year, and the better we institutionalize TQM, the higher will be our annual gains in productivity. The result: we'll be able to buy the same(or more) capability for significantly less.

To summarize, let's look at the results of two surveys, one conducted by the American Society for Quality Control, and the other by Air Force Systems Command (AFSC). Both paint a bleak picture. In the first ASQC survey, results can be characterized by (ASQC, 1990):

> "More than a third (36% private sector employees) ....do not view themselves as participants in quality improvement activities....."

> "....there is a wide gap between their companies' talk and action on quality principles."

> "....only 14% feel completely empowered to make (important) decisions."

In the AFSC survey (Air Force, 1990), government civilian employees indicate that:

> "More than 50% have to rely on "the grapevine" or rumors for information."

> "About 70% believe risk taking goes unrewarded."

> "Less than 60% believe TQM has improved quality in the work area."

> "Less than 60% believe their organization is doing a better job to ensure quality products and services than it did six months ago."

In my opinion, the results of these surveys substantiate the perception that the implementation of Total Quality Management (since 1987) has not met the expectations of very senior DoD and private sector leadership. And why should that concern us? To answer that, we need only to compare the three major economic powers, Japan, Germany and the U.S. In terms of Gross Domestic Product, the U.S. is leading and will remain in the lead for at least several more years, but Japan and Germany are gaining rapidly, mainly because of a large differential in productivity growth. Taking the comparison one step further, it may be important to note what provided the impetus for these two dramatic turn-arounds. Both the Japanese and German economies were essentially "leveled" as a result of WWII, and for the sake of survival, had to improve. What crisis will provide us with the motivation to improve our dismal productivity growth? Will it be economic, social, military or political, or is there another way for us to get motivated toward meaningful change? We don't *have* to experience a collapse, but the only other alternative is leadership, and if this country's government, business and academic leaders don't make the difficult decisions necessary to facilitate a significant increase in productivity growth, before the turn of the century, it will probably be too late.

REFERENCES

Air Force Systems Command Civilian Total Quality Management (TQM) Survey, Human Resources Lab, Brooks AFB, Texas, 1990.

Horgan, Lucille, "A Review of DoD Acquisition Reform Initiatives-1970 to 1987", Oct, 1988, p. 3.

Kennedy, Paul, *The Rise and Fall of the Great Powers*, 1987, p.xv.

McGovern, John P., "The Evolution of Total Quality Management", *Program Manager*, September-October, 1990, p.16.

Mead, Walter Russell, *The Los Angeles Times*, April 22, 1991, pp. M1 & M6.

Quality: Everyone's Job, Many Vacancies, Summary of American Society of Quality Control and Gallup Survey, 1990.

About the author:

Lt Col Mitchel is a Command Pilot with operational tours in Air Training Command, Strategic Air Command and Air Force Systems Command. Since his transition to the acquisition career field he's had assignments as Assistant Chief of Staff for Aeronautical Systems Division and Senior Air Force Plant Representative for Lockheed Advanced Development Projects, as well as duty in several program offices. He's a 1990-1991 RAND Research Fellow, where his research focused on streamlined management and acquisition reform.

ADDENDUM 3

WHY TOTAL QUALITY

"What's all this nonsense about TQM?", Bill mumbled, but Tom didn't answer his office mate. Bill was always upset about something and Tom knew better than to try and answer his questions. Both had been reading an article in the company newsletter where the president of their company was expressing his "strong commitment" to the new TQM effort that the government intended to implement within its agencies and contractors.

"Well, if this TQM thing will win us that new maintenance contract with Peterson AFB, I don't care what they implement–I need this job," Bill continued. "It sounds to me like this is just another one of those Zero Defects or PRIDE programs–'do it right the first time'... 'satisfying the customer'... hey, we've got a Quality Control Department–or are they calling it Quality Assurance these days? Anyway, this stuff about increasing quality and productivity sounds like another way for Callaghan to make us work harder and blame us when the schedule slips. Callaghan wouldn't know what quality was if he saw it–I don't think I even know what it is. The only time he ever talks about quality is when the customer is around. Besides, I don't see him setting any examples regarding 'quality' or worrying about efficiency. It's always 'do it anyway and we'll fix it when the customer complains'–he's a nice guy, but as a boss, he's a real jerk. You know, Tom, if he'd just ask us how to set up those repair jobs, he'd save himself a lot of problems. But no, he thinks he knows it all. I don't give a hoot about how it turns out anyway. It's not my problem, I just do what I'm told. When he tells me how to increase productivity, I will. When he wants to tell me how to increase quality, I will. Until then, I'll do what it takes to get by."

Tom had to agree. "I guess it's always going to be this way Bill, so it won't do any good to complain. I'm tired of hearing all the same old words and music about 'teamwork', 'involvement', 'quality', 'lower cost'–they don't listen to us anyway, so let them say what they want. In the end, all they do is talk and nothing changes–they don't even do what they tell us we should be doing. Oh well, another day, another dollar."

Tom and Bill have heard it all before. They've heard of a number of programs and slogans that exhort employees to increase quality and productivity, to make suggestions and submit ideas for improvements, and to avoid waste and defects. Bill continued with his own philosophy, "So what if the government is pushing a 'new' quality improvement program–it'll go the same way all the others have gone. Besides, if TQM is the song we must sing to win or hold contracts with the government–no problem–we'll sing just as loud as the next guy."

So how's the government going to monitor and control this new set of slogans? If they put it in Tom's and Bill's contract, then they, along with Mr. Callaghan, will find a way to meet just another set of "standards" and make the contract administrators and themselves look good. Bill continued with an observation from his experience. "If they don't put it in the contract, then who's to say we aren't doing 'it', especially when the marketeers and customer relations department are through with them. Besides, the government is only interested in the lowest cost and meeting the schedule–quality is something that happens after that, if ever."

There's another conversation across town between John and Mike who work for Mr. Clements' company. John is reading a similar article in the company newspaper and comments to Mike, "You know, I really don't understand what the big deal is about this 'TQM'. All this talk about quality, productivity, improvements, eliminate waste and rework–we're doing a pretty good job of that already. Since Old Man Clements and his son got out of that ivory tower of theirs and started listening to us, we've really got things turned around. You know, Mike, they're lucky to have us here, we've really made a difference. This job makes me feel important and like I contribute. Old Man Clements seems to care about me and what I have to offer–of course, he's still just as demanding and critical as he's always been, but at least I know he's fair and will listen to me. He doesn't hesitate telling me when I'm wrong either–but I don't mind. In fact, I respect him for that."

"Yeah, I know John. I'm proud of what we do as a company and the service I personally provide to our customer. I know what Clements expects and what our customer expects and I know I'm responsible for seeing that it gets done the way it should. I didn't like this at first, but when I was sure Clements meant what he said about not turning out a product or providing a service that wasn't absolutely right, then I began to develop a real good feeling about working here. Boy, did he take the heat at first when the schedule went all to heck and our costs skyrocketed. But look at it now–we haven't missed a delivery or had any complaints since we revamped the maintenance process ... and we're the ones who did it. I don't think Clements thought we could and I didn't either when I heard the way he wanted us to flowchart out the whole process in such detail. But once we finished, that was a real eye-opener for all of us."

"I'm really glad most of those inspectors on the third floor are gone," John added. "It didn't feel right with them inspecting everything I did. I had no reason to really do it right even though I generally tried to most of the time. I like the way Clements lets us change the way we provide our service. You know, all those steps we cut out using that flowchart really made sense after we got to looking at it. Why did we wait so long? Actually, I really got some good ideas on the SPACETRACK computer replacement process that I'm anxious to make when we start looking at that one. You know, I guess I'm seeing that I can make this job anything I want as long as Clements and his son keep supporting us the way they do."

The difference between the two companies is obvious ... as are the products and services they are currently providing. There will be even greater differences in the products and services they will provide in the future. You don't need to know much more about these companies than the dialogue provides to see the situation with reasonable clarity. One company is proceeding with "business as usual" and will continue to do okay in the near term. The other has made dramatic changes, taken the "hits" with schedule slips and initial increased costs as management changed its behavior, attitude and way of doing business. The resulting changes have created an environment for continuous improvement. The employees are totally involved, quality oriented, and accept responsibility for the results, that is, the customer's satisfaction with their products and services. This company will create the best value for the customer in the future and will consistently win contracts with the customer to the detriment of "business as usual" companies. Which company would you want to be associated with?

If you are interested in making the transition to a different way of conducting business that will make a difference, then this book will help you. As a word of caution, however; you should realize that this book can only provide you with an understanding of what total quality is about and how to implement TQM in your organization. The actual effort to make changes and adapt to a different way of doing business is totally up to you. It's your responsibility to implement change; therefore, you need to have the desire and motivation to make the changes. It is not easy to make changes, but the results will be well worth the effort. In a way, you have no choice as the world is changing around you and change is being forced on those who want to survive. You, however, can choose to lead into the future or be relegated to being a follower.

THE MANY FACES OF TQM IN ACTION

TQM in action does not look the same in every organization. In fact, each organization's implementation of TQM will be unique since there will be a different set of personalities, circumstances, characteristics and situations. As management consultants, we have seen many different implementations of TQM philosophy in organizations because of their unique characteristics. Consider the case of Lincoln Electric.

Lincoln Electric had no formal organizational chart in spite of approximately 3500 employees. The span of control could be up to 100 employees per supervisor and only three management layers from the bottom to the top of the organization. There were no special executive privileges, offices were austere, and company benefits were limited, with an employee association providing many benefits. Pay was generally piece-rate and designed to equal the average income for similar work in the local area. The management style is more authoritative, as supervisors had complete power to assign employees to jobs regardless of an employee's preference. In fact, Mr. Lincoln, the prior CEO, has stated: "We're very authoritative around here. We stress protecting management's authority ... Management has complete power (Lincoln, 1951)."

At first glance, this company would not appear to be practicing TQM or be like the company John and Mike work for in the last section. Yet, this company is using TQM concepts and values in their own way. The company has been extremely successful for the last 90 years and has captured over 40% of the international market in electric welders and associated products and services. Lincoln is effectively meeting the needs and expectations of its customers; their products and services have become industry standards. All this has occurred in a very mature market where there is only 1-2% price variation among similar competing products. Their productivity rate is reported to be twice that of their competitors and reflected in their profits being twice the industry average (Lincoln, 1951).

The employees' performance is exceptional and attitudes seem to be positive. Turnover is non-existent. Generally, the employees are deeply involved in their work, taking no coffee breaks and not spending time in idle chatter. There appears to be almost no supervision or need for management involvement. As a measure of employee productivity, the sales per employee was $157,000 a few years ago (Lincoln, 1951).

Employee basic pay was average for the area, but was often doubled by their annual bonus which was based on their merit rating. Employees were evaluated twice annually in the four areas which directly reflect the values of the company: 1) quality of their work and their products or services, 2) dependability or consistency of effort, 3) ideas (submitted and implemented) and cooperation (i.e., participation and involvement in the efforts of the company), and 4) the quantity of output or results obtained.

The fact that costs of the products have risen only 1/5th as fast as the Consumer Price Index could be attributed directly to employee involvement. They are constantly improving the processes as well as the products and services. The focus is on quality and reducing costs by improving efficiency and eliminating waste. This focus is rewarded individually by merit points. The employees are empowered to identify changes and take issues or problems, as well as opportunities, directly to the individuals or supervisors who can make decisions concerning operational changes.

Each employee is seen as being responsible for making the final product or service better; each is held accountable for their part of the effort. We consider this approach to be the ultimate in participation and typifies the meaning of "participative management" within a TQM environment. Mr. Lincoln confirms this attitude in stating that, while management has complete authority and power and is the "coach who must be obeyed", the employees, however, "are the players alone who can win the games ("TEAM", 1989)." He set the direction and made the major decisions, but listened to his people and empowered them to be deeply involved in the operations of the company.

A final observation that characterizes the TQM orientation of Lincoln Electric: the priorities are absolutely clear. The customers come first, since they must be satisfied to maintain profits and market share. Satisfaction is seen as a function of the quality and value of the products and services which are provided by the employees. Employees, then, are the second priority. The employees must be empowered to create value and continually drive costs down, a major factor in satisfying customers. The last priority is the stockholders. As a result of the first two priorities being well cared for, the stockholders have benefitted greatly in dividends and increased stock prices.

The following provide some additional examples of what others have already done using TQM concepts and methodologies. The point is, TQM works and works extremely well producing outstanding bottom-line results.

- ITT: Using Taguchi methods (see Chapter 9) on a $750,000 automated gold plating machine, saved $1 million a year. In the Electro-optical products division, they were able to ramp up from 1,000 tubes produced per month to

25,500 per month by process improvements and reducing waste. Additional efforts using Taguchi experiments have produced: 30% to 80% savings amounting to $2 million; operations at 30% above previous capacity; 80% increase in market share; overall, the quality of products and services were increased, waste eliminated, cost reduced, and customer satisfaction greatly increased (Duffy, 1989).

— Boeing Aerospace Company (BAC): These examples reflect some of the administrative improvements which have accompanied many manufacturing examples at Boeing. Process improvements in billings on the Inertial Upper Stage Program reduced errors to zero and cycle time from 20 to 3 days. Technical Order Processing was simplified and streamlined, saving $875,000 and 3.5 manhours per technical order. Billing delinquencies on the AWACS contract were reduced by 50% using process improvements. The number of inspectors in the cable shop were reduced by improving quality using statistical process control (SPC) techniques and improved processes (Case Studies). The Calibration and Certification Lab reduced its turn-around of tools from 25 days average to "same day" while the workload doubled ("TEAM", 1989). Overall, BAC estimates savings of $1.5 million per year by emphasizing quality and not quantity.

— Pittron Steel Foundry was on the verge of bankruptcy, but through the use of TQM concepts such as treating employees like people (instead of "assets" or "subordinates") and by listening to them, they have greatly increased their performance and are no longer facing bankruptcy. In just 20 months from the change in philosophy, sales increased 400%, profits were up 30%, turnover has decreased substantially, productivity risen by 64%, and the quality of products is the highest ever.

— U.S. Navy: Several locations in the Navy operations and maintenance areas are reporting exceptional results from adopting TQM methods. The Navy F-14 overhaul program has cut the average cost from $1.6 million in 1986 to $1.2 million per aircraft in 1989. The aircraft failure rates at Cherry Point were reduced by 90% between 1987 and 1988. The overhaul on the USS Saratoga at the Norfolk Naval Shipyard is expected to save $10 million and 22,000 mandays due to the application of TQM concepts and methodologies. The Aircraft Paint section at the Naval Aviation Depot at Cherry Point had problems with poor quality, waste, and morale due to problems detected by final inspections. The Process Action Teams and TQM tools and techniques have produced huge improvements in quality of products and services and lower costs. The Norfolk Navy shipyard reduced a 55% rejection rate in electron connectors to 6% and avoided $500,000 in costs by using improved processes and increased training. The Naval Aviation Depot improved the productivity of Rotor Hubs 29% and a turnaround reduction of 50% using the process analysis techniques and simplification of processes (Burstein and Sedlak, 1988).

– Martin Marietta, using their version of Process Action Teams, made considerable improvements in quality, morale, and efficiency. The Titan IV "boattail" assembly cycle time was reduced from 2500 hours to 1200 hours. A wire crimping process was streamlined, resulting in 11 operations being reduced to 1 with savings of $18,000 per month (Aerospace Business, 1989).

MALCOLM BALDRIGE NATIONAL QUALITY AWARD WINNERS

The most highly publicized TQM success stories are from the winners of the Malcolm Baldrige Award. The award is given annually (since 1988) to those companies that have demonstrated and promoted quality awareness and quality achievements. As many as six awards may be given each year with two each to 1) manufacturing companies or subsidiaries, 2) service companies or subsidiaries, and 3) small businesses of 500 employees or less. The awards are not made unless there is a clear winner. The evaluation process is quite intense with evaluation teams spending an average of 400 hours in the semi-final stage and 4 days during the on-site finals.

In 1989, Xerox and Milliken won the only two awards given. Xerox is a company of 50,200 employees and over $11.4 billion in sales. In a highly intense effort spanning 5 years, Xerox made an internal revolution using quality improvement teams. Their TQM effort was entitled: "Leadership Through Quality". The "Teams" at Xerox spawned the term "Team Xerox" featured in recent TV ads. The teams, however, did much more as the following two examples indicate:

– They reduced the defect rate from 10,000 parts per million (PPM) to 300 PPM in 1989. Based on their continuing improvement programs, they project future defect rates to be measured in parts per billion.

– The vendor base was reduced from 5000 to 400 using a highly structured certification program and "partnership" attitude.

The development and deployment of the Xerox TQM effort required an investment of $125 million (for education) and over 4 million manhours for training. The Malcolm Baldrige application process alone required a 17 member team working 6 days a week for 6 months. The results were 250 binders of documentation. The effort to apply for and be involved in the Malcolm Baldrige Award process paid huge dividends to Xerox. Everyone is now quality conscious and is involved in participating in some way. As the CEO said: "Now we have to live up to the Award". He went on to say the real winners are the Xerox customers (Duffy, 1989).

TQM in action does produce extremely impressive results as other examples throughout this book will demonstrate. But let's next take a look at why TQM is important to us both as a nation and individually. The primary goal of this book is to provide an understanding of TQM. However, understanding TQM is of little value without grasping the importance of the topic to our country, our government, our companies, and to each of us individually. If there is no pressing need for anything different, then there is little reason for you or I to be concerned with some "new way" of doing business. The bumper-sticker which says, "If it ain't broke, don't fix it", is all too classic Americana.

PRODUCTIVITY AND QUALITY

Even though the U.S. can be truly considered a world business leader and we can statistically substantiate our predominance in many areas, the trends are ominous. We each sense the degeneration of our world position from news media and publications that hint at a need for changes. The position of the United States as a nation with a trade surplus a few years ago, but now the largest debtor nation in the world is frightening and intimidating (The Dines Letter, 1987). While we are still a powerful economic force, our dominant world position is eroding.

The number of categories in which the U.S. is the world leader is decreasing, as shown in Figure 1. As an example, 1970 the U.S. pioneered and controlled 90% of the domestic market in phonographs. In 1987, that share had dropped to only 1%. While our business trends in many cases are still positive, they are now increasing at a reduced rate (see Figure 2). The historical trend from 1870 to 1980 for our manufacturing productivity has been steadily increasing and looks impressive until we overlay the productivity increases of Japan and West Germany on the same graph and notice the relative steepness of their gains to ours.

HIGH TECHNOLOGY MARKET – EROSION OF US SHARE

| Technology | Pioneered by | US percentage of US market | | | |
		1970	1975	1980	1987
Phonographs	US	90	40	30	1
Televisions					
Black & White	US	65	30	15	2
Color	US	90	80	60	10
Audio tape recorders	US	40	10	10	1
Video Cassette recorders	US	10	10	1	1
Ball bearings	Germany	88	83	71	71
Machine tools					
Horizontal numerically-					
controlled lathes	US	100*	92*	70	40
Machine centers	US	100*	97*	79	35
Telephone sets	US	99	95	88	25
Semiconductor manufacturing					
equipment 1	US	100	90	75	75
Cellular telephones	Scandinavia/US	N/A	N/A	N/A	40
Facsimile machines	US/Japan	N/A	N/A	N/A	0

Source: Made in America, MIT Press, 1989.

Figure 1

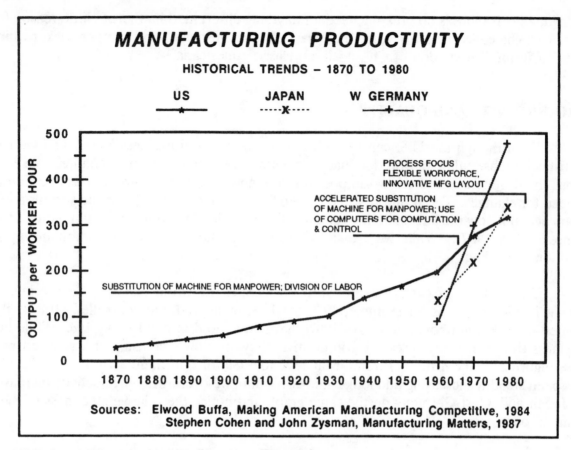

Figure 2

The marketplace today is truly international. Providers of goods and services must now compete on a larger scale and on a quality basis to satisfy the perceived needs, wants and desires of consumers. Buyers are becoming more sophisticated and discriminating. "Business-as-usual" will not meet the challenges posed by the rest of the world. The perception of the quality of U.S. goods and services seems to be changing. Perhaps the actual quality of U.S.-made products has not changed in the last 40 years when "Made in the U.S.A." was considered the standard of quality in the world. At that time, products made in Japan were considered inferior to ours; "Made in Japan" was synonymous with "discardable" and "low quality." Today, however, *relative* to U.S. products, "Made in Japan" seems to characterize the latest in technology, highest quality, best features, and most value for the money.

I remember selling my Toyota Mark II Corolla some years ago to an older Korean man, who was buying the car for his son. He was quite distraught about paying $1100 for what he considered to be an inferior car. His remark stuck in my mind: "... but it's Japanese–not U.S.–it cannot be worth this much". The excellent repair record and the fact that the Toyota had not depreciated as much relative to U.S. cars had no bearing on his perception of quality. The steady increase in market share by foreign car manufacturers at the expense of U.S. manufacturers who dominated world markets a few years ago is a painful reminder of the direction of our competitive edge.

Up until the late 60s, our business environment was relatively stable. But beginning in the 1970s, the environment became more evolutionary and increasingly turbulent with rapidly changing world situations, technological advances, communication enhancements, and increasing standards of living. People are demanding more—both as workers and as consumers. The business environment now appears to be changing even more rapidly, and there seem to be no indications that the rate of change is stabilizing. Managers must accept these changes and adapt rapidly or be left behind. Management styles and adaptive behaviors must be considered; rigidity and inflexibility in management creates an increasing inability to compete.

The usual attitude of a "successful" enterprise (be it a country or a business) is to minimize the impact of potential changes in the external environment. Business-as-usual is anticipated and expected. Changes are typically ignored or minimized because they are not accepted as realistic and the assumption is made that the status quo will continue. If changes are perceived as reality, the assumption is made that the changes will mostly impact other businesses or organizations. The illusion is "others must change, not me." The arrogance of successful organizations is often the underlying attribute that creates the seeds of destruction. The attempt is to maintain the status quo instead of continuously improving to increase competitiveness.

Perhaps the following quote best summarizes the situation within the United States since the end of World War II.

"It takes real talent to withstand adversity, but it takes genius to survive success."

Samuel Rutgers
17th Century

The bottom line is that the productivity and competitiveness of the United States is eroding and there has been no concerted, systematic effort to stem the tide. We need a new orientation toward an adaptive approach to the changing business environment. In expanding markets, such as those existing after WWII, most products and services offered were readily accepted. However, as consumers become more discriminating, and as markets mature or reach levels of saturation, competition becomes more definable and difficult. There are indications from today's market researchers that quality and time to market will be the most competitive arenas in the future.

Defining quality can be difficult as it has different meanings to different people in different settings; that is, there is a situational or contingent aspect to the application of the word "quality". However, there seems to be a definite trend. Quality is associated with value and value is the criterion of discriminating consumers who are demanding more benefits or return for the money they spend. If TQM has an effect on quality, and quality is a competitive factor, then this is a compelling reason to understand what TQM is all about.

BUSINESS ENVIRONMENT ISSUES

The focus for most businesses and government agencies has been on manipulating the operation to meet the short run goals versus an emphasis on the long run growth and development of the organization. In America, we have focused primarily on profits and quarterly dividends. As evidence from an MIT study substantiates, consider the "wave of leveraged buyouts and corporate takeovers that have forced business to focus even more on immediate returns at the expense of long-term sustained growth (Made in America, 1988)." In government agencies, the same problems exist—they are just phrased differently. Historically, it has been easier to eat our "seed-corn" than to plant it and nurture its growth and development for a larger, more productive harvest in later years.

With the increasing intensity of the competitive environment in all sectors (commercial, civil, and government), U.S. organizations must recognize that the way we have done business in the past cannot be maintained. One of the primary points made in the MIT study cited above, concerns the outmoded strategies of American firms which have traditionally focused on producing "standard items for primarily domestic markets, while ignoring foreign markets, technological advances and innovations (Made in America, 1988)."

Foreign competitors have not had this narrow focus and have made considerable inroads to U.S. domestic markets. American businesses, aided by the Government, have attempted to maintain the status quo, sometimes using government mandates, e.g. protective trade barriers and tariffs. This strategy has worked for short term stabilization, but now, even our protective barriers are no longer effective against an increasing number of high quality, foreign-produced goods and services. Our business environments have become chaotic and unstable; business-as-usual will not suffice if we expect to "survive and thrive". The following definition perhaps accurately describes this phenomena.

"Pure insanity: To keep doing the same things and expect something different to happen."

Author Unknown

The need to optimize resources in organizations seems obvious. However, this fundamental objective often seems to get lost in our actual implementation of plans and our daily operations where the emphasis is on expediency and immediate results. Dr. Deming estimates that there is between 20% and 40% waste and inefficiency in our business processes (perhaps even more in the government). This means that up to 40% cost reductions are possible by eliminating waste, scrap, rework, etc. from our operations. Driving out inefficiencies and optimizing our resource utilization will reduce cost, improve quality, and increase profits.

Unfortunately, efficiency alone will not suffice. An organization, business or government agency, must effectively provide value for the consumer. There are numerous examples of successful U.S. organizations that are both effective and efficient and will be discussed in later chapters. Air Force Logistics Command is beginning to discover, through their Blue Ribbon Contractor Program, that the most effective organization will almost inevitably be the most efficient organization in providing the best product or service for the lowest price (Swartz, 1989).

These changes in the business environment are predicted to cause significant changes in the aerospace and defense industries. A major study of these industries and government agencies concluded that one of the top 10 prime contractors would leave the industry or merge in the next 3 to 5 years, and that the same consolidation is likely among major subcontractors and suppliers (Duffy, 1989). General Alfred G. Hansen, Commander, Air Force Logistics Command, USAF makes the point even more strongly by looking at the trends within the defense supporting industries:

"There were 118,000 vendors who sold products (or services) to the military in 1982. Within five years, that number had dropped to less than 40,000 (Hansen, 1989)."

If this is the case, then there is considerable reason to consider a change in the way we conduct our businesses and our government agencies. Unfortunately, these types of changes are not easy to make and require considerable time and effort to implement. Those organizations that consciously and proactively make necessary changes before they become necessary, are almost certain to recoup their costs through increased competitiveness.

THE GOVERNMENT ENVIRONMENT FOR TQM

There are two major forces acting on the government and business environment. One force is the economic decline evident in our productivity and competitiveness as discussed earlier. The government is obligated to respond to this situation. As the major employer and business entity in the country ($175 billion of business a year), the government can create change by the way it does business. In the 1986 Executive Order, President Reagan directed all departments of the federal government to improve the efficiency, effectiveness and the quality of the product and services delivered (Total Quality Management Plan, 1989). TQM seems to have the potential, as demonstrated in some companies (e.g., Xerox, Florida Power and Light) and countries (e.g., Japan), to make substantial improvements in productivity and competitiveness.

The other major force is our fiscal situation, evident in a huge national debt, trade deficits, and budgets that seem impossible to cap. This, coupled with a perceived decrease in the threat to our national security, is resulting in shrinking, or at best flat budgets. The effect on the defense and civil business sectors will result in instability and perhaps increases in costs, stretchouts of existing programs, and postponements of new programs. The future business environment will have fewer opportunities and less money to be shared among existing contractors and suppliers while the need for a strong defense and aggressive civil programs remains just as important, if not more so.

In addition to the declining budgets and our fiscal situation, the perception of the American public is one of excessive fraud, waste and abuse, and general inefficiency in the government's acquisition of goods and services. Former Under Secretary of Defense (Acquisitions) John A. Betti, phrased it:

"There is an overwhelming consensus among (the Defense Department), industry, Congress and the American taxpayer that our Defense acquisition system isn't working. As a matter of fact, some even think it is bankrupt (Aviation Week & Space Technology, 1989)."

The government is responding with attempts to dramatically change the acquisition system with mandates from Congress and government agencies. While there is a great deal of resistance to this change and the bureaucracy is slow to respond, the system will inevitably change. All indicators are that the changes will occur in the direction of TQM.

There is already evidence to support this shifting emphasis. R&M 2000 and Variability Reduction Program are examples of the increased emphasis in reliability and maintainability of government systems. Acquisition strategies such as "Could Cost", although ill-defined and difficult to implement, are a shift in emphasis towards quality and lower costs through government-industry cooperation to eliminate non-value added activities. The increasing use of Source Selections as an acquisition strategy in Operational Maintenance contracts and other service areas emphasizes a trend towards best value and not simply lower cost. Blue Ribbon contractors, the Contractor Performance Certification Program, and Exemplary Facilities are all aimed at identifying quality producers and rewarding their efforts by granting a privileged status. Up to a 20% differential in price can be given to a contractor in such a favored status. The use of Concurrent Engineering techniques and Design to Production Transition are changes in the way of doing business that affect the quality and robustness of systems (DoD's Total Quality Management Plan, 1989).

These programs are excellent, but they are not directed or structured under a common approach. TQM offers the philosophy and methodology to guide and direct these types of efforts. A speaker at the 1st National TQM Conference put it this way, "building the world's most technically sophisticated aircraft, boosters, missiles, satellites and weapons systems is no longer good enough. Now they have to work better and be more reliable, maintainable, and significantly more affordable (1st National TQM Conference, 1989)."

The basic point made by key industry and government leaders alike is the cost of not changing the way we do business, both within the government and outside, is too high to ignore. The cost of maintaining the status quo is rapidly eroding our industrial base and service sector. Not changing might well lead to outright failure and economic extinction. TQM, as a methodology and as a philosophy, has proven its ability to create success in any organization—government or corporate.

KEY AREAS NEEDING CHANGE

In an extensive survey of key individuals in both the aerospace and defense industries and government, some of the key areas identified where changes must be made were (The U.S. Defense Industry, 1989):

1) continued counter-productive relations between government and contractors
2) inefficiency, waste of money, and reduced productivity within government and its contractors
3) increasing defense costs
4) deteriorating quality of products and services
5) erosion of our technological edge
6) loss of global market shares
7) increasing dependence on foreign suppliers
8) erosion of the defense industrial base

These are issues that our nation, our government, and our aerospace and defense companies must address—but not in isolation. They are joint issues and problems that also offer opportunities for substantial growth. But where does TQM fit in? Each problem area can be addressed by using TQM concepts, methodologies, tools, and techniques. Consider each one in turn from a TQM perspective:

(1) A positive relationship between the customer and provider (e.g., the government and the contractors) is essential for a TQM environment. This issue was the greatest concern among all respondents in this study. For any other improvements to occur, the climate between the government and industry must improve. A climate of trust and mutual respect is essential. This is a major concept in the TQM philosophy. Integrity and continuous improvements in meeting and exceeding customers' requirements is a necessity.

(2) The efficiency and effectiveness of an organization are the underlying measures of an organization's productivity and competitiveness. Improvements are achieved through the application of TQM methodologies. In the survey, industry respondents rated changes in productivity made by industry during the last five years as impressive; government and Congress respondents did not agree. The perception, then, of industry's customer is critical to effecting changes. TQM provides tools and techniques to address inefficiency, waste, and low productivity through continuous process improvements. This will affect perceptions over time and create the opportunity for improved relationships based on proactive improvements to the quality of the goods and services.

(3), (4) Lowering costs, while increasing the quality of products and services, is a major focus of TQM methodologies, tools, and techniques. Costs can be in terms of money (e.g., capital, personnel, materials) and time, which applies to government, as well as to business. Obviously, profits are improved through cost savings but the study revealed strong agreement among government and Congress respondents that profit goals must be through productivity enhancements rather than pricing mechanisms. The quality of U.S. "touch labor", as well as fraud, waste, and abuse, were seen as major issues. Industry must prove it can, and will, lower costs and improve quality proactively to create an environment for basing contract awards solely on the "highest and best value". TQM is the best approach for achieving that end.

(5), (6) The results produced by a TQM approach to managing an organization lead to increasing a company's competitive edge and subsequently increasing its market share–or, in government entities, increasing the innate value of a service and the number of people who use and value that service. There was strong agreement in the study that enhancements in cost and quality are essential for competitive survival in the global marketplace. The validity of focusing on TQM within both the government and industry was clearly substantiated.

(7), (8) Dependence on only a few select suppliers, and then the development of that industrial base, is another cornerstone of the TQM approach to business. In summary: TQM directly addresses all the key issues identified.

The conviction of many key people who are convinced of the power of TQM to make the changes necessary for reversing negative trends and creating a base for leadership into the future is evident. As Mr. Bill Scott asserts in a recent article in *Aviation Week and Space Technology* (Scott, 1989):

> "The TQM concept now gaining impetus throughout government, academia and the aerospace and defense industry is being viewed as both a means of corporate survival and a powerful vehicle for revolutionizing American productivity.
>
> The potential bottom-line benefits of reduced costs, improved quality, and better customer satisfaction are prompting major U.S. firms to invest millions of dollars in training, new equipment, and facilities to enhance their own competitiveness on a global scale. In the defense sector, the U.S. military services are pushing TQM concepts through acquisition incentives and DoD guidelines, while simultaneously embarking on a self-assessment process aimed at getting their own houses in order..."

Reversing the negative trends is dependent on domestic companies becoming more efficient, and, to many aerospace and electronics executives, that means converting their organizations' culture to one focused on quality. The end result is that aerospace and defense firms are starting to embrace TQM as the most likely vehicle for surviving a rapidly changing marketplace."

WHY IS TQM IMPORTANT?

The issues noted above are addressed in a Presidential Executive Order. Recall that by signing Executive Order 12552, President Reagan required all departments of the federal government to improve the efficiency, effectiveness and quality of the product or services delivered. A goal of 20% productivity improvement was directed in appropriate functions by 1992 (Total Quality Management Plan, 1989).

In response to that directive, and based on his own convictions, then Under Secretary of Defense Costello initiated a sweeping TQM effort to begin changing the organizational culture and the way the Department of Defense conducts its business and manages its organizations. He created the position of Deputy Assistant Secretary for TQM. The charter was to facilitate and drive this monumental cultural change. Others within the Executive Branch of the government were doing the same in various ways as described in Chapter 13.

In September of 1989, Mr. John A. Betti, then Under Secretary of Defense (Acquisition), increased the visibility of the TQM effort.

"In my review of the TQM initiative within DoD to date, I have concluded that the effort deserves greater visibility in the Department. To demonstrate the importance I attach to the concept of TQM, I have decided to elevate the position of Deputy Assistant Secretary for TQM, which currently reports two levels below me, and have it report directly to me."

"The continuous and comprehensive change required by TQM demands a change in an organization's culture that can only be achieved if top management is firmly committed to the process. I am firmly committed to the principles embodied by TQM, and the Secretary and Deputy Secretary as well (TQM Message, 1989)."

Mr. Peter Yurcisin, the acting Deputy Assistant Secretary of Defense (TQM), has made his position quite clear. He intends to see that DoD takes its leadership role seriously and to ensure that contractors doing business with the government are focused on the quality of the goods and services provided to the government. In TQM Parlance, the intent is to make DoD a "world class customer", as the following quote indicates:

"The DoD has taken on a major leadership role in the focus of quality in this country. We are faced with ... difficult challenge[s] ... The only way we can meet [these] challenges in an environment of budget reductions, increased technological complexity, a growing diversity of threats, and an eroding industrial base is to significantly improve not only our own quality, but the quality of our contractors (Yurcisin, 1989)."

Mr. Yurcisin has initiated a Process Action Team with representatives from the Office of the Secretary of Defense and the defense agencies to consider changes to the Federal Acquisition Regulation and the DoD supplement as well as regulatory impediments to implementing TQM. As a part of the efforts of this team, they will "develop specific language that can be used in government contracts to integrate TQM into the source selection process (Duffy, 1989)."

Preceding quotes and references may provide an understanding for what others feel is the potential of TQM and what they are doing about it, but that does not necessarily explain "why" they feel as they do and what makes TQM so important. The answer can be deduced fairly simply with the following four points.

1.   TQM WORKS! There are many success stories within the government and industry.

2.   The Japanese and other countries have created their successes by using a TQM-type approach to managing their organizations.

3.   TQM is basically a set of fundamental principles and concepts which are structured with specialized tools and techniques into an overall philosophy of managing—they are basic, believable, understandable and proven.

4.   TQM is instinctively appealing. Success occurs by creating a structure and environment that empowers the latent abilities and capabilities of people to continually improve quality and satisfy customers.

So, why is TQM important? Simple—it "answers the mail." Today, there are problems, issues, and opportunities facing us that need to be addressed. Corporate and government leaders have concluded TQM can effect real and meaningful change, create an environment to find causes of problems, develop solutions, and activate the untapped potential in our organizations.

Okay, so now your question may be: "TQM sounds impressive, but how does all this effect me personally?" Read on.

WHY DO I HAVE TO KNOW WHAT TQM IS ABOUT?
(i.e., HOW DOES TQM AFFECT ME PERSONALLY?)

TQM is inevitable and you will have to face it. As a manager, you have two choices. You can either get out of the way of change, or you can change and adapt to a new way of managing and personally lead to the future. Changing is not easy. It takes self-discipline and a desire to effect change in yourself and in the way you do things. The director of Total Quality Improvement at Boeing Commercial Airplanes (BCA) indicated that the middle managers probably had the toughest time with the cultural change. About 20% of the managers at BCA responded with enthusiasm and quickly adopted the changes. This group was seen as the potential leaders and senior managers of the future for the company. Another 60% were mostly "on the fence", waiting to see what would happen. Then there were the last 20% that either openly or quietly resisted the changes. Depending on the situation, they were either fired, moved to positions of little influence, or by-passed by structural organizational changes and made powerless (Schwartz, 1989).

As a non-management member of the organization, the effects of TQM are just as profound. Your involvement in the organization will change as will your visibility. You, too, have the same choices: participate or get out of the way. The TQM philosophy stresses that each member of an organization is responsible for the results or objectives of the organization, while each is fully accountable for their part in the process of producing products or services. Each will be held responsible and fully accountable, as well as given sufficient authority to do their job in a team environment. Each is expected to fully participate to the level they are capable of performing—and to be fully rewarded for their level of performance. No longer can individuals simply "do their job" routinely with minimum involvement. Creative and critical thinking, continuous learning, and constant growth will be required.

HOW DOES TQM AFFECT MY JOB AND MY COMPANY?

The government does not seem to be content to allow a peaceful evolution of the TQM philosophy in industry or its own departments and agencies. The government is looking for ways to "increase the speed of adoption (Yurcisin, 1989)." *Aviation Week,* notes that DoD is taking a leadership role in developing a "selection bias" for quality-oriented firms and thus, at the moment, is creating "encouragement" towards TQM versus requiring TQM in contracts (Scott, 1989). However, that could easily change if the government becomes frustrated in its efforts to effect quality and productivity. The message is clear: either change the way you do business or have it mandated in regulations and legislation and that will directly affect your company and your job.

Assumptions concerning how business should be conducted by both industry and government have to change. Industry's attitude seems to be "we'll give the government customer whatever they want—give us the specifications and we'll cost it, bid it, build it as specified (maybe with a few waivers, ECPs and variations as necessary) but without regard for how smart or good the product or service may be for the customer or even if there is a better way." Government's attitude seems to be "I have to specify exactly what I want (and that's a continuously moving target) in great detail and watch the contractor constantly with a heavy hand or else I'll get ripped off." These sort of attitudes will change in a TQM environment—not by mandate, but by active and involved leadership within government and industry.

But there is still a choice in how an organization responds—one can proact or react. This can best be illustrated in two scenarios of the "Victim" and the "Enhancer". In the Victim scenario, management reacts to federal budget cuts, and the subsequent requirement to cut operating costs by cutting people, organizational components, reducing the scope and depth of operations, and generally decrying the terrible situation that has been forced upon them. "The organization's not to blame," it tells its people, "it's the sorry state of affairs, the Japanese, the government, and Congress—we're just a helpless victim at the end of the government's rope." The result is decreased morale, deteriorating product quality and service, and barely passable customer satisfaction.

The Enhancer, on the other hand, assesses its strengths and resources and expands where it is most capable into voids left by other companies. Enhancers proactively respond by improving the processes that produce the goods and services. Wastes are eliminated, non-value added steps are removed, processes are simplified, and the customer's needs and expectations are met. Instead of laying off people who are affected by increasing efficiency, they attempt to use them to increase the scope and depth of operations and by expanding the service and business quality. The result is, they do the same job better, for less money, with increasing customer satisfaction and greatly increased employee morale.

So how does TQM affect my organization and my job? The two scenarios above suggest you can either continue in a "business as usual" mode, setting up your organization as a future victim, or you can institute positive changes and transform your organization into an enchanced operation. Victim organizations will lose business, lay off employees and eventually become extinct, while enchancer organizations will prosper. The choice is really a personal one. As the song says: "The times, they are a changin'" and how you respond is up to you.

REFERENCES

"Aerospace Business", *Aviation Week and Space Technology*, December 1989.

Aviation Week & Space Technology, December 4, 1989, p. 70.

Berg, N.A., and Fast, N.D.,"Lincoln Electric Case Study", Harvard Business School Publishing Co.: Massachusetts, 1976.

Burstein, C. and Sedlak, K., "The Federal Productivity Improvement Effort", *National Productivity Review*, Spring 1988.

"Case Studies", #8, #11, #15 and #19, Boeing Aerospace Company.

DoD's Total Quality Management Strategy, 1989 draft.

Duffy, C., "TQM Efforts Mean Survival at ITT Defense", *Washington Technology*, November 22, 1989, p.9.

Duffy, C., "Xerox, Milliken Honored for Quality", *Washington Technology*, November 22, 1989, p. 12.

Earnest & Young, "The U.S. Defense Industry: Key Issues for the 1990s", October 1, 1989.

1st National TQM Conference, Denver, Colorado, November 1989.

Hansen, Alfred G., "Are We Destroying the Arsenal of Democracy?", *Leaders Magazine*, July 1989, p. 43.

"Made in America: Regaining the Productive Edge", MIT Press, 1988.

Schwartz, Richard E., "Total Quality Implementation", Boeing Commercial Airplanes, Seattle, WA, June 1989.

Scott, William B., "TQM" expected to boost Productivity, Ensure Survival of U.S. Industry", *Aviation Week and Space Technology*, December 4, 1989.

Swartz, R., Major General, Speech delivered on October 14, 1989.

"TEAM", *BCA Quality Newspaper*, May 1989.

The Dines Letter, James Dines and Company, Inc., Belvedere, CA, December 1987.

Total Quality Management Plan, DCASR, NY, September 1989.

"TQM Message", *DoD* publication, June/July 1989.

"TQM Message", *DoD* publication, September 1989.

"TQM Message", *DoD* publication, November 1989.

Yurcisin, Peter, "The Way to Quality", *Contract Management*, November, 1989.

Chapter 2

WHAT IS TOTAL QUALITY?

WHAT IS TOTAL QUALITY?

When first hearing the term "total quality management" or "TQM", many people think total quality is just another program. They often associate TQM with the quality control or quality assurance functions in organizations. They even may believe quality is excessively expensive or dependent on the attributes or features characterizing a product or service. Their concept of quality holds that there are acceptable levels of quality which may contain defects and errors. These acceptable levels of quality are typically achieved through inspection of the end-product or service.

However, total quality brings to organizations a new definition of quality: quality is the satisfaction experienced by the customer in using products or services. "Quality encompasses improvement in cost position, delivery performance, time to market, and responsiveness to changes in the marketplace (Fortuna, 1990)." It brings tools and techniques to organizations that make achieving quality products and services *less* expensive, while also insuring the customers' needs are met. TQM philosophy proposes quality must be built in, not "inspected in". Many of the philosophies, concepts, principles and techniques of TQM are not new. Some organizations and individuals claim credit for "inventing" total quality management, but this is an immodest claim at best. Today coming together under the umbrella of TQM are many traditional philosophies and tools. What is unique about TQM is the disciplined and structured way in which these concepts are integrated and applied.

The term "Total Quality Management (TQM)" is used frequently by both industry and government, but still may not mean the same thing to everyone. Many government agencies and companies create unique definitions of total quality management which reflect their own organizational emphasis. These efforts are called a variety of names such as "total quality control (TQC)", "total quality leadership (TQL)", "total quality", and "continuous quality improvement (CQI)". Thus, there are a multitude of definitions of TQM; some examples include:

Department of Defense:

"Total quality management is both a philosophy and a set of guiding principles that represent the foundation of a continuously improving organization. TQM is the application of quantitative methods and human resources to improve the material and services supplied to an organization, all the processes within an organization, and the degree to which the needs of the customer are met now and in the future. TQM integrates fundamental management techniques, existing improvement efforts and technical tools under a disciplined approach focused on continuous improvement."

Federal Quality Institute:

"TQM is a strategic integrated management system for achieving customer satisfaction which involves all managers and employees and uses quantitative methods to continuously improve an organization's processes."

Martin Marietta (Norm Augustine):

"TQM is a philosophy and a strategy for continuously improving performance at every level and in all areas of responsibility. TQM combines fundamental management techniques, existing improvement efforts and specialized technical tools under a disciplined structure focused on continuous improvement of all processes. Improved performance is focused on satisfying such broad cross-functional goals as quality cost, schedule, customer satisfaction and mission need and suitability."

General Dynamics (Ft.Worth):

"TQM is a fundamental change in the way of doing business. It is the creation of an attitude that results in real employee involvement, initiated by a commitment and involvement of top management. TQM is an environment that promotes innovation, leadership, creativity, individual responsibility/authority, and acceptance of accountability at all levels."

Productivity Press:

"TQM is a global phenomenon which represents fundamental change in the way we think, educate, manage and operate today's organizations. It is more than a management system. It involves new strategic and cultural techniques in addition to new quality technologies to achieve customer satisfaction. It is concerned more with the quality of management than the management of quality. TQM is a new approach to managing companies for the continuous improvement of products, services, and productivity of an organization. In applying TQM, each company learns from the experience of world class organizations, better understands its own strengths and weaknesses and designs its own TQM based on its own national, regional and specific company strengths."

These definitions are similar, and yet they contain differences in emphasis. The same is generally true of the total quality philosophies and approaches of the "TQM gurus". There is no one immutable definition or correct approach to total quality. The principles underlying total quality are generally agreed to, but there are subtle differences in philosophies and approaches. As the world changes, total quality itself may evolve and continuously be improved to insure it continues to fit the needs of the organizations, employees and conditions of the future.

WHAT ARE THE GENERALLY AGREED TO PRINCIPLES OF TOTAL QUALITY?

- **Top management commitment to TQM.**

  Management bears the primary responsibility for deploying total quality concepts throughout the organization. Everyone in the organization must be involved, but without the commitment of top management, a TQM effort will achieve little more than isolated process improvements and cost reductions. What does commitment mean? Dedication to behaving in ways that are consistent with total quality philosophy, values and principles is an important aspect of commitment. Active involvement in transforming the organization is another aspect of commitment. Genuine belief in the values upon which total quality is based is also essential to commitment.

- **Employee belief in management's commitment to TQM.**

  Some managers spend a lot of time issuing TQM plans, posting slogans, and training employees without really changing their behavior or the organizational culture. Employees are likely to see right through this. Lack of belief in top management's commitment to total quality as a new way of managing the organization is a frequent reason for TQM faltering (and even failing) in organizations.

- **Employees that are empowered versus tightly directed and controlled.**

  TQM philosophy is based on two fundamental beliefs about people: 1) individuals have a natural inherent desire to improve and be successful, and 2) the people closest to the work know best how to improve it to achieve customer satisfaction. No longer is the executive or manager thought of as being the resident expert on all operations. No longer are employees looked upon as only "hands and feet", but are recognized for their brains and their knowledge of their processes. No longer are workers assumed to be stupid, lazy, or requiring constant supervision. TQM concepts recognize that workers don't need to be closely watched or checked in order to produce quality work. In fact, from the TQM perspective, close scrutiny from above is more likely to inhibit rather than enhance productivity.

- **Leadership: executives and managers who see their role as coaches, enablers, customer advocates, strategic planners, barrier removers, and "walkers of the talk".**

  TQM concepts and principles threaten some managers who see their primary roles as being directors, checkers, approvers, and controllers. However, TQM philosophy provides managers more complex, and ultimately more successful, roles as coaches, enablers, customer advocates, strategic planners, and barrier removers. Their role is to transform the organization. They lead by setting an example of total quality in action. These leaders have a vision, and are followed because their employees share their vision.

- **An unending, intense focus on customers' needs, wants, expectations and requirements, and a commitment to satisfying them.**

  TQM begins and ends with the customer. Many organizations think TQM is just about continuous improvement, and start improving processes without focusing on customers (either internal or external – see Chapter 3). We have a tendency to assume we know what our customers want, without asking them. This is not TQM; it is business as usual. Customer satisfaction is not the same thing as "the customer is always right." Sometimes satisfying the customer requires educating the customer about what will best satisfy their need. TQM concepts suggest this be done through a dialogue and partnership with customers, rather than by making assumptions.

- **Decision-making based on data, measurement, and statistical inference, rather than opinions.**

  Objective measurement is a fundamental underpinning of TQM philosophy. American managers spend a great deal of time discussing things, and frequently the most powerful opinion prevails. TQM enables many opinions to be heard, but then focuses on test, measurement, and statistical inference as methods for confirming what works best.

- **A view of process control that embraces reduction of variation, rather than just meeting the specification, to create customer satisfaction.**

  "Close enough for Government work" is no longer close enough. Another all too popular expression of government employees also applies: "If the minimum weren't good enough, it wouldn't be the minimum." A great many of our quality, reliability and maintainability problems come from variation between upper and lower specification limits. TQM concepts require focus on minimizing this variation in the attempt to achieve the target value. This is discussed in more detail in Chapter 9.

- **A commitment to continuous improvement, that is, "if it ain't broke, improve it."**

  For years management philosophy has been "If it ain't broke, don't fix it." We now know that the world is changing too quickly for us to be able to rest on the laurels of past success. We can be fairly certain someone else will be working to increase the value added and/or decrease the cycle time required to produce the product or service.

- **Focus on process improvement versus product inspection.**

  Attempting to inspect quality in after a product or service is completed is very expensive. The discovery of defects after processing causes delivery delays, scrap, re-do, rework and/or costly repairs. Inspection is also a very ineffective method for detecting defects, and takes problem identification away from the production line.

- **Focus on prevention of problems rather than fixing problems.**

  Our heros have always been cowboys and fire fighters. However, the philosophy of TQM focuses on incremental, small steps to improve processes to *prevent* problems, rather than on rewarding heroic actions to fix problems.

- **An organizational climate based on collaboration and trust instead of competition.**

  In order for process improvement to thrive in a inter-related, inter-dependent organization, we must be able to submerge concerns for the benefit of the overall organization. This requires an organizational climate of trust and teamwork.

- **A lean organizational structure which depends on cross-functional teamwork, not vertical organizational hierarchies.**

  Quality depends on more than one department or functional area; it is a result of cross-functional activities requiring involvement of all departments and functions. To facilitate communications horizontally between functions, multi-layered, vertical organizations are becoming less hierarchical, and are focusing on processes and activities rather than on specialized functions.

- **Managers who spend more time listening than they do transmitting.**

  To achieve quality products and services requires knowledge of internal and external customers' needs, wants, expectations and requirements. Acquiring this knowledge requires listening, not transmitting; a difficult skill for many managers who became successful by giving directions and orders.

- **Managers who focus on creating quality rather than being driven by schedule, bottom-line and short term financial gain.**

  In a world driven by short term results (bonus programs, three year tours, shareholders need for return on investment, etc.) it is often difficult to sacrifice schedule for quality. However, in the long run, profits, safety, and cost will be more favorably affected by a focus on quality, rather than on the immediate schedule.

- **Messengers who are rewarded for being realistic and honest, rather than being "shot" for identifying problems.**

  In an operational environment of total quality, every problem or difficulty is viewed as an opportunity for improvement. If these opportunities are not found, they cannot be capitalized on. In a total quality culture, the only reason to kill the messenger is willful deception.

- **Management that cares about employees as opposed to viewing them as an expendable commodity.**

  Total quality management requires investment in workers through training and education. Managers know (rather than just "believe") members of their organization have an inherent desire to produce quality work and be successful. Consequently, they provide training and education to enable their members to satisfy their natural desire to produce quality goods and services.

  Management's failure to demonstrate loyalty to the employees has bred an employee lack of loyalty toward the company. This is evident by the frequent company changes that many employees are pursuing. The end result is when times get tough, the tough move on to another company rather than rally to make things better.

- **An approach to product/service development which is more concurrent than sequential and uses cross functional groups working as a team.**

  Spending more time-up front in the product development/definition phase can have three benefits:

  1) increasing the quality of products and services,
  2) decreasing their development time, and
  3) reducing their production cost.

  Rather than having functions develop products sequentially, TQM employs development teams consisting of research, development and design engineers, manufacturing, purchasing, marketing and field service personnel and even suppliers and customers from outside the company. Under this approach, you minimize the phenomenon of "throwing it over the wall" so prevalent in organizations today.

● **A view of customers and suppliers as partners, not adversaries.**

Competition is the American way. Yet TQM philosophy suggests forming partnerships with vendors and suppliers to improve quality and lower cost. Not only do we waste resources in the competition activity itself, but we miss the opportunity to reduce the variability of our products and services when we acquire materials from many vendors.

● **An effort on everyone's part to not only be world class suppliers, but world class customers as well.**

TQM philosophy creates a partnership between customers and suppliers that is two-way. Just as suppliers must focus on their customers needs and continuously improve the products and services they deliver, customers have obligations as well (Heystead, 1990). World class customers focus on adding value, not providing grief, to their suppliers. They clearly and completely articulate their needs, wants, expectations and requirements to their suppliers. They eliminate unnecessary paperwork and inspections, don't shoot messengers, admit what they don't know, and limit changes to those that add value and are necessary to mission accomplishment.

● **Management focus on long term results rather than short term profits and schedule.**

This is sometimes referred to as "doing the *right* things" right the first time. It is what Dr. W.E. Deming refers to as having "constancy of purpose".

● **Values which embrace integrity rather than the end justifying the means.**

Total quality is more about substance than about style. An organization which focuses on continuous improvement and customer satisfaction won't have to dupe customers into believing their products and services are what customers need.

Effectively deploying TQM concepts requires balancing the technical and the human/social aspects. The human side of TQM is often underestimated by managers and executives with technical backgrounds. They focus on the technical tools of TQM (such as statistical process control and design of experiments) and underestimate the importance and complexity of developing effective teams, empowering employees, and truly focusing on customer needs. Similarly, some managers over-focus on teamwork without adequate emphasis on measurement and statistics. There are many ways to enhance organizational climate without improving the effectiveness of processes or focusing on quality. Such human relations may be necessary, but they are not sufficient to insure success in the long run. The key is to achieve and maintain balance.

FOUNDATIONS OF TOTAL QUALITY MANAGEMENT

The number of "practitioners" in the field of total quality management has grown exponentially over the past 10 years. There are many individuals who have brought valuable ideas, approaches and tools to TQM. Some of the most notable of these are Dr. W. Edwards Deming, Dr. Joseph Juran, Dr. Walter Shewhart, Dr. Armand Feigenbaum, Kaoru Ishikawa, and Philip Crosby.

DEMING PHILOSOPHY

Dr. Deming has made many contributions to total quality but is best known for his Fourteen Points (Walton, 1990):

1. Create constancy of purpose for improvement of product and service.
2. Adopt the new philosophy.
3. Cease dependence on mass inspection.
4. End the practice of awarding business on price alone.
5. Improve, constantly and forever the system of production and service.
6. Institute training.
7. Institute leadership.
8. Drive out fear.
9. Break down barriers between staff areas.
10. Eliminate slogans, exhortations, and targets for the work force.
11. Eliminate numerical quotas.
12. Remove barriers to pride of workmanship.
13. Institute a vigorous program of education and re-training.
14. Take action to accomplish the transformation.

Dr. Deming's philosophy is explained in more detail in Addendum 1 of this chapter.

JOSEPH JURAN: 10 STEPS TO QUALITY IMPROVEMENT

Dr. Juran's philosophies are used world wide. He created "The Juran Institute" in 1979 to provide training and consulting to those wanting to pursue total quality. A summary of his ten practical steps to quality improvement include (Juran, 1988):

1. Build awareness of the need and opportunity for improvement.
2. Set goals for improvement.
3. Organize to reach goals (establish a quality council, identify problems, select projects, appoint teams, designate facilitators).
4. Provide training.
5. Carry out projects to solve problems.

6.   Report progress.
7.   Give recognition.
8.   Communicate results.
9.   Keep score.
10. Maintain momentum by making annual improvement part of the regular systems and processes of the organization.

SHEWHART CYCLE

Dr. Walter Shewhart, who worked at Bell Labs, is quite well-known for his Shewhart cycle, "Plan-Do-Check-Act". This will be covered in Chapter 7.

FEIGENBAUM PHILOSOPHY

Dr. Armand Feigenbaum of General Systems Co. is credited as the originator of total quality control (TQC), and promulgates ten ways to boost quality (Feigenbaum, 1991):

1.   Make quality a company-wide process.
2.   Quality should be what the customer says it is.
3.   Quality and cost are a sum, not a difference.
4.   Quality requires both individual and teamwork zealotry.
5.   Quality is a way of managing.
6.   Quality and innovation are mutually dependent.
7.   Quality is an ethic.
8.   Quality requires continuous improvement.
9.   Quality is the most cost-effective, least capital intensive route to productivity.
10. Quality is implemented with a total system connected with customers and suppliers.

KAIZEN

Masaaki Imai's brought the "Kaizen" philosophy of Ishikawa and Ohno to the United States in the early 1980's. Briefly summarized, it includes (Imai, 1986):

- Kaizen means continuous improvement involving everyone.
- Improvement is made in gradual, small steps.
- Emphasis is on process, not product.
- Quality improvement is the responsibility of management.
- Kaizen's benefits are realized in the long term.
- Kaizen focuses on satisfying internal and external customers.

- Kaizen starts with the recognition that problems exist. The starting point for improvement is a problem.
- A thinking worker is a productive worker; encourage workers to make improvement suggestions.
- Cross-functional teamwork is essential to improvement.

CROSBY APPROACH

Philip Crosby packaged total quality in books and articles utilizing anecdotes and examples that many people could relate to easily. He is most well known for his concepts of "zero defects", "Do it right the first time", and "Quality is free". He submits there are four absolutes of quality (Crosby, 1979):

1. Quality means conformance to requirements.
2. Quality is achieved through a system of prevention. Processes are analyzed to identify opportunities for error.
3. The only standard for performance is zero defects: Do it right the first time.
4. To measure the cost of quality, measure the process of non-conformance, that is, how much it costs when you fail to do it right the first time, and then compare this to the price of conformance.

Crosby also promulgated 14 steps to quality improvement:

1. Management commitment to quality.
2. Form quality improvement teams.
3. Quality measurement.
4. Evaluate the cost of quality.
5. Raise the quality awareness of all employees.
6. Take actions to correct problems.
7. Establish an ad hoc committee for the zero defects program.
8. Train supervisors.
9. Hold a "zero defects" day.
10. Set improvement goals.
11. Encourage employees to communicate problems to management.
12. Provide recognition of participants.
13. Establish quality councils to provide information on status of the program.
14. Do it all over again.

Although the philosophies of Deming, Crosby, Shewhart, Juran, Imai and Feigenbaum are all different, there are fundamental tenets on which they agree. They affirm that achieving quality reduces long term costs; prevention is a preferred strategy to inspection; conformance should be measured using objective statistical data; managers are responsible for improving quality; education and training in quality improvement are necessary for both workers and managers; achieving quality requires a systems approach to organizational activities and processes; there are no short cuts to quality; improvement efforts must be continuous; and focus on the customer is essential.

WHAT TQM IS NOT

TQM is often accused of being just another management program. Sometimes its implementation is accompanied by all the trappings of a fad, with "hype" campaigns of posters, handbills, lapel pins, quality days, etc. If there is no enduring, systemic change in an organization, then TQM can indeed become "just another fad".

TQM is sometimes compared to zero defects. Zero defects was a DoD program which focused on avoiding product defects. It defined quality as the absence of defects and often used multiple inspections to achieve this goal. TQM on the other hand is not a program, it is a management philosophy. In practice, TQM avoids defects through motivated and capable employees working together to control and improve all work processes. However, TQM defines quality as the presence of value (customer satisfaction) with a focus on continuous effort to enlarge, enhance and create greater value.

TQM is also not another quality assurance (QA) program vested in the hands of one department. In TQM, the goal is to replace inspection, rework and repair with prevention by effective and efficient processes. Each individual is responsible for the quality of their output and will not accept anything but quality in their inputs. Statistical testing of end products is replaced with statistical measures of key process parameters to insure quality is built in, not inspected in. TQM requires everyone be trained in the tools and techniques of quality, not just the QA department. QA focuses on quality as conformance to specifications, whereas TQM defines conformance quality as continuous reduction in variation to achieve target value.

Finally, TQM is not the same as Management 101, which consisted of planning, organizing, staffing, directing, and controlling. TQM views the role of the manager as an advocate for removing barriers and obstacles so customer satisfaction and process improvement are possible. No longer is she/he required to be an expert in one particular functional area, but rather to become an expert in facilitating cross-functional teamwork to optimize the whole organization. Management 101 places the responsibility for productivity on the workers; TQM suggests that at least 85% of productivity rests in the process capability, not the individual. Management owns the processes, and is therefore responsible for creating an environment where improving the processes is possible.

DISCUSSION QUESTIONS

1. What does the term "TQM" mean?

2. Compare and contrast the old and the new definition of quality.

3. Who is responsible for TQM implementation?

4. Why is doing the *right* things right important?

5. Which of the principles of total quality do you think will work best in your organization, and which will work the least?

6. Customer satisfaction is key to TQM. What do you do when you feel the customer is wrong and doesn't really know what he wants?

7. Who are internal and external customers?

8. Give some examples of what TQM isn't.

9. Give a brief example of an incidence of customer satisfaction or dissatisfaction that happened to you recently.

REFERENCES

Crosby, P.B., *Quality is Free*, McGraw Hill: New York, 1979.

Feigenbaum, Armand, "10 Ways to Boost Quality", *Management Review*, January 1991, p. 5.

Fortuna, Ronald, *Total Quality: An Executives Guide for the 1990s*, Business One Irwin: Homewood, IL, 1990.

Heystead, John, "In Search of Quality", *Defense Electronics*, Sept. 1990.

Imai, Masaaki, *Kaizen: The Key to Japan's Competitive Success*, McGraw Hill: New York, 1986.

Juran, Joseph, *Juran on Planning for Quality*, The Free Press: New York, 1988.

Walton, Mary, *Deming Management at Work*, G.B. Putnam's Sons: New York, 1990.

ADDENDUM 1

TOTAL QUALITY MANAGEMENT: A LEADERSHIP REVOLUTION[1]

In TQM, quality is defined as **providing the customer what he/she expects to receive.**[2] One must therefore be able to define the customer and understand his/her desires., expectations, and preconceived notions. No customer expectation is too strenuous, too extreme, or too outrageous. Within this framework, anything is possible.

Quality expectations are achieved through a focus on five elements:

1. People
2. Equipment
3. Materials
4. Methods
5. Environment (Stuelpnagel, 1988)

Each element is focused on the business operation and organized to meet customer expectations through a process of continuous improvement. These products, whether internal or external (Figure 1) will have robust designs, and, when measured against standards, will be grouped close to the mean[3] with very little variability.

PRINCIPLES AND KEY CONCEPTS

TQM is an all-encompassing concept that combines technical aspects of quality, qualitative methods, and human resources in a system designed to provide the customer with the very best product. Processes and techniques are integrated within a system that is

---

[1]This addendum was written by Lt Col Michael Prowse.

[2]Dr. Tribus, Myron, *Quality First: Selection papers on Quality and Productivity Improvement* (Cambridge, Mass: Massachusetts Institute of Technology, 1987) defines quality as "... giving people what they have the right to receive." I have chosen to orient the focus on quality to assert that customers must first clearly establish what their requirements are. After that has been done, quality is what they expect.

[3]Variability distribution is the distribution of defects grouped around a center point. The closer the defects to the center point, or mean, the better the quality. The better the quality through variability reduction, the lower the cost of quality.

---

focused on continuous improvement through highly trained and motivated system members.[4]

PRINCIPLES

TQM principles serve as the foundation for managers and other system members to use in analyzing decisions and future planning actions. They provide a framework to assess outcomes and appraise behavior. TQM's nine principles guide the work done by each member of the system, and they force accountability of the system on management:

1. Continuous Process Improvement
2. Process Knowledge
3. User Focus
4. Commitment
5. Top-Down Implementation
6. Constancy of Purpose
7. Total Involvement
8. Teamwork
9. Investment in People

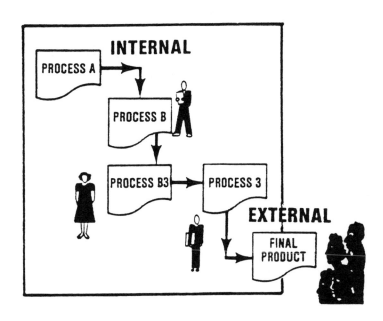

Figure 1 Internal and External Customers

---

[4]System members are any employees in an organization, work group, or team that share common processes and goals. System members are labor, staff and/or management. In the broadest sense, system members include the customer.

WHAT IS TOTAL QUALITY

KEY CONCEPTS

Management Involvement

An important fundamental of TQM is that managers at the highest level of the organization must initiate a quality revolution throughout the organization. TQM will succeed only with the constant commitment of senior leaders. If top management is totally committed to a cultural change and, if that is believed by everyone in the organization, achievement can be realized. Without active and actual top management involvement in TQM, the organizational culture will not change. This idea was expressed by James Harrington when he said, "The improvement process starts with top management, progresses at a rate proportional to their demonstrated commitment, and will stop soon after they lose interest in the process (Harrington)."

Continuous Improvement

The hallmark of the TQM process is continuous improvement (Department of Defense). The continuous improvement concept relies on developing systems and processes that *build* quality into a product, not *inspect* it in. Continuous improvement requires that improvements occur *beyond* an "acceptable" quality level; it puts quality first, before cost and schedule; and continuous improvement never ends (DoD 5000.51-G, 1989). TQM focuses on seven areas of continuous improvement:

1. Management must be of such quality that, throughout the organization, managers find ways to inspire, motivate, and educate employees in the continuous improvement process.

2. The quality of all processes, at all levels, must be assured at all times.

3. TQM focuses the efforts of the entire operation on customer satisfaction.

4. TQM relies heavily on cross-functional teams. The TQM organization is made up of process teams that are a part of larger functional teams which are a part of end-product teams.

5. TQM requires the total commitment of top management.

6. TQM relies on statistical process control to determine where any problems are, to evaluate cause-and-effect relationships, and to assist in a systematic decision-making process designed to solve these problems.

7. TQM requires more training than other systems because TQM is an unending process.

A continuous improvement system cannot be established overnight. It takes a long time to implement it fully, and it should be developed in a time-phased approach designed to keep the attention and interest of both managers and employees.

Management of Outcomes Versus Management of Processes

The typical management approach is to react to events that occur in the system; the TQM approach is to continuously work on the system itself. The first approach corrects problems topically, without understanding systemic causes. In many cases the topical correction causes problems in other parts of the system. The TQM approach is to first understand the system and how it functions. The manager must determine the cause of problems before he/she corrects them. TQM formalizes this process and makes it routine. The formalization occurs in seven major areas:

1. **Planning and Goal Setting**. Planning through goal-setting attempts to forecast the future. It sets the organizational course. Effective planning forces the system to review customer requirements concerning people, equipment, methods, materials, and the environment (Figure 2).

2. **Promoting Improvement**. The best way to promote an improvement program is to live and breathe it every day. Quality and improvement should be the first things system workers think of before they initiate any action and the last things they think about when they evaluate any change. Current reward programs should be rewritten to reflect improvement efforts as the single most important criteria.

3. **Process Improvement**. Process improvement is the practice of breaking down all the organization's processes into well-defined activities and then improving each activity.

4. **Signals**. The right signals go a long way toward keeping the attention of system workers. Any slackening of senior management commitment will cause erosion of confidence throughout the organization and TQM will wither and die.

5. **Communication**. Constructive and uninhibited communication up and down the organization is critical to the success of TQM. One of the first processes reviewed is that of communication within the organization.

6. **Skill-Building**. TQM is initially not free, but investment in it can return great rewards. The predominant cost of TQM is in training and skills building.

7. **Resource Optimization**. Part of the payback in TQM is that processes and resources are less costly to operate and maintain than in a traditional

organization. TQM frees individuals to look at each process and determine the optimum amount of resources at just the right time (Feigenbaum, 1983).

Deming, Juran, Feigenbaum, and Philip Crosby appreciated the need to go beyond the quality inspection charts and incorporate the essentials of human dynamics, organizational development, and motivational theory in TQM. The key concept is that management must take responsibility for the system. As Deming said, "It is management's responsibility to work *on* the system, while the worker labors *in* the system."

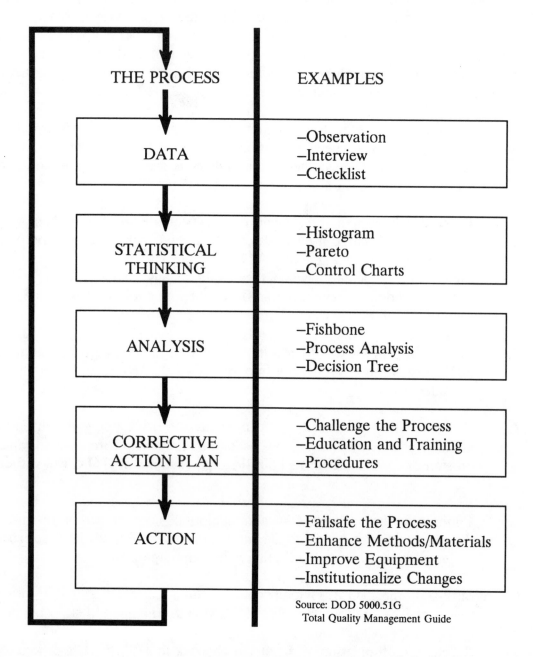

Source: DOD 5000.51G
Total Quality Management Guide

Figure 2 Improvement Cycle

The Fourteen Obligations of Top Management

The goal of TQM is quality. One aspect of ensuring quality is the elimination of obstacles that hinder quality improvement, many of which were established by management. To underscore the importance of the management change needed, Dr. Deming developed "the Fourteen Obligations of Top Management."[5] They are the basic elements taught to the Japanese. The fourteen obligations of top management are (Feigenbaum, 1983):

1. **Create constancy of purpose toward improvement of product and service, with the aim of becoming competitive, staying in business and providing jobs.** Management must do everything possible to eliminate the quarterly profit and loss mentality, which is one of the biggest detriments to long-term growth in our country.[6] Managers and leaders must establish a structure that will be around for the long run. The practice of moving managers and leaders frequently must be stopped; frequent movement causes them to come into jobs with a short-term attitude and to leave with the same attitude. Promotions should be based on all their past positions in the organization, not just the last one. The continuous improvement process should also include better methods of production, better application of materials, revitalized training, retraining, continuous updating of training aids, and training funds for the future. Part of today's funds must go toward research and development to improve products, maintenance, and services; without an understanding of the customer's future requirements, an organization will not be prepared to meet the challenges.

2. **Adopt a new philosophy. We are in a new economic age. Western managers must awaken to the challenge, learn their responsibilities, and take on the leadership for change.** According to Nancy R. Mann, "This goal will only be achieved if we demand high quality, dependable products, and/or services (Mann, 1987)." Too often shortsighted managers allow lower quality and unreliable products. Some managers actually plan for low quality, less dependable products, defects, workers who don't know their job, poor training, worse supervision, slipped schedules, and cost overruns. *If you plan for poor quality, you will get poor quality.*

3. **Cease dependence on inspection to achieve quality. Eliminate the need for inspection on a mass basis by building quality into the product in the first place.** *Build* quality in–don't try to *inspect* it in later. The best way to build quality into the product is through robust design and the elimination of variability. To understand variability, one must use statistical process control techniques. Statistical design has not been used much in the United States; but where it is used extensively, that industry

---

[5]Deming has been revising his fourteen points. I was able to find three different sets.

[6]Quarterly financial management is used here to mean the system employed by many American manufacturers that focuses all activities on the quarterly profit and loss statement.

---

dominates the world market.[7] Statistical process control uses such tools as flow charts, Pareto diagrams, cause and effect diagrams, run charts, scattergrams, and histograms. Workers who know how to apply these techniques are better able to find the problems an inspector might find. When the system worker finds problems and corrects them, it is looked at as part of the job; when an inspector finds errors, it is considered a failure. Blame is generally assigned to the system worker, not management. As quality improves, inspection should decrease. Lack of inspections can even be used as a reward for units that are producing quality products and/or services. In addition to eliminating the reliance on mass inspection, replacing military quality standards with a statistical process control system geared to continuous improvement would go a long way to recognize producers who know quality and not just the quality standards.

4.   **End the practice of awarding business on the basis of the price tag. Instead, minimize total cost. Move toward a single supplier for any one item, building a long-term relationship of loyalty and trust.** Dr. Deming's feelings on this subject are presented in the following quotation. He is referring to the purchase of municipal buses from the lowest bidder.

> To have somebody that knows something about quality, they'd have to pay money. Such people are high priced. But they would save untold sums of money. It requires only a third-grade drop-out to observe which price is the lowest, and he's the one that gets the job.
>
> There's a better way today. We're in a new economic age, which requires that suppliers give statistical evidence of quality in the form of control charts and evidence that they are working on all 14 points. Quality and competition are not directly related when the goal is the low-bidder. All bidders for a product or service should be required to prove that they employ statistical process control and that the products they are offering are in statistical control. When this happens bidders will be forced to look for the best with the lowest cost of ownership cost. Additionally, this will force bidders to develop long-term relationships with their suppliers who are in statistical control and able to provide quality parts, not low-priced parts. In the long term, high quality parts in statistical control will be low cost parts (Mann, 1987).

5.   **Constantly improve production and service system to improve quality and productivity and thus constantly decrease cost.** Don't wait for things to go wrong. Put the entire work force in a posture to find problems before defects occur. Plan for a system that is forever in control, forever getting better. Retrain quality inspectors to become teachers of statistical control and facilitators of experimental design. Make them a part of each work unit.

6.   **Institute training on the job.** An employer cannot expect to hire fully trained employees. Company training is therefore mandatory. Training is a continuous

---

[7]Mann, in *The Keys to Excellence*, makes the point that the Agriculture industry has used statistical design of experiments for years and is dominant in the world food market.

process that matches the needs of the worker to the requirements of the system. Both benefit through increased satisfaction and productivity. Statistical methods should be used to determine what training is needed, and when it is complete. As training becomes effective, product quality improves. In those rare cases where the proper training has not improved the output of a unit or individual, the system needs to be re-examined. In some rare cases, the unit or individual may have to be relocated or discharged.

7. **Institute leadership (see point 12a). The aim of leadership should be to help people and machines do a better job.** Too little attention is given to training supervisors and ensuring they are managing in statistical control. Management must teach supervisors what their jobs are and allow them to ask questions. The supervisor should serve as a coach, helping system workers solve problems. Foremen and mid-level supervisors are essential to quality education. And top leaders must recognize that continuous improvement is the means to achieve customer satisfaction. The leaders of organizations must find ways to reduce the amount of time foremen and supervisors spend doing nonproductive work. Some activities and situations that are commonly found in organizations and that might be classified as nonproductive are:

- Weekly sign-off of time cards verifying attendance
- Inspection of incoming parts between divisions
- Clerks in approval cycle of manager's travel request
- Work measurement system
- More quality standards
- An acceptable quality level
- Ineffective communications systems
- Travel instead of teleconferencing
- No preferred suppliers list
- Required second sourcing
- 400-page requests for proposal (RFPs) and 800-page proposals

8. **Drive out fear, so that everyone may work effectively.** Dr. Deming estimates that probably 80% of American workers do not know and are afraid to ask what their jobs are (Mann, 1987).

> And why is the American worker afraid? Well, somebody trained him, maybe the foreman. But he still doesn't understand what to do. Or there is some material that is unsuited to the purpose. He asks for help two or three times, but the foreman never has any time or tells him, 'Well, it's the way I told you.' So the worker doesn't wish to be a trouble maker. He works in fear (Mann, 1987).

Top managers are not only responsible for other components of the system, but also for supervision. Supervision that instills fear and fosters ignorance is intolerable. Like other parts of the system, supervision must be trained in statistical process control techniques so they can identify quality costs and help workers eliminate barriers to quality. Supervisors must not be afraid to ask questions, flag problem areas, and make suggestions.

9. **Break down barriers between departments. People in research, design, sales, and production must work as a team.** The time has come to break down the walls that nurture parochialism within the system. These walls prevent cooperative work between and across functions. The lack of cross-functional assignments has contributed to worker ignorance of the total organization. This must change! Everyone must contribute to the system's goals. Multifunctional teams with common goals and objectives should be the goal of every senior executive officer, divisional manager, supervisor, foreman, and worker.

10. **Eliminate slogans, exhortations, and targets for the work force asking for zero defects and new levels of productivity.** If the company president wouldn't hang the poster in his office, it doesn't belong on the shop floor. Posters should reflect company goals, the status of the work being done, and work that is not yet under statistical control but is getting there. Give the workers a map of where they have been, where they are, and where they are going. (A slogan like "Zero Defects" tells them what is expected but not how to get there.) "The slogan advertises to the work force that management is helpless to solve the problems of the company. Do they need to advertise? The workers already know it (Mann, 1987)."

11a. **Replace work standards (quotas) on the factory floor with leadership.** Work standards have a way of limiting improvement because the workers know that their every movement is measured and gauged. The best form of work measurement in a production operation is statistical process control. Once a process is in control and the efficiencies found, no work measurement system will improve the process. Quotas emphasize quantity over quality, leading eventually to higher cost.

11b. **Eliminate management by objective. Eliminate management by numbers. Substitute leadership.** Management by objectives is the misapplication of a good concept. Objectives are established by management and forced to lower levels where lower level objectives must be created to support the higher level ones. This imposes a requirement on system workers without giving them a means to satisfy it. Further, the documentation required–along with the cheating that occurs in reporting the progress–is counter-productive. Managing through the use of vision, goals, and objectives can be effective, however. If two levels of the organization reach a clear understanding of the organization's vision, the documentation can be the same as that used to measure and maintain process control.

12a. **Remove barriers that rob the hourly worker of his or her right to pride of workmanship. The responsibility of supervisors must be changed from numbers to quality.** Satisfied workers do not set out to produce bad products or provide poor service. If they do a poor job, it is because the system failed to ensure they had the support they needed or clearly understood what was required. To ensure they know when a worker is about to fail, managers must establish communication lines through which information can freely pass. These lines of communication are critical; through them come warnings of approaching dangers. Teamwork requires communication and inspires pride in daily work.

12b.   **Abolish the annual merit rating.** TQM offers a replacement for annual ratings: statistical process control and teamwork. Bill Scherkenbach said the performance system "destroys teamwork and cooperation, fosters mediocrity, increases variability, and focuses on the short term. In addition, it treats people like commodities and promotes fear and loss of self-worth (Mann, 1987)." But, an annual performance system can work if the areas of measurement are changed to teamwork, long-term goals, and continuous process improvement. Too often, annual appraisals are based on outcomes not under the control of the individual, but rather the system. Only about 15% of a company's processes are under the control of workers; the other 85% are under the control of management (Hayes, 1985). Appraisal systems will work if they are applied fairly consistent with the goals and objectives of the organization, and provide information the worker can use for continuous self-improvement.

13.   **Institute a vigorous program of education and self-improvement.** TQM is effective when everyone in the organization is trained in basic statistical process methods. They must understand these methods and use them to solve problems. As the entire organization is trained in statistical process control, it frames the way the organization looks at problems and corrects quality deficiencies.

14.   **Put everyone in the company to work on the transformation.** It is not only important to put in a system for continuous improvement, but it is also important that everyone be involved in making the system better.

If there is one thing different between TQM and previous management programs, it is that TQM is for everyone.

CONCLUSION

Total Quality Management is not new. The basic concepts presented have been with us since the 50s. They include such business practices as focusing our efforts on customers, both internal and external; training our people to do the job we expect, eliminating barriers that inhibit good performance, and continuously improving every task we perform.

Successful leaders recognize that a total quality transformation of their organizations will not happen over night. They establish long-term visions, prepare their companies and employees for a quality change through training and education, and then systematically and consistently begin the journey toward total quality.

REFERENCES

Department of Defense, "Total Quality Management," Washington, DC, Brochure, p. 2.

Department of Defense, "Total Quality Management Master Plan," August 1988, p. 1.

DoD 5000.51-G, Final draft, *Total Quality Management Guide*, 23 August 1989.

Feigenbaum, A. B., *Total Quality Control*, New York: McGraw-Hill, 1983, p. 6.

Harrington, James H. "A Guideline to Improvement," This unpublished paper is distributed
    by OSD. Dr. Harrington is President of Harrington, Hurd & Reiker.

Hayes, Glenn E., *Quality and Productivity: The New Challenge*, Hitchcock Publishing:
    Wheaton, IL, 1985, p. 106.

Mann, Nancy R., *The Keys to Excellence*, Prestwide Books, 1987.

OASD (P&L) TQM-IPQ Fact Sheer, Subject: Total Quality Management, 4 May 1989.

Stuelpnagel, Thomas R., "Improved US Defense Total Quality Control," *National Defense*
    72, May/June 1988, pp. 43-48; and "Total Quality Management", *National Defense*
    72, November 1988, pp. 57-62.

ADDENDUM 2

LEADERSHIP, POWER, AND THE MISSING LINK: THE BASIS OF TOTAL QUALITY MANAGEMENT[1]

The corporation of today did not spring whole from the head of Peter Drucker. Like everything else, it is the product of an evolutionary process. Having evolved through a "machine" stage and an "organism" stage, the corporation has now reached the *organization* stage (Ackhoff, 1981).

Therefore, to understand today's corporation, one must first understand what an organization is:

A purposeful system that is part of one or more purposeful systems ... parts of which, people, have purposes of their own (Ackoff, 1981).

Purpose, then, is a key element of today's corporation. An organization's purposes are usually multileveled–societal, organizational, and individual–and interrelated. The people who are part of the organization also have purposes which are multileveled and interrelated. The premier purpose of the organization, however, is to achieve some level of *performance*. To do that, the organization evolved a supervisory or *management* function.

Like an organization, the management function has interdependent types of responsibilities: 1) the system they manage–control, 2) the people who are part of the managed system–humanization, and 3) the containing system and other systems that it contains–environmentalization (Ackoff, 1981).

If today's management falls short of the ideal–and little about the present corporate environment would suggest otherwise–then the bulk of the blame may fall upon the way management executes its responsibilities in the *human* sector. Success in the other two areas–control and environment–will not overcome shortcomings in the human side. One can manage things, but one must *lead* people; otherwise, supervisors will never be able to channel the corporation's people with their many purposes toward accomplishment of the organization's objectives.

Today's managers are better at managing than they are at leading. This ability gap must be filled if we are to evolve today's corporations into tomorrow's organizations: ones which *respect* and *value* their people, *enable* and *encourage* them to meet their own goals and, at the same time, *achieve the organizational mission*.

In this paper we shall examine the humanization aspect of management, explore the differences between management and leadership, and identify the "missing link" between management and leadership. These are all integral to the successful development of Total

---

[1]This addendum was written by Tasso Christie.

Quality Management (TQM)–which challenges executives to manage firms in a completely new way.

The challenge of TQM is achievable if executives view the human assets of their firm not as things to be managed, but as people who contribute to their own as well as organizational purposes. This change in perspective compels a change in tactics. Instead of using external stimulants such as money and incentive plans to motivate people to work harder or smarter, today's executives must motivate employees with job satisfaction and the feelings that result when people know they are valued and respected. Such motivation comes from a leadership culture which encourages employees to contribute, systematically provides the training they need to do so, fosters an environment that rewards such contributions, and maintains a climate of dignity and respect.

The ultimate issue is not management, but leadership.

WHAT IS LEADERSHIP?

There are no simple answers. Many authorities speak of leadership and leaders in other-worldly tones, and comment as much about the *absence* of certain characteristics as they do on the *presence* of certain others.

L. P. Williams, for example, believes that leaders radiate an inspirational aura, and that leadership

> ... is the ability to tie men and women to one's person and cause. But how is that done? Leadership is obviously a combination of many things ... When pressures increase, we turn to those we trust to act in the general interest .... Some people simply seem to have an aura around them that inspires trust and confidence. We have faith in them and in their ability to deal with matters in a way that will be satisfactory to us. They inspire our confidence and we grant them our loyalty. These are the qualities that unite followers and that leaders, somehow, in some mysterious way, are able to call forth. Quite simply, we know leadership when we experience it (Williams, 1980).

WHAT ARE THE CHARACTERISTICS OF A LEADER?

Perhaps our corporations lack leadership and leaders precisely because there is so little understanding of what these things are. James McGregor Burns echoed this sentiment when he said,

> The crisis of leadership today is the mediocrity or irresponsibility of so many of the men and women in power .... The fundamental crisis underlying mediocrity is intellectual .... we know far too little about leadership. We fail to grasp the essence of leadership that is relevant to the modern age .... Leadership is one of the most observed and least understood phenomena on earth (Burns, 1978).

We could describe leadership as the effective use of self to influence the thoughts and actions of others, but this is only part of the task. Leadership is a multidimensional phenomenon; we must therefore specify the attributes of leaders in the context of many of these dimensions, such as those presented in Figure 1.

Dimensions	Leaders
Attitudes Toward Goals	Personal
	Active in shaping ideas instead of responding to them
	Change way people think about what's desirable, possible, necessary
Conceptions of Work	Projects ideas into images that excite people
	Translates images into understandable concepts
	Divergent, creates options
	Cannot tolerate mundane
	Creates shared ideas
	Seeks out risk and danger
	Arouses expectations and mobilizes action
Relations with Others	Prefers solitary activities
	Relates intuitively and empathetically
	Focus on "what" events and decisions mean to participants
Sense of Self	Feel separate from his/her environment
	Depend on personal ability and mastery of events for identity
	"Twice-born" development through personal mastery
	Establish and breakoff intensive one-to-one relationships

Figure 1 The Dimensions of Leadership Characteristics (Burke, 1985)

These may be the ideal. The reality, however, is likely to be quite different, as anyone with experience in a corporate environment will testify. This is because, as corporations evolved, a new power ethic emerged: an ethic which favored collective over individual leadership, and the cult of the group over personal expression; an ethic which ensured competence, control, and a power balance among competitive groups, but did not "... ensure imagination, creativity or ethical behavior" in corporate life (Zaleznik, 1977).

This new power ethic spawned by corporations is "a new breed called the manager (Zaleznik, 1977)."

MANAGERS DIFFER GREATLY FROM LEADERS

Managers differ greatly from leaders in terms of goals, careers, relations with others and with themselves. When one compares the attributes of managers with those of leaders, it is obvious that this "new breed called the manager" did not develop in response to the need for a system that would stimulate effectiveness or create excitement. It emerged as a way of avoiding confrontation with the issue of *power*. Figure 2 provides a comparison of the characteristics of leaders and managers:

Dimensions for Comparison	Leaders	Managers
Attitudes Toward Goals	Personal	Impersonal
	Active in shaping ideas instead of responding to them	Reactive and passive
		Develop from necessities (not desires)
	Change way people think about what's desirable, possible, necessary	Embedded in history and culture of organization
		Tinkerers re-innovation; no grand design
Conceptions of Work	Projects ideas into images that excite people	An enabling process of coordinating and balancing
	Translates images into understandable concepts	Shifts balance of power toward solution and compromise
	Divergent, creates options	Negotiates and bargains
	Cannot tolerate mundane	Limited in visualizing purpose and value
	Creates shared ideas	Limits options
	Seeks out risk and danger	Employs coercion
	Arouses expectations and mobilizes action	Perpetuates group conflict
Relations with Others	Prefer solitary activities	Prefer to work with people (solitary makes them anxious)
	Relate intuitively and empathetically	Relate to roles
	Focus on "what" events and decisions mean to participants	Requires people to operate at levels of status and responsibility
		Attends to "how" things get done
		Focuses attention on procedure, not substance, how to make decisions not what decisions
		Low level of emotional involvement
		Uses "signals" instead of "messages"
		Tries to turn win/lose to win/win
		Seeks compromise
		Establishes balance of power
Sense of Self	Feel separate from his/her environment	Belong to environment (controlled by it)
	Depend on personal ability and mastery of events for identity	Depend on membership, role, for identity (conceive of self as role)
	Establish and breakoff intensive one-to-one relationships	Form moderate and widely distributed attachments

Figure 2 A Comparison of Leaders and Managers (Burke, 1985)

POWER

Power: the ability to make things happen in the way one wants them to; the force that makes things happen in an intended way; the ability to get others to do what one wants —or, as Rosabeth Moss Kanter puts it, "America's last dirty word (Kanter, 1979)."

People avoid confronting the issue of power because they are uncomfortable with the concept of power–even, in many cases, offended by the very notion. Many believe that power is inextricable from coercion and exploitation. They believe, further, that power in the hands of an individual entails too many human risks–including the risk of equating power with the ability to get immediate results; the risk of ignoring the many different ways people can legitimately accumulate power, and the risk of losing self-control in the pursuit of power (Zaleznik, 1977).

To have and use power is to possess the ability and the willingness to transform. This *transformational* use of power, which is the central element of leadership, makes many people uneasy. The risks attendant to such power seem far too great; to avoid them, a new, lower level was created: the *transactional* level: management.

The ultimate result of this compromise has been highly unsatisfactory. We weakened our ability to shape the corporation's people, purposes and processes toward performance. In many cases, we have seriously limited the firm's productive life-span.

THE ROAD TO LEADERSHIP

The road to leadership begins with an acceptance of an enlightened and positive perspective on power. Power is a pervasive; it exists everywhere. It is basic to all organizations, to all human interaction. Power is not by definition good or evil. It is neutral.

From a more practical perspective, power alone does not necessarily lead to results, but lack of power most certainly prohibits them. Power may not always overcome inertia, but the absence of power sustains it. Furthermore, power is central to leadership. It is, in fact,

> ... the reciprocal of leadership ... the basic energy needed to initiate and sustain action ... the *capacity to translate intention* into reality *and sustain it* ... Leadership is the wise use of this power: *transformative* leadership ... Vision is the commodity of leaders, and power is their currency (Bennis and Nanus, 1985).

If leaders are to lead, then the issue and impact of power can not be avoided, they must be confronted and understood. Leadership inevitably requires using power to influence the thoughts and actions of others. It includes effective use of self and others in arriving at collective goals for the benefit of the group. An open acceptance of power, and its resultant constructive use, is what separates leaders (who are transformational) from managers (who are transactional). This comparison is presented in Figure 3.

Dimensions for Comparison	Leaders	Managers
Theme	Heroes & Ideologues Leadership/Transformation	Group leadership Bargainers/Bureaucrats
Emotional involvement	With the institution, ideas and vision Charismatic Transforms, never leaves things as found	With the task and people associated with the task Goal oriented
Personal life	Work and personal/private life not too distinguishable	Separates work from private life
Achieves commitment	By inspiration, positive other-regard	By involvement
Holds people accountable via	Implicit, guilt induction Wants whole person Movement toward a purpose	Explicit, contractual transactions ("deal") Wants task accomplishment
Value emphasis	Terminal End-state	Instrumental Means
Problems	Create them (problem finding)	Fix them (problem solving)
Plans	Strategic and long range	Tactical and short range
Appreciates from followers/subordinates	Contrariness Thinking	Conformity Response
Engenders in followers/subordinates	Intense feelings—love, sometimes hate Desire to identify Turbulent	Feelings not intense Reactions smoother and steadier
Style	Use themselves as instruments of learning and acting Intuitive flashes Do the right things	Use their accumulation of collective experiences Tinkerers, problem solvers Do things right

**Figure 3 A Comparison of Transformational (Leaders)
and Transactional (Managers) (Burke, 1985)**

LEADERSHIP COMPETENCIES

However, the differences go beyond power, as demonstrated by a study of 90 corporate executives (Bennis and Nanus, 1985). This study identified four leadership competencies. Let us examine them:

Management of attention. This is the ability leaders have to draw others to them. Leaders have a vision, a dream, a set of intentions, a frame of reference; they attract and enroll people with these. Leaders also manage attention by communicating an extraordinary focus of commitment, and have an abiding faith in people's need for excellence (Hall, 1980).

Management of meaning. Leaders know that people will work at their highest level when they find meaning and challenge in their work. Leaders strive, therefore, to communicate their visions, dreams, intentions and commitments effectively, and to make them real and meaningful to their followers. What sets leaders apart is that they communicate these things not simply through words, but also through action: by appreciating the needs of others for personal worth and self-respect; by recognizing the work people do as an important means to their self-expression, development, and health; by organizing work in a way that encourages the expression of individual competence (Hall, 1980).

Management of trust. When a manager faithfully exhibits reliability or constancy, when "you always know where she's coming from or what he stands for" (Bennis and Nanus, 1985), there is trust: an essential component to all organizations. Leaders initiate trust, intuitively understanding that trust is a catalytic process, that trust begets trust, and that "... when trust is high ... people and people-systems function well (Gibb, 1978)." Leaders are acutely conscious of the effect of social transactions on both the quality and productivity of working relationships. They set a personal example of open, authentic and collaborative interpersonal practices. Workplaces so led are characterized by mutual reliance, candor, trust, and fun (Hall, 1980).

Management of self. A leader has a clear view of his/her limitations as well as strengths, and seeks to overcome personal weaknesses, but always deploys her/his existing skills effectively. This effective "management of self" enables the leader to move beyond role-behavior and role-expectations and to create a collaborative, interactive and creative job environment (Gibb, 1978).

These four competencies of leadership, then, describe a leader as someone who is committed to an ideal or vision; a person who can explain to those with whom she/he works the essence of that vision; one whose reliability or constancy is persistent (someone you can depend on); and, finally, a leader has an awareness of self and an ability to use self constructively, in exchanges with others.

But one senses something missing from this roster of attributes. Alone, they do not explain how leaders make the difference between achieving goals, or only moving toward them; between a work force composed of people who are excited about going to work as opposed to those who show up because they need the money.

This missing link—to which all the others are a subset—is the ability leaders have *to empower those around them*. To enable people to accomplish their tasks more readily. To permit them to experience the excitement that comes from successfully shepherding a project to completion.

Empowerment is the ability to create power; to enable or to permit. For leaders, empowerment is an act of building, developing and giving away power; it is "freedom from self (Ackerman, 1984)," an ability to consider the needs of others. Empowerment must be interactive to be effective.

Empowerment can be described as consisting of six components: (Murrell, 1984)

- *Educating* is the way power is created by sharing information and knowledge in an interactive process between expert and seeker.
- *Leading* is the act of inspiring, rewarding, directing others in a less intensive form than mentoring.
- *Structuring* is the creation of structural, opposed to personal, factors which produce empowerment.
- *Providing* resources needed for people to get their jobs done and feel good about themselves in the process.
- *Mentoring*, a close personal relationship by a more senior person that leading cannot usually provide.
- *Actualizing*. The sum of the above, the synergistic result, the *gestalt* under the control of the person.

The idea of empowerment is not universally embraced. Some believe that power is a finite quantity and therefore cannot be created, only redistributed. However, power is, in fact, an unlimited resource that exists in every human exchange, in varying degrees. Its existence may not be recognized, or if it is, it may not be an issue between the parties to the exchange (Murrell, 1984).

Empowerment is also shunned by those with power who are threatened by the idea of creating power, or empowering others. This is the fear which led to the creation of "the new breed called managers," a fear we must eliminate to create effective leaders.

It is necessary to look at TQM more carefully in order to see how leaders and managers can set in motion the required new management paradigm. It should be increasingly clear that the present attributes of managers do not fit the model of supervision that encourages self-management and project activities that require the work of a team.

None of this is to claim that the role for the transactional manager in today's organization is obsolete. Clearly, there are roles in some functions of certain organizations which are better fulfilled by a transactional manager than a transformational leader. It is even possible for managers to practice empowerment–though the effects of the empowering process for managers based on role differ significantly from those of leaders. Some of these differences are shown in Figure 4.

Empowering Process for Followers and Subordinates	Leaders	Managers
Providing Direction	Via ideals, vision, a higher purpose, super-ordinate goals Pulls	Via involvement of subordinates in determining paths toward goal accomplishment Pushes
Stimulating	With ideas and meaning Make dreams apparent	With action Things to accomplish
Rewarding	Informal Personal recognition Trust, reliable, constant	Formal Incentive systems
Developing	By inspiration to do more than they thought they could Through self, enabling others	By involving them in important decision-making activities Providing feedback for potential learning
Appealing	Of followership and dependency	For autonomy and independency

**Figure 4 Differences in the Empowering Process
As a Function of Role-Leaders Compared with Managers** (Burke, 1985)

As the corporation continues to evolve, the responsibilities of executives will intensify; and nowhere will this intensification be felt as acutely as in the utilization of the corporation's human resources. In response to this intensification, our supervisory function must transform itself from a transactional management style to a transformational leadership style, which requires the adoption of the four competencies of leadership described earlier.

Yet, as we have seen, even these will not be enough. The promise of Total Quality Management–and the corporation of the future–can only be achieved by the transformational leader who has the vision to mobilize the human assets of the organization through personal empowerment.

REFERENCES

Ackerman, Linda S., *The Transformational Manager: Facilitating The Flow State, The 1984 Annual: Developing Human Resources*, San Diego: University Associates, Inc., 1984, pp. 252.

Ackhoff, Russell, *Creating the Corporation Future: Plan or Be Planned For*, New York: John Wiley & Sons, 1981, pp. 29-49.

Bennis, Warren, and Nanus, Burt, *Leaders: The Strategies For Taking Charge*, New York: Harper & Row, 1985, pp. 16-18.

Burke, Warner, San Diego, 1985.

Burns, James McGregor, *Leadership*, New York: Harper & Row, 1978, pp. 1-2.

Gibb, Jack, *Trust: A New View of Personal and Organizational Development*, Los Angeles, CA: The Guild of Tutors Press, 1978, pp. 15-16.

Hall, Jay, *The Competence Process: Management For Commitment and Creativity*, The Woodlands, TX: Teleometrics International, 1980, p. 219.

Kanter, Rosabeth Moss, *Men and Women of the Corporation*, New York: Basic, 1979, p. 65.

Murrell, Kenneth L., *Empowerment: New Concepts and New Thinking About Power* (Unpublished, Mimeographed, 1984), pp. 8-10.

"The Total Quality Management Story", *Harris Conversations for the 90s*, Chicago: Harris Trust & Savings Bank, 1991.

Williams, L.P., "Parallel Lives", *Executive 6*, 1980, pp. 8-12.

Zaleznik, Abraham, "Managers and Leaders: Are They Different?" *Harvard Business Review* May/June 1977, pp. 67-78.

Chapter 3

CUSTOMER FOCUS

IMPORTANCE OF CUSTOMER FOCUS

Customer focus is the entrance and exit to TQM (Ishikawa, 1985). The reaction of many people to this idea is that paying close attention to customers' needs, wants and expectations is just common sense. The only difficulty is, in this case, "common sense" is not all that common in organizations and businesses in the U.S. Think of your own recent experience purchasing products and services: how many times have you had to return or repair items, how many times have you waited on lines to receive "service", how many times have you been treated by store personnel like they were doing you a favor by waiting on you?

There are many reasons why customer focus is frequently a weakness in many organizations:

1. We like to believe we know what customers want better than they do. The approach of American business has often been to develop products/services and then convince customers they want them, through slick marketing techniques.

2. An arm's length relationship has existed between customers and suppliers, imposed by the American obsession with competition. This phenomenon has been particularly prevalent in Government contracting.

3. Listening to the customer often means we have to hear negative feedback to which we would really rather not be exposed. Opening oneself up to criticism by the customer is difficult and requires personal courage.

4. Effective techniques for discerning customers' needs, wants and expectations have not been developed or taught. We must develop better techniques to focus on customers' needs, and make sure our work force is trained and motivated to use these techniques.

5. Managers have made the assumption all they need to do is tell their employees to treat customers well and it will happen. What happens more frequently, however, is employees treat customers the same way management

treats employees. In many organizations, this translates to customers being treated like second class citizens, as this is the way employees have been treated by management.

6. It is easier for management to blame lack of clearly defined customer requirements on the customer, than it is to take responsibility, and work hard to define customer needs/requirements.

7. Some organizations believe they have so many different customers with differing needs (that sometimes conflict) that to attempt to discern what "customers" need and satisfy their needs is difficult, if not impossible.

8. Some government organizations have difficulty recognizing "customers" and prefer believing they only have a "mission."

9. Individual or group performance is rarely appraised on customer satisfaction, especially internal customer satisfaction. This is especially true in organizations with "TURF-TYPE" systems.

WHO ARE CUSTOMERS?

We are used to thinking about our customers as the ultimate user of our product or service. However, within organizations we are used to thinking about individuals with whom we work as headaches. We often think of them as people for whom we have to do unreasonable things in unreasonable timeframes. Total quality recognizes two types of customers: internal and external. External customers are the ultimate users of the organization's products and services. Internal customers are those individuals within an organization to whom you supply a product or service. Finance personnel supply project cost information to their project manager customers. Personnel supplies new hires to their organizational customers. Payroll supplies paychecks to employee customers. The training department supplies training to its trainee customers as well as the trainees' parent division. Within organizations, everyone is a customer of the preceding operation. Even the most simple processes usually have several customer and supplier interactions.

Many employees think they have only two customers: "their boss", and the outside customer who buys or uses the product or service. They are correct in considering the purchaser/user of their product/service to be an external customer, however, their boss should more often be considered a supplier, not a customer. The boss is a supplier of strategic direction, boundaries, resources, time, rewards, training, materials, etc. This is a very difficult conceptual transition for many employees and managers.

INTERNAL CUSTOMERS - Those within your organization to whom you provide inputs, materials, products, services or information.

EXTERNAL CUSTOMERS - Those outside your organization to whom you provide products and services.

Within an organization there are many "chains" of customer-supplier relationships. As each "customer" receives something from his "supplier", their role changes from customer to supplier to the next individual in the chain. Each individual is the customer of the preceding operation.

CUSTOMER-SUPPLIER PARTNERSHIPS

To create an environment where customer focus is possible requires establishing a non-adversarial, partnership relationship between customers and suppliers. This requires building trust where, quite often, significant distrust used to exist. Just as a total quality orientation requires management's behavior towards its employees to be based on trust; so also it requires management's behavior towards its suppliers to be based on trust.

There has been a lot of emphasis on businesses becoming "world class". This means becoming the best in the world at whatever it is you do, that is, consistently delivering goods and services which fully meet or exceed customers' needs and expectations. The expression became popular as global competition increased and American businesses began to suffer market losses to other countries. Although suppliers need to relentlessly pursue customer satisfaction excellence, customers have obligations to be world class also.

"World class customers" take an active role in the customer-supplier partnership. They don't portray the attitude: "I am the customer. Customers have more rights and are more important than suppliers. Service me." To be a world class customer means doing the following:

- Inviting suppliers to participate in strategic/long range planning.

- Assisting suppliers to achieve total quality, process control, and process improvement by sharing training and/or providing coaches.

- Eliminating the practice of awarding contracts to the lowest bidder. Ensure total acquisition costs are considered.

- Sharing relevant performance data with suppliers. Some prime contractors take materials/sub-assemblies provided to them by subcontractors and install them in higher assemblies. When these higher level assemblies are tested and the suppliers sub-assembly fails, some primary customers may trouble-shoot and fix the defect themselves, without feeding these data back to the sub-assembly supplier.

- Providing a clear definition of requirements, derived from needs, wants and expectations.

- Inviting interchange and comments to clarify requirements.

- Managing and improving customer satisfaction processes (e.g., the process of requirements definition can be defined and continuously improved just like any other process).

- Not accepting marginal quality (from either internal or external suppliers), that is, quality which doesn't fully meet needs or expectations.

- Rewarding (not shooting) messengers who are taking responsibility for the problem and who's intent is to improve the process. A problem exposed is an opportunity for improvement. A hidden problem is an invitation to disaster.

- Doing it right the first time. Don't drag your suppliers through the knot hole of unnecessary changes.

- Investing in and pursuing continuous learning and skill development.

- Benchmarking with other world class customers.

Many organizations give awards/recognition to their best suppliers. Some companies are talking about giving their best *customers* a "Customer-of-the-Year" award to encourage customers to behave in world class ways as well.

GUIDELINES FOR FOCUSING ON CUSTOMERS' REQUIREMENTS

Requirements from the customer can be categorized in four ways: basic, performance, mandated and excitement.

- **Basic** requirements are those which are so fundamental to the product or service they are rarely mentioned. For example, when purchasing an automobile, if a salesperson asked you what features you were looking for, rarely would you mention such basic features as a rear view mirror, capability to vent fresh air into the car, or a glove compartment. These are the things that customers and suppliers assume are required—but often our assumptions don't match.

  Aleta Holub, Vice President of Quality Assurance, First National Bank of Chicago, Illinois, ordered a ham and cheese sandwich at a cafeteria at the University of Texas in Austin. She assumed it would be made with american cheese because that's how she always gets it in Chicago. However, in this UT cafeteria, ordering "ham and cheese" gets you swiss, not american. Both the customer (Aleta) and the supplier (UT) assumed the basic requirement of cheese to mean two different things. The result: customer dissatisfaction.

- **Performance** features relate to what you want the product or service to do: an auto which gets at least 40 miles per gallon, a hamburger cooked medium rare, or light starch in your shirts.

- **Mandated** requirements derive from regulatory agencies, for example the requirements for emissions systems, safety glass, and seat belts in autos.

- **Excitement/Delight** requirements are those that we may not perceive as necessary, but that really turn us on. All other things being equal, they frequently make the difference in why we purchase one product or service over another. In a speech to the Association for Quality and Participation in October 1990, Tom Peters suggested requirements in the excitement category would provide the competitive advantage of the next decade, "The consumer wants glow and tingle (Peters, 1990)."

Identifying customer requirements isn't difficult conceptually. However, it can be difficult to accomplish due to:

- Geographically diverse customers.
- Adversarial relationships between you and your customers. Customers who don't trust their suppliers may not want to be very open about their requirements.
- Investment in your product or service.
- Poor listening skills.
- Arrogance.
- Not seeing yourself as a true partner.
- Unwillingness to change or adapt.

In focusing on your customers and their requirements, you should keep the following things in mind:

- It is important to ask the right questions:

    1. What are you in business/existence to do or serve?

    2. Who are your customers?

    3. Who are you supporting?

    4. Who else should you be supporting?

5. Who are you supporting that you shouldn't be?

6. What are your customers' needs, wants, expectations and preferences?

7. How do they measure if your product/service satisfies them?

8. How do you measure if your product/service satisfies them?

9. How well does your product/service currently satisfy them?

10. What are opportunities for improving customer satisfaction?

- You should ask questions to get the answers you need, not the answers you want. Nobody likes bad news and criticism, but unless problems are discovered they cannot be eliminated. The alternative to learning bad news may be far more unpleasant: stick your head in the sand and watch your business/job disappear to a competitor. Sometimes it is easier for customers to describe what they don't want/like, rather than what they do want/like. If you are having difficulty getting customers to identify their requirements, try asking them to characterize what makes a "bad" product or service. A contingency diagram can be used to brainstorm what makes a bad product or service.

- Form partnerships with your customers. Develop a relationship of trust so your customers will share information about their present and anticipated needs and wants with you.

- Anticipate changes in customers' needs. Don't focus on the present to the exclusion of the future. Get to know your customers so well that you are able to anticipate needed changes to products and services. Include identification of changes to future needs, wants, and expectations in your planning. Anticipating changes to your customers' needs is as important as satisfying their present needs.

- Put in place a method to gather feedback from customers whenever products and services are provided.

- Listen well. Conceptually, this is the most simple and yet it is often the most difficult to practice.

- Walk in your customers' shoes. Try to be your own customer. Call your office and see how customers are treated on the phone. Order something from your company, and see how long it takes, and in what condition it arrives. Eat in your own restaurant, stay in your hotel, or execute a transaction in your bank, insurance company, etc. Do what ever you can to experience the perspective of your customer.

- Analyze your own behavior when you are in the role of "customer." Are you demanding, unreasonable, difficult to work with, focused on price? This says something about how you view your customers.

CUSTOMER FOCUS TOOLS & TECHNIQUES

The following section presents several tools and techniques which can be helpful in focusing on customers and their underlying needs and requirements:

- Group Interviews/Focus Groups

- Active Listening/Rogerian Feedback

- Questionnaires/Surveys

- Requirements Breakdown Structure

- Brainstorming/Crawford Pink Slips

- Contingency Diagram

- Gymnastic Scoring Technique

- Quality Function Deployment

GROUP INTERVIEWS/FOCUS GROUPS

Purpose:

- To gather data from customers on their requirements

- To obtain feedback on customer satisfaction

- To obtain benchmarking data

How Used:

Group interviews are simple in nature, but can be quite difficult to execute well. If the issue, requirement or problem spans across more than one area, be sure the group is cross-functional, (i.e., is composed of representatives from appropriate functional areas). It is important to establish an environment of trust and openness, and to state the objective of the group interview clearly. If you are facilitating a group interview, it is a good idea to have a non-participant scribe dedicated to recording the data generated at the interview.

A good way to get the conversation rolling is to ask the group to brainstorm what makes "bad" products. For example, what makes "bad" software systems? Or what makes "bad" program management? Often it is easier to enumerate how something makes you dissatisfied, than it is to identify what you really want.

If your purpose is to identify customer requirements, be sure to invite your customers' comments on basic, performance, mandated/regulatory and excitement/delight categories of requirements.

Data Collected By This Method Can Include:

What are the customers' requirements?
How severe is a customer satisfaction problem?
How many customers does it affect?
What is the impact of the problem?
What are the potential causes of the problem?
When does the problem occur?
Can/has data been collected to verify opinions?
Where does the problem occur?
Have efforts to solve it already been undertaken?

Invite representatives of all those affected by a problem or issue. If the purpose is to generate and discuss requirements, ensure representatives are invited from marketing, design engineering, manufacturing engineering, research and development, field services, customers, finance/capital assets, procurement, technical documentation people, and personnel.

If you are a managerial intermediary between your customer and your supplier, you must **make sure the supplier is part of the group process** for two reasons: 1) their interaction is critical to achieving an optimized system, and 2) the more direct communication is, the more effective it is.

Key Skills Needed To Use This Tool:

Good Facilitation Skills
Gatekeeping Skills
Clarifying Skills
Listening Skills
Non Defensiveness
Ability To Ask Good Follow-up Questions

When Used:

When requirements, issues, and problems are multi-disciplined and cross functional. To gather data for further analysis.

Advantages:

Interaction can lead to great synergy
Can aid in promoting teamwork
Low cost technique
Greater acceptance of changes

Disadvantages:

It is hard to be as objective and non-defensive as this forum requires.
If trust is lacking, meeting can generate bad data. Bad data are sometimes worse than no data.
It is hard to get groups used to competing against each other, to work with each other.
The process is unstructured and requires a good facilitator.

ACTIVE LISTENING/ROGERIAN FEEDBACK

===

"I know you believe you understand what you think I said, but I am not sure you realize that what you heard is not what I meant."

Anonymous

Purpose:

- To ensure effective listening

How Used:

This is a well-known technique of the humanist psychologist, Carl Rogers. Known as active listening, it is not often used because most people believe it is unnecessary. No one wants to believe he/she is not a good listener. Very simply, it involves repeating back or re-phrasing what you thought the speaker said. It is more effective to use varied techniques to re-phrase, not just "what I think I heard you say is ..."

Key Skills Needed To Use This Tool:

Patience
Mental Alertness
Courage

When Used:

Should be used all the time, but it is especially critical when it is important you "get it" like the customer really meant it.

Advantages:

Only costs you time.

Disadvantages:

If done like an automaton, it will drive your customer or supplier crazy.

QUESTIONNAIRES/SURVEYS

===

Purpose:

- To obtain customer data on requirements or performance

How Used:

Must be constructed with great care, so that you get the answers you need, as opposed to the answers you want. If you are constructing a rating scale, it is best to use one to five. Agree-disagree scales can be useful. Always include space for comments so that respondents can add input not effectively solicited by the questionnaire. Always explain the purpose of the questionnaire/survey right up-front in terms that will make the respondent want to answer the survey.

Be sure to plan ahead concerning how the data will be processed and used. Keep the survey as short as possible, and be sure to "pilot" the survey before producing the final form.

Surveys are most often conducted anonymously, to encourage negative comments. However, including an option for the respondent to provide his/her name and phone number will give you an opportunity to clarify or obtain follow-up input.

Key Skills Needed To Use This Tool:

Clear And Concise Writing Ability
Automatic Data Processing Scoring Capability Is Helpful

When Used:

Especially useful when you need input from many sources, especially from large numbers of individuals.

Advantages:

Anonymity allows people to tell it like it is.
Less time consuming than interviewing, if done with large numbers.
Easier to summarize numerical scores than subjective interview data.

Disadvantages:

Response rates are often low and may not be representative of all customers.
Questions are often interpreted differently by different people.
You can easily get carried away. Maintain focus and don't ask for data you won't use.

REQUIREMENTS BREAKDOWN STRUCTURE (RBS)

Purpose:

- To ensure all elements of a requirement are identified

- To clarify the relationship between requirements

- To clarify responsibility for satisfaction of requirements

How Used:

You can use traditional work breakdown structure (WBS) format (with each succeeding level representing a greater degree of detail) or a tree format (where branches go left to right). Starting with the highest level of requirement, break into its component pieces. This breakdown should be based on customer input. Legs of the structure should be as mutually exclusive as possible, and entire structure should be collectively exhaustive (see example).

You can use affinity diagram technique as a first step toward compiling an RBS.

Key Skills Needed To Use This Tool:

Conceptual Ability
Analytic Ability
Ability To Listen

When Used:

To document components of a complex requirement.

Advantages:

Forces you to really think through all the pieces and how they relate.

Disadvantages:

For complex requirements, structure becomes very complicated. May have to use many pages to adequately cover all the levels.

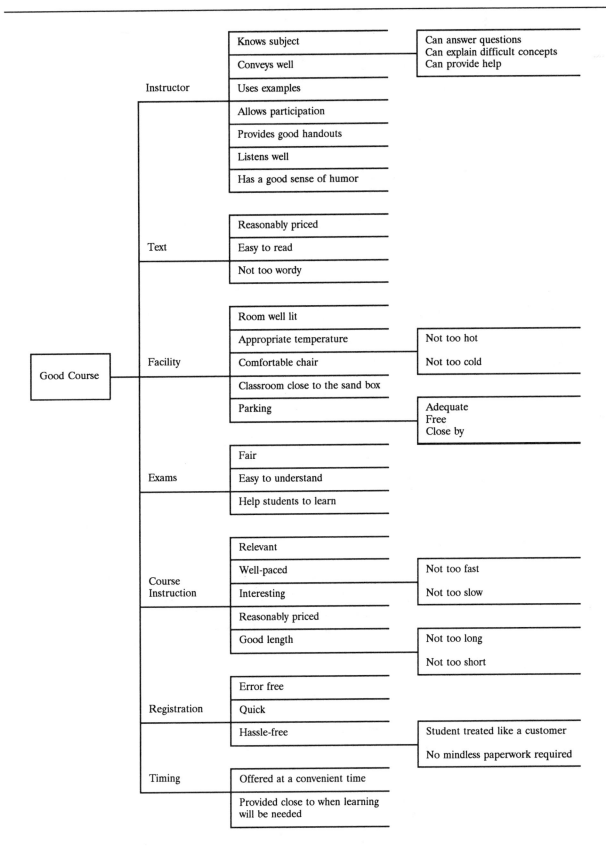

Example: Requirements Breakdown Structure (RBS) for a Good Course

BRAINSTORMING/CRAWFORD PINK SLIPS

==

Purpose:

- To quickly generate, clarify and evaluate ideas

- To obtain new ideas about process problem causes, ways to satisfy the customer, process problem solutions, etc.

- To obtain involvement and commitment from cross-functional groups

How Used:

Invite all participants that have something to offer or whose buy-in is needed.

1. Explain Ground Rules

Free-wheeling generation of ideas
No criticism or evaluation of ideas at the start
No hogging the floor
No using the meeting as an exercise in ego satisfaction or showing how
    smart you want everyone to think you are
If taking turns, it's ok to skip
Stick to the subject, leave baggage at the door

2. Generate Ideas

Use either turn taking or open floor. Record ideas on blackboard or flip charts. Try to get true essence of the idea, if you re-word to shorten, make sure contributor agrees that you have captured the thought. Ask for clarification of any ideas you don't understand.

Encourage creative thinking:

New Viewpoints
Making the Familiar Strange
Tangential Thinking
Building on the Ideas of Others
Analogy and Metaphor
Disrobing the Emperor
Discarding Limitations
Piggy Backing

3. Combine/Clarify Ideas

With group participation, try to group ideas that are very similar. Eliminate duplications. Ask if anyone needs clarification of an input. Always go back to the person who gave the input and let them explain their idea, don't you try to do it. Limit discussion to clarification rather than arguing.

NOTE: Crawford pink slip method is named for its originator. This technique uses small slips of paper (usually pink) to record ideas. Participants are asked to generate one idea per slip and pass them in. Slips can be taped to the wall, inputs re-written, or data analyzed and collated off-line.

Key Skills Needed To Use This Tool:

Good Facilitation Skills
Good Listening & Recording Skills
Good Idea Combining Skills

When Used:

Used to get cross functional input to identify opportunities for process improvement, to identify potential causes of process problems, to identify ways to better satisfy customers.

Advantages:

Promotes synergy and ownership.
Pink slips can be used to gather data from quite large groups in a very short period of time.
Pink slips can maintain anonymity.

Disadvantages:

Can be time-consuming.
Frustrating for people who think they already know the answer.

CONTINGENCY DIAGRAM

==

Purpose:

- To brainstorm factors upon which a condition, problem, or requirement is contingent

How Used:

The condition for which you want to identify contingent factors should be written in a circle on the right hand side of a page, flip chart, etc. Contingent factors are brainstormed and written on lines feeding into the circle (see example).

Key Skills Needed:

Brainstorming

When Used:

Especially useful to look at problems, requirements from a perspective in reverse from the usual: "What makes bad software?", "What makes bad service?", etc. Once having done this, you will have identified both "what to do" and "what not to do" to better satisfy customers.

Advantages:

Very easy to use.

Disadvantages:

For complex conditions, diagrams can get very complex.

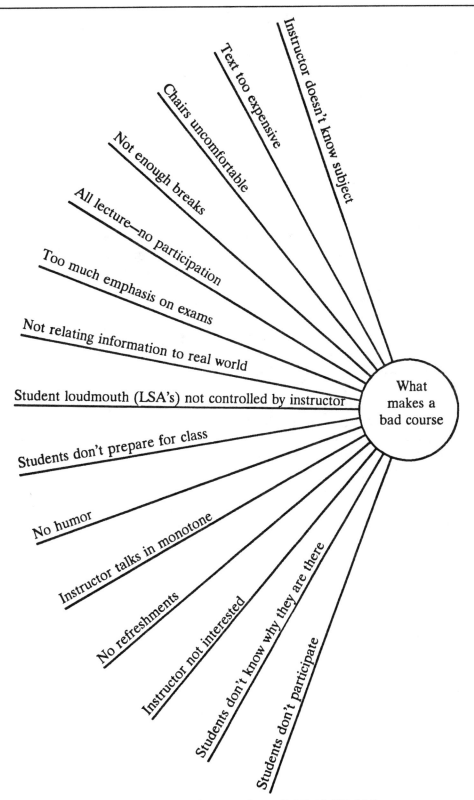

**Example: CONTINGENCY DIAGRAM
for "What Makes a Bad Course"**

GYMNASTIC SCORING CARD TECHNIQUE

Purpose:

- To gather customer data regarding the importance of known or hypothesized customer requirements

- To gather data from customers as to how well you are meeting their requirements

- To create a forum in which customers and suppliers can compare evaluative measurement ratings and the reasons for the differences, if they exist

How Used:

Construct cards (with legible numbers, 1 to 10), make as many sets as you have customer and supplier representatives. Limit your session to no more than 10 total people or you won't be able to allow participants adequate discussion time.

Prepare scoring sheets to gather data. Scoring sheets should accommodate both numerical ratings and comments. Put customers and suppliers on opposite sides, so they can see each other's ratings. Be sure to explain the purpose of the exercise, and establish an environment of trust and non-attribution. Ask everyone to put up their card at once, rating each requirement one at a time and entering scores on the scoring sheet. Rate each factor on importance and then on your performance. Note significant differences in customers and suppliers ratings. Discuss differences and be sure you understand the reasons behind both importance ratings and performance ratings before you proceed to the next item. The dialogue you have to elucidate the ratings is one of the most important aspects of this technique. A "7" may be a good score from one individual, but not from another.

It's a good idea to give the customer a chance to suggest items for rating as well, if you limit yourself to your own agenda of items, you may miss key items of importance to your customer.

Key Skills Needed To Use This Tool:

> Listen Well
> Don't Be Defensive
> Ask Good Follow-up Questions
> Keep A Sense Of Humor

When Used:

> When you are providing a product or service to an internal or external customer and want to measure how well you understand the requirement and how well you are satisfying your customer. Especially useful for white collar, internal customers and suppliers, for things that are difficult to measure.

Advantages:

> Easier and more fun than questionnaires.

Disadvantages:

> Tool is only as good as the participants ability to listen. Can result in hard feelings if participants are defensive (or become overly competitive as we've all witnessed during Olympic contests).

QUALITY FUNCTION DEPLOYMENT (QFD)

==

Note: QFD is covered in detail in Chapter 8. The following is a very brief summary.

Purpose:

- To comprehensively identify customer's requirements.

- To focus and coordinate skills within an organization, first to design, then to manufacture and market products/services that customers want to buy and will continue to buy.

- To facilitate customer, marketing, design engineers, manufacturing and support personnel to work together from the time a product is conceived.

How Used:

Quality function deployment uses a somewhat complex matrix to produce a conceptual map of customer requirements and engineering characteristics. It requires you to address the following questions in a fairly structured, disciplined manner:

1. What are the customer requirements?

2. What are their requirement priorities?

3. Are your competitors able to satisfy these requirements with current/emerging products/services?

4. What engineering characteristics are required to satisfy customer requirements?

5. How does each engineering characteristic affect each customer expectation?

6. How does each engineering characteristic affect other characteristics?

7. What is the relative cost of satisfying each customer requirement?

Key Skills Needed To Use This Tool:

Good Customer Focus Skills

When Used:

Most frequently used in the initial design of a product/service.

Advantages:

Ensures products/services are designed to optimize customers desires, engineering feasibility, cost and competitive advantage, simultaneously and in a timely fashion.

Disadvantages:

Matrix can get very complex. Several computer programs have been developed to alleviate this problem.

REFERENCE: (Hauser, p. 63).

DISCUSSION QUESTIONS

1.   Why is customer focus an area of weakness in many U.S. companies?

2.   What is the difference between an internal and an external customer?

3.   What are "world class customers" and what kinds of things must they do?

4.   Explain the four categories of customer requirements and give an example of each.

5.   Why is identifying customers' requirements difficult?

6.   What customer focus tool is best used with very large groups?

7.   What customer focus tool enables you to obtain a numerical score from your customer on both the importance of requirements and how well you are meeting them?

8.   What customer focus tool facilitates customer, marketing, design engineers, manufacturing and support personnel to work together from the first time a product is conceived?

REFERENCES

Hauser, J. & Clausing, D., "House of Quality", *Harvard Business Review*, May-June 1988, p. 63.

Ishikawa, K., *What is Total Quality Control?: The Japanese Way*, Prentice Hall: Englewood Cliffs, NJ, 1985.

Peters, Tom, Speech to the Association for Quality and Participation, Denver, CO, Oct. 1990.

Chapter 4

COST OF QUALITY[1]

INTRODUCTION

"Quality is free. It's not a gift, but it is free (Crosby, 1990)." Even if quality products and services are not free, each year increasing numbers of authors seem to agree that TQM concepts do make sense. As TQM philosophies are implemented, an organization strives to satisfy its customers' needs at the lowest possible cost. Simultaneously its managers search for means of measuring this goal. In essence, these managers are trying to determine their cost of quality.

Improved profit and cash flow would seem to be inevitable as a company cuts costs, increases productivity and eliminates waste. This is what TQM methodologies can offer and explains in part the excitement they have created. But beyond the obvious benefits of TQM, eventually somebody needs to determine exactly how they have added value to the company's bottom-line. Developing an answer to the inevitable question, "How much does transforming an organization to TQM cost?" cannot be accomplished by simply touching the cost of quality button on an organization's accounting system. As industry, government and academia scramble for a universal definition of quality, the seemingly futile task of identification, measurement and control of the costs of achieving quality seems to be causing anxiety in the accounting community.

BACKGROUND

Generally, quality related cost data are not easily extracted from existing cost data. Even though most cost systems have matured over the years and are now fully automated, few show any difference in philosophy than they did thirty years ago. Consequently, questions about the costs of quality are either not answered or are satisfied with available and often inaccurate data.

Complicating this requirement is that top management seems to consistently demonstrate they best relate to dollars, not management philosophies. Consequently, in order to successfully introduce TQM, there is a need for an easily identifiable link between

---

[1]This chapter was written by Major Steve G. Green.

quality and cost. This obstacle is a fundamental issue that managers should address before attempting to implement TQM philosophies.

How to define and develop the cost of quality is not without controversy. TQM philosophies, if conscientiously implemented, can afford management increased control at bargain basement prices. But, to successfully initiate TQM philosophies, not only is there a need to calculate the cost of implementation, there is also a need for on-going measurement and evaluation. This system-wide cradle-to-grave perspective demonstrates that perhaps the best means of implementing TQM philosophies, is to use the very same TQM philosophies.

Other problems arise because costing TQM philosophies cannot be accomplished in a vacuum. Looking at internal costs without examining external implications is estimating only the cost of quality up to the factory door. Also, traditional cost accounting systems may not be capable of accurately accumulating the costs of quality. A comprehensive analysis is required to derive the costs of implementing TQM. A reluctance to experiment with implementing TQM philosophies is not always an aversion to TQM, but may simply be an indication that an organization is not prepared to commit the resources required for such an analysis.

To describe the cost of quality and how this information can be managed, this chapter will be divided into five sections. After an operational definition of the cost of quality is explored, the conventional wisdom on the matter will be presented. While these prevailing views will not be all inclusive of the many available sources, they will represent the perspectives of government, industry and several noted experts. Next, the cost of conformance and nonconformance will be identified. Also viewed as internal and external costs, they represent the most frequently cited costs of quality. This discussion will be followed by a description of cost information management and evolving costing methodologies involving quality. An emphasis on Activity-Based Costing (ABC) will demonstrate current initiatives. Finally, issues concerning the derivation and uses of the costs of quality will be discussed.

- Definition of the Cost of Quality
- Conventional Wisdom Perspective
- Conformance and Nonconformance Costs
- Cost Information Management
- Issues

DEFINITION OF THE COST OF QUALITY

Asking ten people to define the cost of quality will predictably result in ten different answers. Webster's Dictionary defines "cost" as: "Something that is sacrificed to obtain something else (Grove, 1976)." This helps to demonstrate that in order to accurately accumulate all of the cost of quality, not only must all processes and activities be identified, but the breadth and depth of the firm's TQM approach must be clearly delineated. Both internal implementation costs and external costs of not implementing TQM philosophies must be addressed. Complicating this task is that each organization is unique. It might be easier to define the cost of quality by examining why it is so hard to describe. Besides the unique nature of organizations, there is confusion with other management initiatives, incompatibility with traditional cost accounting systems, absence of a unifying cost theory, lack of validated estimating tools, and problems with accumulation and measurement. All of these issues are major obstacles to deriving a common operational definition of the cost of quality:

- Confusion with other management initiatives
- Incompatibility with traditional cost systems
- Absence of a unifying cost theory
- Lack of estimating models
- Problems with accumulation and measurement

Difficulties arise when operationally defining the cost of quality due in part to the confusion created when quality management is equated to quality control. While the two concepts are not unrelated, they have fundamental differences in scope and timing. As described in previous chapters, TQM (with its prevention approach) encompasses much more than quality control (which is corrective in nature). More confusion is possible when TQM is lumped together with other management initiatives that also have three letter acronyms. For example, Management by Objectives (MBO) and Zero Based Budgeting (ZBB) which rose to prominence on the management scene, only to fade after a few years, have been known to cause people to think TQM may do the same.

A natural place to start defining the elements of the cost of quality is to look at traditional cost accounting systems. But further investigation will usually show there is considerable incompatibility. A firm's cost accounting system is usually an intangible entity which most people avoid or see as something run by accountants for accountants' informational needs. On the contrary, top managers often use accounting information to structure strategic plans and policies. Specifically, they use cost data for functions including determination of pricing policies, capital investment decisions and marketing strategies. These decisions, made with misleading or distorted information, could be disastrous to a firm. Also, common quality related cost categories such as rework and scrap, are not always specifically reflected in traditional cost accounting systems. Managers tend to distrust cost data that is not readily available or which does not originate from the organization's existing cost accounting system. Costs that are vague or of mysterious origins may be considered by some managers as valid grounds for a reluctance to invest dollars in TQM.

Developing an operational definition of the cost of quality is also difficult because individual companies define their own costs. Without the existence of a unifying cost theory and conceptual framework, such as financial accounting's Generally Accepted Accounting

Principles (GAAP), guidelines for defining the cost of quality are scarce. For these reasons alone it would be inappropriate to define the cost of quality in any one particular context. But, witnessed by the many operational definitions, many would argue that conceptually there is probably enough commonality among production and service organizations to derive a definition.

For example, there are specific costs associated with achieving quality products and services that can be identified and measured. The costs of making, finding, repairing or avoiding defects are usually cited as costs of quality. Each has quality related costs which can be uniquely identified and traced. Complement this cost information with more subjective cost data from intangibles such as lost opportunities, goodwill and morale, and a total cost of quality begins to materialize.

Another reason the cost of quality is difficult to define is because of its fundamental inconsistencies with existing cost estimating and analysis methodologies. When an organization is involved in estimating the costs of quality, traditional cost analysis tools are often inappropriately employed. Parametric or analogous methods will generally prove to be inaccurate because these approaches rely heavily on historical data bases or experiences developed from activities not specifically associated with quality. Even though sophisticated management accounting models have been developed, they tend to work best in simplified, stylized, production settings (Johnson and Kaplan, 1991).

While cost analysts may eventually agree that TQM related cost estimating relationships will evolve, information for decisions are needed today. To be accurate and useful, initial costs of quality need to be developed through bottom-up or engineering methods. This grass-roots approach to cost analysis is very accurate, but extremely time consuming and expensive. Consequently, when cost of quality data is requested, "rules-of-thumb" are often hastily created.

A primary reason these "rules-of-thumb" fail to provide valid costs of quality is they usually have as a foundation a common misconception that cost of quality is somehow related to cost-cutting. But cost cutting, usually in the form of indiscriminate reductions in the organization's spending, could in fact result in exact opposite results. Studies show that in the 1980s, American manufacturers attempted to regain their lost competitive edge by resolutely chipping away at waste and inefficiency. This action, however, proved not enough to restore competitive health. In fact, a focus on only cost reduction actually proved harmful (Skinner, 1986).

There are many other issues to consider when defining the cost of quality. These issues are especially apparent as these costs are accumulated and measured. The complexity of the effort is illustrated when an organization attempts to accumulate costs for measurement and control purposes for evaluating periodic performance. For example, once the costs of quality are identified, they are spread by traditional volume-based overhead allocation techniques. These newly identified and allocated costs can create havoc with predetermined budgets, actual costs and most importantly for control purposes, variance between the two.

Also, internal conflicts on how to classify the cost of quality, validity of estimates, and completeness of figures, can result in late and inaccurate reports. A preoccupation with organization-wide totals can actually create delays in the undertaking of important projects (Juran and Gryna, 1980). It would seem that few managers would tolerate this and deriving the actual costs of quality may not even be attempted.

Even if the costs of quality are well defined, a fundamental step toward measuring and managing them would be to extinguish mind-sets regarding quality itself. Beyond the idea that TQM is repackaged or rebundled quality control, people equate quality to "goodness" and it becomes impossible to measure. If quality is not measurable, an argument can be made that it is also not manageable.

Similarly, if there is a quality problem within an organization, many managers might associate it with the quality department, if one exists. If one doesn't exist, they may create one so there will be a single point of responsibility for the problem. This idea is contrary to TQM philosophies which suggest that quality problems should be associated with the process that creates them, not a separate body. Further, TQM philosophies would also suggest that the people who work daily with the product or service, not a detached staff organization, can best report, address and improve the derivation of the cost of quality.

In summary, because TQM should be pervasive throughout an organization, the true costs of quality are difficult to identify and quantify. If the costs of quality are ambiguous, accumulation and measurement become difficult. Without measurement of the correct items, there is no control and even the most sophisticated management system will break down. Consequently, TQM is difficult to institutionalize within the framework of traditional cost accounting systems. Faced with these vague decision parameters, management has yet another reason to be reluctant to invest dollars in TQM.

CONVENTIONAL WISDOM PERSPECTIVE

Both government and industry TQM experts are addressing this predicament by developing their own operational definitions of the cost of quality. Throughout these definitions, however, are common themes of process identification and improvement, management commitment, employee involvement and customer satisfaction. Using current methodologies, all of these concepts are difficult to identify and measure and developing the cost of quality becomes a formidable and expensive task. However, knowing what it actually costs to produce quality products and services is something modern managers cannot afford not to pursue.

Relative to other management theories, TQM is in its infancy. Consequently, authors outside of a handful of TQM experts, lack the credibility and wide-acceptance needed to devise a universally accepted definition of the cost of quality. However, the perspectives of some experts, along with government's and industry's views, can be considered representative of conventional wisdom's position on the cost of quality.

Expert Perspective

A person often associated with the cost of quality is Philip B. Crosby. He begins his cost definition formulation by describing quality as conformance to requirements. His perspective includes addressing the cost of quality as the expense of nonconformance or, the costs of doing things wrong (Crosby, 1980). Basically, he categorizes costs by activities of prevention, appraisal and failure. Several years after Crosby's first quality related book, *Quality is Free*, he took this generalized description a step further in what he refers to as his Fourth Absolute of Quality Management. Referring to the meaningless nature of some quality related cost data and measurement parameters, Crosby describes the measurement of quality as the price of nonconformance, not meaningless indices (Crosby, 1984).

Crosby may have been referring to efficiency indices or ratios similar to those described by Joseph M. Juran. Juran identified cost of poor quality (COPQ) indices with dollars as the numerator and such items as operating hours, dollars of operating hours, standard operating costs, processing costs, sales or units produced as the denominator. Juran's perspective is these indices could provide parameters to observe trends and compare performance (Juran, 1988).

From an engineering perspective, the cost of quality can be viewed as the losses incurred when a product's functional parameters deviate from a target value. By decreasing variability around a target value, reduced costs and increased customer satisfaction should occur. Dr. Genichi Taguchi is often associated with this phenomena referred to as the "loss function." Taguchi feels that product and process design can have a significant impact on quality and cost. He states that the total loss to society to produce a product with specific values would be the production cost to the manufacturer and the inferior quality cost (Gitlow et. al., 1989). The loss function takes these actual and intuitive costs of quality and graphically represents them on a parabolic curve.

With this loss function, if an activity is on target, the process has been optimized and the conformance cost of quality is zero. If it is determined that this point of zero cost is unachievable, improving the process, reviewing specifications and tolerance variations, or creating an environment more conducive to personal accountability might be in order. (For more details on the Taguchi loss function, see Chapter 9.)

But the notion that loss only occurs when the product is outside of specification limits is obsolete. Loss is not constrained to scrap and rework. Other considerations such as excess inventory, capital investment, customer dissatisfaction and eventual loss of market share, must be identified and managed. Crosby, Juran, Taguchi and others agree that the magnitude of nonconformance costs such as repeating work, scrap, warranty, inspection, test and all the clerical and administrative expenses associated with these costs, will usually raise eyebrows in corporate board rooms.

Government Perspective

The United States Government, particularly the Department of Defense (DoD) seems to favor a blend between Crosby's and Taguchi's definition of the cost of quality. The DoD perspective, as well as other's, is that the payoff is maximized when quality is addressed during the early phases of developing a product or service since costly problems can best be prevented during the design phase. Thereafter, the leverage of prevention is reduced as the more costly corrective actions prevail (DoD 5000.51-C, 1990).

Poor conformance quality can be viewed as waste or something that does not add value to a product or service. This waste perspective is used by the DoD to conclude that much of the cost of poor quality is from processes that are permitted to be wasteful. In the past, this waste was often considered chronic and accepted as a business norm. Avoiding the need to address chronic waste was accomplished by "putting out fires" in an attempt to prevent the situation from getting worse. Today, the environment DoD wants to create is one of reduced chronic waste through continuous process improvement, not merely quick-fixes.

With increased public awareness of government inefficiency, many see implementing TQM methodologies as demonstrating a commitment to improvement. Consequently, as witnessed by the numerous highly publicized quality improvement campaigns, TQM methodologies are being widely embraced by the government and particularly the DoD.

For example, before the United States Air Force (USAF) formally institutionalized TQM in the late 1980s, it had formalized an approach to increasing capability through improving reliability and maintainability practices with their R&M 2000 Process. At its foundation, this program uses a parabolic curve approach (similar to Taguchi's loss function) to graphically illustrate how management assesses the true cost of production process improvement (USAF R&M 2000 Process, 1989). The similarities between R&M 2000 and TQM are numerous because it is actually the same TQM methodologies. For example, both view continuous process improvement as a means of reducing variability around a target specification to minimize loss and associated costs, and both advocate the use of specific process improvement techniques.

An example of how TQM and the cost of quality are changing the way the government does business can be seen with how they deal with new programs. Since TQM methodologies are most effective when implemented in the early stages of an activity, future programs and projects that require many years and billions of dollars are prime targets for implementation. Also, in early concept definition phases of programs, TQM is easier to "sell" to management because the up-front conformance costs are trivial relative to the program life cycle costs of a major undertaking. Finally, the TQM methodologies that managers sense might have been hastily implemented for existing programs, are "part of the design" of future efforts and are more acceptable.

For example, DoD and the National Aeronautics and Space Administration (NASA) turned to TQM philosophies as a means of meeting strict budget constraints. After the Apollo era, our nation developed a space program around the Space Shuttle. After the 1986 Challenger tragedy, DoD, NASA, and the aerospace industry returned to the drawing board to reassess the feasibility of the country's goal of assured access to space. The result of the Shuttle's tarnished safety record and growing popular demand for increased reliability was the development, testing and deployment of a new generation of heavy lift, unmanned launch vehicles, the Titan-IVs. However, these systems were recognized as only a stepping stone for the next generation of space "trucks" referred to as the Advanced Launch System (ALS).

In a textbook TQM application, both government and contractors working on the ALS, implemented system-wide quality programs with an emphasis on high reliability to reduce costs in order to meet specific budget constraints. The focus was on designing quality, reliability and maintainability into the system from the beginning. TQM was also emphasized in order to continuously improve all processes and sub-systems to further reduce costs throughout the ALS program life (Scott, 1989).

Another TQM related lesson learned from the Challenger disaster was that non-conformance quality costs can be prohibitively high. The government and public alike have demonstrated that they will not tolerate the lengthy down-times and the possibility for loss of human lives associated with a catastrophic failure. Putting a dollar figure on the cost of quality is made much more difficult when human lives are at stake.

Several other references to the cost of quality can be found in current literature, in applications and embedded in regulations or policy statements. Even the Internal Revenue System claimed a $630,000 savings in the 1990 tax filing through a TQM related effort (Shoop, 1991).

As TQM implementation becomes a standard for doing business with the government, industry has emerged as an invaluable source of cost of quality information.

Industry Perspective

Xerox Corporation, through an intensive company-wide quality emphasis, has become an industry benchmark. The highlight of their Leadership Through Quality Program was the winning of the 1989 Malcolm Baldrige National Quality Award. Among other initiatives, Xerox initiated a Quality Cost Management effort with their United States Marketing Group. This organization produced a corporate publication dedicated to informing and instructing employees on the application of a cost of quality management system. Their primer, *The Cost of Quality*, defines the cost of quality from Xerox's perspective and demonstrates measurement procedures and techniques. Like others, Xerox used cost of conformance, nonconformance and lost opportunity as the framework for discussion. Xerox graphically describes the trade-off of the need to increase conformance costs such as training inspectors to reducing nonconformance costs such as waste and unnecessary extras in Figure 4.1.

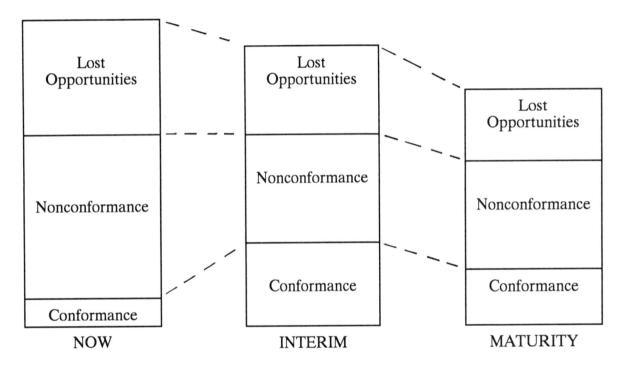

Source: XEROX   IMPLEMENTATION OF TQM

Figure 4.1 Evolution of Cost of Quality

Finally, by addressing these costs, lost opportunities such as missed profits can be reduced (Rand et al, 1987). An example of Xerox's cost of quality worksheet and instructions is found in Figures 4.2 and 4.3.

Other large corporations have similar programs that emphasize the importance of the cost of quality. Organizations have developed these management information systems to meet specific needs for timely, accurate cost of quality data. Effective decision making in today's dynamic business environment becomes very difficult without it.

COST OF QUALITY WORKSHEET
(INSTRUCTIONS FOLLOW)

Name of Output _____

Project Leader _____ Location _____

Cost of Non-Conformance: (Annualize all costs):

1. Replacement materials / supplies _____ x ___ = _____
Cost per month   Annualized subtotal

2. Rework Labor _____ x _____ x ___ = _____
Labor & benefits/hr   Total manhours / mo   Annualized subtotal

3. Exceeding
Requirements _____ x _____ x ___ = _____
Excess Labor &   Excess materials/mo   Annualized subtotal
benefits/hr

4. Other _____ _____ = _____
Annualized subtotal

5. **Total Non-Conforming Cost**
(Add subtotals from lines 1, 2, 3 & 4 above)

▸ $ _____

Cost of Lost Opportunity: (Annualize all costs):

6. Potential Lost Revenue _____ x 12 = _____
Estimated revenue   Annualized subtotal
lost/month

7. **Total Lost Opportunity Cost**
(Subtotal from line 6 above)

▸ $ _____

8. **Total Non-Conformance and Lost Opportunity**
(Subtotal from lines 5 and 7)

▸ $ _____

Cost of Conformance: (Annualize all costs):

9. Training/meetings
Communications _____ x _____ X 12 = _____
Labor & benefits/hr   Total manhours / mo   Annualized subtotal

10. Inspection _____ x _____ X 12 = _____
Labor & benefits/hr   Total manhours / mo   Annualized subtotal

11. Other _____ _____ = _____
Annualized subtotal

12. **Total Conforming Cost**
(Add subtotals from lines 9, 10, & 11)

▸ $ _____

13. **Annualized Cost Of Quality Savings / Opportunity**
(Subtract Total on line 12 from Total on line 8)

▸ $ _____

Figure 4.2 Worksheet (Reproduced with permission from Xerox)

COST OF QUALITY WORKSHEET
INSTRUCTIONS / EXAMPLES

Name of Output   Identify Output Using Noun/Verb Format - (5090
                 Sales Order Processed

Project Leader   Manager / Leader's Name   Location   District Name

Cost of Non-Conformance (Annualize all costs):

1. Replacement materials / supplies
   Add up all materials and supplies used on a monthly basis as a result of doing the job over, and annualize by multiplying by 12. Example: Average extra billing forms used per month due to errors = $35 X 12 = $ 420 per year.

2. Rework / Repair
   Add labor plus benefits (loaded labor rate - see DBM for standard) for time to correct errors. Example: $10 per hour plus $2.30 benefits = $12.30 per hour, times 15 hours per month rework time = $184.50 per month, X 12 = $ 2214 per year.

3. Exceeding requirements
   Cost of producing a 5-page report when only one page is required. Other examples are people performing duplicate functions, overly detailed work processes being used, or unnecessary people attending meetings. To calculate cost, identify materials and labor costs associated with excessive activities and annualize for 12-month period as in Steps 1 and 2 above.

4. Other
   Any other Non-Conforming costs such as rescheduling rigger, sales returns due to wrong product, accommodations to customers and the cost of writing off bad debts. Be sure to include any travel, labor or materials expense for a 12-month period as in Steps 1 and 2 above.

   5. *Total Non-Conforming Cost* $ _____
       (Add subtotals from lines 1, 2, 3 & 4)

Cost of Lost Opportunity: (Annualize all costs):

6. Potential Lost Revenue
   The estimated loss of revenue such as trial equipment aged over the standard policy (including our cost to carry this inventory). Other lost opportunities are: orders not processed promptly and accurately, shipping delays, equipment cancellations, and FSMAs not being locked in at order time or renewed at expiration. Estimate these costs based on past performance data.
   $ _____

   7. *Total Lost Opportunity Cost*
       (Subtotal from Line 6 above)

   8. *Total Non-Conformance and Lost Opportunity* $ _____
       (Add totals from Lines 5 & 7)

Cost of Conformance (Annualize all costs):

9. Training/Meetings/Communications
   Add portion of labor and benefits associated with developing or presenting training or communication sessions that are intended to inform people how to perform their job more effectively. Include labor and benefits of anyone presenting or receiving the information.

10. Inspection
    Add portion of labor and benefits of people who inspect or check partial or completed work to insure the output meets specifications, including proofreading memos, reviewing incoming materials or requirements and surveying internal or external customers about the results of the output.

11. Other
    Add any other cost associated with inspection or prevention activities such as the cost of the meeting room, travel expenses, consultant fees, training materials, or any other equipment intended to prevent errors.

    12. *Total Conforming Cost* $ _____
         (Add subtotals from Lines 9, 10, & 11)

    13. *Annualized Cost of Quality Savings/Opportunity* $ _____
         (Subtract total on Line 12 from total on Line 8)

Figure 4.3 Worksheet Instructions (Reproduced with permission from Xerox)

Even smaller firms recognize the importance of the cost of quality. From the world of consultants and small businesses come many unique perspectives on describing the cost of quality. One firm, ODI, views the cost of quality as a great untapped reservoir of opportunity. They feel every dollar saved from avoiding the cost of poor quality can be added directly to the "bottom line (Labovitz and Chang, 1989)."

ODI created a paradigm by decomposing the cost of quality into three distinct categories: prevention costs, inspection and correction costs, and field failure costs. Based on cost behavior, they tritely refer to these categories as the "good", the "bad" and the "ugly." Prevention costs are categorized as "good" and are preventive in nature. "Bad" costs include traditional quality control activities associated with inspection and checking. Finally, "ugly" costs are expended only after the customer receives the product or service, and a firm's reputation is damaged (Labovitz and Chang, 1989).

These costs earn their dubious names from what is described as the "1-10-100" rule. This heuristic guideline suggests that for every dollar spent on prevention (good costs), ten dollars might have been spent on inspection (bad costs) or one hundred dollars will have to be spent on correction (ugly costs) (Labovitz and Chang, 1989).

As time passes, research will provide empirical evidence to support or refute theories such as the 1-10-100 rule. Until then, managers will mostly rely on intuition to determine cost of quality or turn again to traditional costs systems and treat these costs as overhead. In either case, costs of quality may be inaccurate and lead to wrong decisions. To increase accuracy, after the costs of quality are identified, a measurement system must be devised.

Whether the organization's orientation is production, service, or not-for-profit, the cost of quality should be measured and reported. However, it may not be the organization's traditional cost accounting system performing this measurement function. If the cost of quality is determined, improvement goals in the form of reduced costs can be initiated. While this represents conventional wisdom's cost of quality goal, a means to this end has not been identified. Managers are turning to cost classification, such as conformance and non-conformance, to guide their measurement and control efforts.

CONFORMANCE AND NONCONFORMANCE COSTS

Similar to conventional wisdom's definition of the cost of quality, there is commonality in most contemporary views regarding quality cost classifications. If all organizational activities are portrayed as processes, costs of quality are incurred before, during and after each event. Costs occurring before actual production of goods or services, or anytime during the process, are considered prevention costs. These conformance costs are aimed at minimizing failures that would need to be eventually identified and corrected (Figure 4.4).

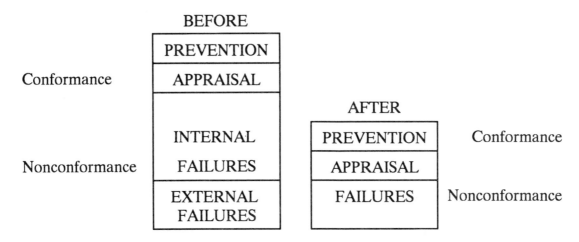

Source: DOD 5000.51 C

Figure 4.4 Cost of Quality

It is up to management to permit the people actually working in the activity to develop methods of collecting and reporting the cost of quality throughout the entire process. This type of management commitment and employee involvement is a fundamental TQM philosophy. Once this is accomplished, the most significant costs must be identified and cost reduction or elimination plans must be developed. Pareto Charts (see Chapter 7) are specifically used for this purpose.

The conformance costs associated with TQM that seems to attract the most management attention are the ones that require capital expenditures. This is particularly true if these usually large investments need to be immediately addressed. These conformance capital investments are associated with any activity an organization initiates that will help it avoid or prevent future costs. Crosby defines prevention costs as the cost of all activities undertaken to prevent defects in design, development, purchasing, labor and other aspects of beginning and creating a product or service (Crosby, 1980).

Examples of these conformance costs include design verification, specification reviews, comprehensive training, orientations, statistical process control activities, process studies, supplier evaluations, preventive maintenance and all associated administrative costs. Also identifying the implementation costs of TQM techniques and the administration of its processes must be considered.

Another perspective is to return to the loss function and consider all of these activities as aimed at reducing overall costs. The potential effects of conformance costs are not trivial. Taichi Ohno, a renowned Toyota Motor Company executive put these costs into perspective, "Whatever an executive thinks the losses of poor quality are, they are usually six times greater (Taguchi and Clausing, 1990)."

Other conformance costs recognized by many authors are appraisal costs. These costs are incurred as product or service conformance is determined. The appraisal process could include costs incurred while conducting inspection and test or the transfer of specifications from customer to vendor. Crosby cites several examples of these types of costs including, prototype, receiving, packaging, inspection, test, production specification conformance analyses, supplier surveillance and status measurement and reporting (Crosby, 1980). Other costs, including the administrative costs of all of the other appraisal activities, should be considered.

Nonconformance costs, on the other hand, are best associated with the costs of traditional quality control inspectors. If this activity could have been avoided, there would not be a need for this function and its associated costs.

Motorola Corporation, the recipient of the first Malcolm Baldrige National Quality Award in 1988, has as a stated corporate goal the achievement of virtually defect-free operations. They use the engineering term, six sigma, to demonstrate that they will only tolerate 3.4 defects per million parts produced. Put another way, the company wants to be perfect 99.9999998 percent of the time (Gill, 1990).

The virtual elimination of nonconformance costs by Motorola will not be easy or cheap. While the firm estimates that the cost savings of not having zero defects at $800 million a year, they failed to cite the conformance cost associated with this savings (Gill, 1990). Perhaps they did not have a means of collecting these quality related costs?

There have been other preliminary cost savings and results from application of TQM philosophies. Hewlett-Packard, which a dozen years ago received the lowest quality ratings possible, now estimates $600 million annual savings in warranty repairs and five times that much in production costs (Gill, 1990).

An example of a government organization that has realized savings is the Strategic Defense Initiative Organization (SDIO). Through TQM management initiatives, the cost of a $500 million target and sensor experiment was reduced by half (Scott, 1990). Even though programs that report mammoth cost savings rarely mention associated conformance costs, numbers such as these are impressive. Whether these same programs can determine these costs may never be known.

With documented proof that implementation of TQM philosophies can produce impressive savings, the question still remains as to why TQM has not been universally accepted. The answer may be revealed by looking at what information is used by managers to make decisions and where this information comes from.

COST INFORMATION MANAGEMENT

Accountants are constantly under pressure to provide accurate and timely information for decision makers. Today, managers are faced with increasing demand for products and services of high quality and low cost. Cyclical business slumps and rapidly changing technologies are making matters worse. All of these factors have made an already fiercely competitive atmosphere even more so.

This dynamic and unpredictable business environment has created a need for the greatest possible accuracy when dealing with costs used to base decisions of capital investment, management incentives, pricing or market strategies. The result is a need to continuously improve already sophisticated cost accounting systems. To complicate the situation, now there are new requirements to measure, justify and evaluate elusive costs of quality.

Until recently, traditional cost accounting systems which primarily focused attention on unit costs, could satisfy management's needs. However, the added requirement of the cost of quality has made some accounting systems obsolete. The costs of quality, which were usually hidden in overhead accounts not measurable or unavailable for management action, now need to be identified, measured and controlled.

Traditional cost accounting methods are time-proven at accurately defining unit costs as either labor, material or overhead. But they fall short, in many instances, of meaningfully allocating overhead. Without an accurate measure, control is lost and accounting information is less useful. However, like other disciplines, management accounting is witnessing a revolution of sorts. Requirements to address high technology systems and management philosophies such as TQM, have put a strain on traditional cost systems and the conservatism characteristic of accountants.

Accounting historians agree that modern cost accounting is a consequence of the industrial revolution (Johnson, 1981). These accounting systems, whose descendants are still in use today, were developed earlier in the century for a different environment. They best accommodated mass production of a few standard items with a fairly high labor content. As firms evolved and became more specialized, or changed product lines or services, these generic cost systems became inadequate.

Even as automated systems permitted the accurate accounting of several different products from the same assembly line, they still had some inherent limitations. For example, an accounting system stressing efficiency and the ability to produce many units would be inappropriate for a firm with an emphasis on research and development.

The overriding objective of any accounting system should be a reliable measurement system that is supportive of and consistent with the organization's overall strategy. If the strategy changes, the accounting system must be adaptive enough to still provide accurate and timely cost data for decision making. TQM is putting the flexibility of some of the traditional accounting systems to the test.

A contemporary cost system also needs to be able to accommodate changes in management philosophy. TQM application, for example, requires an increase in management attention toward the processes involved in the organization's product or service. Like TQM, this type of emphasis is not new. Over 25 years ago, Peter F. Drucker, a noted management theorist, stated that an organization could not make good, solid strategic management decisions with inefficient cost information. He wrote what is surely an early description of TQM in a context of effectiveness, "And while the job to be done may look different in every individual company, one basic truth will always be present: every product, every operation, and every activity in a business should, therefore, be put on trial for its life every two or three years. Each should be considered the way we consider a proposal to go into a new product, a new operation or activity (Drucker, 1963)."

This need to continuously improve an organization's processes and activities along with its means of measurement and control, has been advocated by two of contemporary accounting's most prolific authors. Robin Cooper and Robert Kaplan are credited with taking rather revolutionary perspectives on the collection and uses of cost information.

Robin Cooper suggests that management should periodically evaluate a firm's cost system to answer the question, "Do I really know what my products cost?" His answer is that a firm should look for symptoms that usually accompany a poorly designed or obsolete cost system. Cooper feels it is time to redesign your system if conditions exist that demonstrate a loss of control. Some of his warning bells sound when: functional managers want to drop seemingly profitable lines, profit margins are hard to explain, departments have their own cost systems, you have the high margin niche all to yourself, competitor's prices seem unrealistically low and potentially most embarrassing, customers do not mind price increases (Cooper, 1989).

Cooper explains that many of the situations that sound warnings can be avoided if a firm's cost system is kept current with respect to a changing environment. His position is that a cost system may be obsolete if a firm experiences a number of different situations including: increased automation, simplification of manufacturing processes, un-bundling of products, deregulation, technological improvements or changes in strategies or goals (Cooper, 1989). Many of these same phenomena are characteristic of an organization implementing TQM philosophies.

Robert S. Kaplan has recognized the importance of direct measurement of quality as well as a more accurate measure of the actual costs of resources. In several of his publications his position is that activity-based cost systems, as opposed to traditional volume-based absorption systems, can assign the cost of indirect and support resources to the specific products and activity that benefit from the resources. He feels that this approach to costing is particularly suited for complex, technologically advanced environments (Kaplan, 1989).

Many see Kaplan as leading the charge for Activity-Based Costing (ABC). ABC is a relatively new concept, making its debut about the same relative time TQM arrived on the management scene. While some see this emergence as more than coincidence, others argue that ABC's time had arrived independent of TQM.

Activity-based systems prove more useful than traditional volume-based systems since instead of using volume to trace costs and assign overhead, they use activities. This is particularly significant since overhead is becoming one of the biggest elements of cost. Basically, ABC traces costs to products according to the activities performed on them. It seeks to assign costs either to the products or to the "activities" that "cause" the costs. ABC concentrates on these activities and refers to them as cost drivers. Another way to look at the fundamental principles of ABC is to set aside the traditional construct that products or services absorb resources. Instead visualize activities absorbing resources and products or services absorbing activities.

For example, one of John Deere's manufacturing facilities was designed to produce parts in high-volume quantities. "They felt their existing traditional cost system was sophisticated because it used three volume-related cost drivers; direct labor hours, machine hours and material dollars. Not surprisingly, they realized they were probably systematically under costing low-volume products. When they initiated an ABC system, they kept their original three cost drivers and added four volume-independent allocation bases: set-up hours, number of production orders, part numbers and number of production loads. The result was that low volume products' overhead doubled and high volume products' overhead fell 10%. In addition to better accountability, these new product costs also seemed to agree with management's intuition (Cooper, 1989)."

Simply put, management identifies the "cost drivers" for each activity and assigns overhead costs to products based on cost driver information rather than solely subjective, volume-based measures. Consequently, ABC lends itself to multi-product, varying volume processes much better than traditional costing approaches.

Another argument for ABC is that traditional cost systems lull managers into believing direct labor is the most controllable cost factor. Consequently, many managers try to reduce this labor cost, only to see overhead costs in the form of tooling, engineering and maintenance skyrocket. Knowledge and its associated control over activities is critical to successful operations. ABC's biggest attribute is that it makes costs more identifiable, measurable and controllable. As TQM philosophies are implemented, conformance costs are usually dumped into overhead for lack of a more suitable home. ABC helps to properly allocate these costs.

But most importantly, ABC helps answer one of the most important production questions, "which product is making money and which is not?" By more accurately allocating overhead, including TQM related costs, action can be taken to eliminate unprofitable product lines. In many cases, these overhead costs are becoming one of the largest cost elements. Also, ABC programs like TQM philosophies, help managers and employees alike concentrate on true cost reduction activities through the identification of non-value added work.

Finally, ABC's acceptance is being fueled by TQM and vice versa. Traditional cost systems stifle TQM. Not only do they fail to report the true cost of quality, they camouflage them in variance. In only a few rare instances is the cost system directly linked to the quality system, permitting managers to know how much nonconformance costs really are (O'Guin, 1990).

If ABC and TQM are so compatible and if they emerged at the same relative time, questions might arise as to why both have not been widely implemented. The answer involves both fact and conjecture. Peter Turney, approached this question by looking at why managers and academics are "afraid" of ABC. He divided what he referred to as his ten myths about implementing ABC into four common themes. His major myth categories are: ABC systems are too difficult to implement and use, improving existing systems will do the job, more accurate product costs are not needed and cost systems only play a limited role (Turney, 1990).

ISSUES

The cost of quality is powerful information. In today's business environment, an organization must be able to identify, measure and control costs including the costs of quality products and services. But even with ABC and other emerging costing methodologies, managers should be cautious about how they use cost of quality data. There will be inconsistencies with existing costing methodologies, laws and regulations and how this cost information is used throughout the organization.

If nothing else is clear about developing the cost of quality, it must be that accountants must change the way they do business. Even though accountants by convention are conservative, they must explore innovative and dynamic costing approaches. Accountants and controllers must leave the front office and get to know the organizations' processes. These processes and activities, and the elimination of non-value added work, must replace traditional cost accounting systems as the focus for cost of quality development.

Today, in part due to the limitations of traditional cost systems, rising overhead costs are causing unnecessary retention of some direct and indirect employees at the expense of others. There is also unwarranted pressure to reduce these same people regardless of the value they may be adding to the process. The resulting rising overhead, and the associated stigma of inefficiency, is hardly an incentive for outsiders to invest capital. All of these manifestations contradict fundamental TQM principles because they do not identify and eliminate non-value added work, they simply cut costs.

Another issue that must be addressed when developing any cost of quality will be the inconsistencies with TQM philosophies and existing laws and regulations. For example, Cost Accounting Standards (CAS) associated with government contracting, dictate specifics on accountability, reporting, allocating, and capitalizing costs. These standards and other laws outlined in the Federal Acquisition Regulation (FAR) and by the Internal Revenue Service (IRS) must not inhibit process improvement efforts and accurate development of costs of quality, but sometimes do. For example, early communication between engineers, production people and operators is in line with TQM philosophies, but competition implications often make this type of interaction impossible.

Finally, an issue arises with how cost of quality is used in the decision process throughout the organization. For example, the cost of quality used by management for TQM implementation decisions may be fundamentally inaccurate. Unless activity-based cost systems are in place, accurate conformance and nonconformance costs are difficult to determine. Deciding which should be implemented first, TQM or the costing systems needed to cost it, perhaps is the real implementation decision for managers.

Since the proverbial bottom-line is, has been, and will continue to be, the focus of management attention, the effects of TQM on the bottom-line should be determined. Instead of viewing TQM as a cost that reduces profits, view TQM as an investment with the potential for increasing profits. Instead of asking what the cost of quality is, perhaps the question that should be asked is what is the return on quality. Management would be hard-pressed to turn down an investment that will provide increased efficiency, reduced waste, enhanced customer and employee satisfaction, and eventually an improved bottom-line.

Note: The ideas and opinions expressed in this chapter are those of the author and do not necessarily reflect the views of the United States Air Force Academy or any other agency of the Department of Defense.

About the author:

Steve Green graduated from the United States Air Force Academy in 1980 with a Bachelor of Science Degree. While working as an acquisition officer and cost analyst for several major satellite system program offices in Los Angeles, he completed a Master of Science Degree from the University of Southern California and a Doctor of Business Administration from the United States International University in San Diego. He returned to the Academy and is currently an Associate Professor in the Department of Management.

REFERENCES

Cooper, Robin, "You Need a New Cost System When ..." *Harvard Business Review*. Jan.-Feb. 1989, pp. 77-82.

Cooper, Robin, "ABC: Key to Future Costs", *Management Consultancy*, October 1989, pp. 42-44.

Crosby, Philip B., *Quality is Free*, Mentor: New York, 1980.

Crosby, Philip B., *Quality Without Tears*, McGraw Hill: New York, 1984.

Drucker, Peter F., "Managing for Business Effectiveness", *Harvard Business Review*, May-June 1963, pp. 33-60.

Gill, Mark S., "Stalking Six Sigma", *Business Month*, January 1990, pp. 42-46.

Gitlow, Howard, Shelly Gitlow, Allen Oppenheim, and Rosa Oppenheim, *Tools and Methods for Improvement of Quality*, Irwin: Boston, 1989.

Grove, Philip Babcock, Editor, *Webster's Third New International Dictionary*, G&C Merriam Co.: Springfield, 1976.

Johnson, H. Thomas, "The Evolution of Management Accounting", *The Accounting Review*, Vol LVI, No 3, July 1981, pp. 510-531.

Johnson, H. Thomas, and Robert S. Kaplan, *Relevance Lost, The Rise and Fall of Management Accounting*, Harvard Business School Press: Boston, 1991.

Juran, Joseph M., *Juran on Planning for Quality*, The Free Press: New York, 1988.

Juran, Joseph M. and Frank M. Gryna Jr., *Quality Planning and Analysis*, Second Edition, McGraw-Hill: New York, 1980.

Kaplan, Robert S., "Management Accounting for Advanced Technology Environments" *Science*, August 29, 1989, pp. 819-823.

Labovitz, George H. and Y. S. Chang, "Quality Costs: The Good, The Bad, and The Ugly", Unpublished Manuscript, ODI: San Antonio, 1990.

Rand, A. Barry et al, *Cost of Quality: A Guide for Application*, Xerox Corporation: Rochester, 1987.

Scott, William B., "ALS Cost, Efficiency to Depend Heavily on Process Improvement", *Aviation Week and Space Technology*, October 23, 1989, pp. 41-43.

Scott, William B., "Aerospace/Defense Firms See Preliminary Results From Applications of TQM Concepts", *Aviation Week and Space Technology*, January 8, 1990, pp. 61-62 .

Shoop, Tom, "Uphill Climb to Quality", *Government Executive*, March 1991, pp. 17-19.

Skinner, Wickham, "The Productivity Paradox", *Harvard Business Review*, July-August 1986, pp. 55-59.

Taguchi, Genichi, and Don Clausing, "Robust Quality", *Harvard Business Review*, Jan.-Feb. 1990, pp. 65-75.

Turney, Peter B.B., "Ten Myths About Implementing an Activity-Based Cost System", *Journal of Cost Management*, Spring 1990, pp. 24-31.

"Total Quality Management Implementation Guide", Volume 1, DoD 5000.51C, Final Draft, January 15, 1990.

"USAF R&M 2000 Process", AFP 800-7, January 1, 1989.

Chapter 5

HOW TO GET STARTED

FOCUS ON THE PROCESS

In Chapter 3 you learned focus on satisfying the customer is key to total quality. Some organizations starting the TQM journey forget this, and try to implement total quality using the same methods and practices they have used for years. They create a special TQM office, put someone "in charge", develop a schedule, write a plan, and announce a "program." A far better approach to transforming an organization to total quality is to apply the principles of total quality to the process of transformation itself. This requires management to learn some new principles, methods and techniques up front, but will greatly improve the probability of success. There is not one single best "recipe" for transformation of organizations to total quality. The inputs to the process are different for every organization, and therefore transformation should not be approached by either strictly copying what worked for someone else or buying someone's canned, step-by-step prescription for TQM "success."

What will be presented in this chapter, therefore, is not a cook-book approach to transformation, but a process approach. You may find this approach frustrating, but remember total quality requires us to think about things in entirely new ways.

The activities involved in a process approach to transforming an organization should include the following:

PHASE 1:   Learn about total quality and establish an environment of continuous learning.

PHASE 2:   Start transformation activities.

      Step 1:   Assess customers (internal and external)
      Step 2:   Perform strategic planning: develop/refine mission and vision
      Step 3:   Identify key opportunities
      Step 4:   Develop executive commitment visibility
      Step 5:   Define training strategies and start training
      Step 6:   Start process action teams
      Step 7:   Develop partnerships with suppliers
      Step 8:   Measure process effectiveness and continuous improvement

PHASE 3:   Manage the transformation process.

Each of these phases will be described in more detail in the following section. The phases are inter-related and inter-dependent. You should start Phase 1 first, however, you don't "finish" one phase before going on to the next one. The activities of all three phases will be going on at the same time and should be iterated continuously.

PHASE 1: LEARN ABOUT TOTAL QUALITY AND ESTABLISH AN ENVIRONMENT OF CONTINUOUS LEARNING.

To perform an analysis of the transformation process will require substantial learning on the part of management. There is no substitute for this learning, and the transformation process cannot be delegated to a "TQM coordinator." TQM is not a quick fix, nor is it an overnight panacea. TQM methods require investing time and effort on prevention up-front, rather than racing prematurely into design and production resulting in the inevitable need for rework and repair. The same is true of applying total quality to transforming an organization. Racing into establishing steering committees, process action teams, statistical process control, etc. before spending adequate time identifying your customers' needs and requirements, metrics, and the relationship between inputs and outputs, will result in "rework and repair" to your transformation effort.

That is not to say you must learn everything ever written on TQM before you act. However, you should learn enough about total quality to enable you to apply its principles and practice what you preach as you pursue the transformation to total quality. Perhaps most importantly, you must establish an environment in your organization that values continuous learning. Transformation and profound knowledge cannot be acquired through only reading a few books or taking a few courses.

Sources of learning

There are many sources of learning about total quality; it does not have to cost you a lot of money:

> Visit other organizations implementing total quality (not with the intent of *copying* their approach, but to learn from them)
> Books
> Magazine articles
> Audio tapes
> Videos
> Consultants
> College courses
> National Institute of Standards and Technology (who administer the Malcolm Baldrige award: (301) 975-2036
> Federal Quality Institute: (202) 376-3753
> American Society for Quality Control: (800) 248-1946
> Association for Quality and Participation: (513) 381-1959

See K.D. Lam, *Total Quality Management: A Resource Guide*, 1990, for a detailed listing of books, videos, audios, software programs, college courses, organizations, etc.

This phase is started first, but should never end. Continuous learning is the bedrock upon which total quality can be built.

PHASE 2:   START TRANSFORMATION ACTIVITIES.

Activities frequently pursued to accomplish the transformation include:

Step 1:   Assess customers (internal and external)
Step 2:   Perform strategic planning: develop/refine mission and vision
Step 3:   Identify key opportunities
Step 4:   Develop executive commitment visibility
Step 5:   Define training strategies and start training
Step 6:   Start process action teams
Step 7:   Develop partnerships with suppliers
Step 8:   Measure process effectiveness and continuous improvement

These activities comprise many of the "mini-processes" or "sub-processes" within the overall transformation. They should be tailored to fit the philosophy and culture change required at your organization. These activities should continue on an on-going basis; first steps are not "completed" before other later steps are begun.

Step 1: Assess customers (internal and external):

The first "mini-process" within the overall implementation process is that of assessing what your customers like and dislike about your products and services. Many organizations try to skip this step using the logic "We know what our customers want better than they do." This is very dangerous thinking, as customer focus is why total quality works as well as it does. If you skip over going "face-to-face" with your customers, you run the risk of undermining your entire TQM effort. This effort (described in more detail in Chapter 3, Customer Focus) should include assessing both current and anticipated needs, wants and expectations of your internal and external customers. The effort should include analysis of customers' needs from the perspective of the customer, not what you imagine those needs to be. Try to experience what your customers experience when they do business with your organization.

Customer assessment should include both external and internal customers. Internal customers can be assessed using the same methods as those used for external customers: surveys, interviews, gymnastic scoring technique, active listening, brainstorming, etc. It is crucial to identify and work to resolve key internal customer issues such as lack of trust between employees and management, perceived lack of commitment to long term viability of the organization, and perceived lack of commitment to total quality.

Step 2: Perform strategic planning:

This second mini-process within the overall process is another step which managers frequently want to skip in order to "just get on with it." This activity is frequently skipped in organizations who put someone from the quality department "in charge" of the TQM effort. The resulting perspective is frequently narrow, and focused on quality of products and services, to the exclusion of the overall big picture of the organization. They frequently produce a "Quality Plan," which enumerates all the things that need to be done in the name of quality. Just as frequently, these "Quality Plans" are not well integrated with the overall operations and planning of the organization. As a result, individuals in the organization may tend to perceive quality as something extra, not a concept/strategy necessary for the survival of the organization.

A much preferred strategy is to step back, and use the total quality transformation as an opportunity to re-evaluate where you are as an organization, where you want to be, and how you are going to get there. This process should be engaged in by the "key leadership team" of the organization. That is to say, the head of the organization should not go off in a room and invent this alone, neither should it be delegated to a planning department or to the "TQM coordinator". Participation of all the key managers is critical to 1) ensure you tap the ideas and knowledge of this group, and 2) to create ownership of the outcomes of the session.

It is essential that planning for quality be integrated with the overall planning for the organization's business, operations, capital equipment, overhead, human resources, and technology.

A planning technique called "Hoshin" planning is being used by companies such as Hewlett Packard. It derives from the Japanese term "Hoshin kanri" which means "shining metal" and "pointing direction." Hoshin planning is a system that helps to point an organization in the right direction. Top management sets two or three most important goals for the year, and every manager knows these goals. Each manager identifies the two or three most important tasks they must accomplish to help achieve the overall goals. Measurable milestones are set for these activities and milestones are audited and documented and reported up through the organization to enable diagnosis and improvement (King, 1989).

Outputs of strategic quality planning frequently include:

- A new/updated customer-based vision
- A new/updated customer-based mission
- A visible commitment to a transformation to total quality as essential to achieving the vision
- A training strategy
- An employee involvement strategy
- A reward/recognition strategy
- A communications strategy
- A benchmarking strategy
- A resource commitment plan
- A supplier/customer involvement strategy

Prioritized goals and objectives are frequently developed to translate the commitment to total quality into specific actions, time tables and individual responsibilities. The vision and mission statements can be supplemented with a statement of values or guiding principles to clarify those philosophies and behaviors the organization believes are essential to achieving the vision.

The most important output of strategic quality planning is not a nicely bound document, but rather ownership of a common vision and commitment of the key leadership team to work to make it happen.

Step 3: Identify key opportunities

Where do you start with your process improvement efforts? Some organizations starting the TQM journey establish process action teams and let them choose what and how they want to improve. In the very early stages of the transformation, this may or may not result in important customer satisfaction issues getting addressed. An alternative strategy is to use the external and internal customer assessment data, and have the key leadership team prioritize these opportunities using criteria such as:

> Importance to customer
> Cost to achieve
> Accomplishability

A detailed list of project selection criteria is presented in Chapter 7, Process Improvement. The output of this activity should be a list of prioritized opportunities around which the organization can then plan to create process action teams. Finding time to learn and use new process improvement tools and techniques is a frequent complaint of managers and supervisors. For this reason, top management may want to consider starting some of the first teams themselves to identify activities which they may be requiring of their employees that don't add value. Elimination of these non-value added activities (e.g., certain meetings, reports, etc.) will then free up some time for employees, and make it a little easier for employees to learn and implement process improvement (see Chapter 6).

As the organization gains experience, it can transition to self-managed or self-directed teams, which require employees to be quite skilled in process management, process control and process improvement.

Step 4: Develop executive commitment visibility

An important activity necessary to transform to total quality is a tangible, visible commitment by the key leadership team to do things *differently*. Most often it is just assumed that after creating a new vision and agreeing to start the TQM journey, executives and managers will just somehow magically change. Often, many managers seem to assume it is just the other person that really needs to change.

The key leadership team should invest time in delineating what they personally need to do differently to accomplish the transformation at their organization. One technique is to create a written contract that all executives sign. This contract identifies the behaviors required in order for management to set an example or "walk the talk." Examples of items you might include in such a contract include:

"We agree ...

>... not to shoot messengers who take responsibility for the problem and whose intent it is to improve the process.

>... to strive for consensus, that is, being able to live with a decision and support it when we leave the room.

>... to strive to be better organizational ambassadors, as opposed to bickering, finger-pointing, and undercutting peer functions.

>... not only to stop gossiping, but help others to stop.

>... to confront rather than subvert other's activities that may or may not threaten one's turf.

>... to behave honoring the value "we have a job to do," rather than engaging in bureaucratic warfare.

>... to always go to the source to clarify issues.

>... to start all meetings with an agenda and to start and end meetings on time."

Step 5: Define training strategies and start training[1]

A common strategy for total quality management training is to establish an approach which has as its major thrust the training of the entire work force prior to initiating operational total quality shifts and practices. Proponents of this approach believe that the entire human system needs to make mental shifts before they can make the necessary quality shifts in work systems and processes. They point to the necessity for people to understand that quality improvements in one area may cause harmful consequences in other areas without system-wide integration steps. They rightfully maintain system-wide integration is most difficult if the proponents of a quality shift are talking with people who do not share their views nor understand the total quality management philosophy. Additionally, proponents of the train-the-entire-work force-first school make a case that individuals can be encouraged to start the total quality journey without waiting for formal total quality initiatives from senior management. Each individual in the organization would start quality management behaviors at their separate work stations, rather then waiting for the completion of the training cycle.

---

[1]This section contributed by Theodore L. Bloomer, Defense Systems Management College.

The concern for the train-the-entire-work force-first strategy is the obvious impact of time. Large organizations will find that an effective training cycle could take a year or more. They then have the problem of sustaining interest. The dynamics of most work places is that we move with a flow of crises and work requirements increasing the probability that energy and knowledge dedicated to total quality will deteriorate at a rapid rate. Many believe that the gap between training and implementation should be kept as short as possible, preferably with no gap at all.

Another approach is to train the work force incrementally. That is, conduct top leadership training, then train top-down in vertical slices of the organization. For example, after training the top people, select an advocate who has leadership over a functional slice of the organization (where total quality methodologies will likely work very well) and enrich the training in that area only. This allows the organization to run prototype activities and opportunities to conduct fairly rigorous "lessons learned" evaluations. This approach has two other significant results. The first is that the organization implements total quality activities rapidly. The organization realizes benefits, people have a sense of gratification. The second is that the early movement into total quality is used as the show-place for other organizational activities. The "test-bed" approach is less threatening and the "de-bugging" aspects reduce the personal and organizational risk normally associated with change.

A hybrid of these two approaches is to train top management in depth, provide a short awareness training course to everyone, and proceed to train the organization in depth using a strategy supportive of those process improvements you want to pursue first.

The Training Content

Training content should be tailored to fit the implementation strategy designed by the organization and should include the following areas:

Overview of Total Quality
Customer Focus
Teamwork
How to Facilitate Teams
Problem Solving Skills and Tools
Cost of Quality/Price of Nonconformance
Process Improvement (PDCA)
Statistical Process Control
Communications Skills
Graphical Tools
Design of Experiments
Quality Function Deployment
Benchmarking

The training content is not only influenced by the implementation strategy, but must be designed to meet its target groups. A case could be made training content should address specific layers of the organization differently. For example, one way to stratify an organization would be the following:

- Corporate/executive/general officer team. Their training might focus upon the integration of the total quality initiative within overall corporate plans. Not to do so would send a message to others that the total quality initiative is not a "main stream" corporate effort.

- Senior management team. Their training might include references to the corporate interface, but would begin to focus somewhat more around the operational definition of the transformation process and a closer look at total quality management methodologies and tools. The senior management team may also be trained to train others, to develop revised reward systems, to develop revised accounting systems, to manage and improve their own processes. Frequently, at this level it is difficult for managers to see "how all this applies to what I do."

- First line supervisors. These supervisors (rather than outside consultants) can have a significant role in the total quality effort, and must be very articulate in methodologies and tools. They are in a position to sandbag total quality or help it survive and prosper. Their training should include facilitator skills, process definition, measurement and inference, process improvement, use of the many problem solving tools and techniques, and skills to initiate and maintain positive efforts toward continuous process improvement.

- The work force. The work force can be trained by a number of approaches, for example, by their supervisors, by a training department or through outside sources. The advantage to training done by supervisors from their own department is they can frequently better relate the principles and tools of total quality to examples related to the specific job duties.

Step 6: Start process action teams

Many organizations implementing TQM make a case for only starting a few process action teams at first, in order to guarantee success of these first efforts. Proponents of this approach suggest you should choose these first few teams and the process problems on which they will work carefully to ensure success. See Chapter 7 for suggested project selection criteria. Some organizations call these initial efforts "pilot projects." Calling them "pilots" may send a message to the work force that TQM is just being tried out, and if it fails it will not be pursued.

Process action team members should be "selected" as much as possible using volunteers. In some cases, an individual's participation may be *required* as they bring a critical perspective to the group...try to encourage that individual's participation rather than "drafting" him or her. Ensure you have all the required cross-functional interfaces represented. Try to keep teams a manageable size: too small and you may not get the input you need, too large and teamwork becomes very difficult to manage. See Chapter 6, Teamwork.

Step 7: Develop partnerships with suppliers

Essential to the transformation is to develop partnerships with suppliers. If your suppliers are already knowledgeable of TQM, you may want to pursue transitioning to more of a partner relationship fairly soon. If your suppliers have not yet started the TQM journey, you may want to first accomplish some of the TQM transformation internally before you suggest it to your suppliers.

Step 8: Measure process effectiveness and continuous improvement

Remember, transforming an organization to total quality can be viewed as a process similar to other work processes. Therefore, it should be measured and continuously improved just like other organizational processes. For example, a measurement strategy should be put in place for measuring the effectiveness of training. The extent to which the organization culture is changing can also be measured (albeit subjectively). Executives can measure their own behavior such as numbers of messengers they shoot, minutes they arrive late to meetings, etc.

PHASE 3: MANAGING THE TRANSFORMATION PROCESS

The key leadership team must pay close attention to the transformation. Again, it is a responsibility that should not be delegated to a "TQM coordinator."

Key ingredients for successful transition to total quality include:

- Teamwork and authenticity of leadership team

- Focus on customers' real needs (current and future)

- Ownership and commitment of key leadership team

- Integration of total quality with everyday operations

- Safety net for displaced employees (not a guarantee of a job, but rather a commitment to ensure employee "employ-ability")

- A reward structure consistent with total quality principles and philosophy

  - collaboration versus competition
  - problem prevention versus fire fighting
  - teamwork versus individual, where appropriate

- Investment in continuous learning/training

- Empowerment of employees – with information and resources, not just responsibility

- Measurement of the right things – accomplishment versus activity

- Focus on keeping the momentum going – ensure adequate reward, recognition and coaching of team efforts

WHY TOTAL QUALITY MAY THREATEN EMPLOYEES

There are many reasons why TQM may threaten employees. Some of them include:

- "If I'm measured, I will look bad and everyone will know."

- "Process improvement may show that my job is no longer needed."

- "My bonus/performance award will be in jeopardy, as it rewards my individual performance."

- "TQM requires me to communicate, I'm more comfortable with numbers, circuits, and designs."

- "TQM is work."

- "TQM requires me to give some of my power away. I don't like that."

- "TQM involves too much discipline."

- "TQM will mean we have to spend extra time listening to the customer. Everyone knows they don't know what they want."

Employees experiencing these feelings are in many cases responding appropriately within an environment which is fear or competition based. The management of the organization must take action to drive out fear and competition that creates destructive sub-optimizing behavior.

IMPLEMENTATION PITFALLS TO AVOID

There are many pot-holes in the road on the long total quality journey. Some of them include:

- Over or under emphasis of the technical tools

- Not integrating total quality planning with overall business planning

- Lack of support from top/senior management

- Putting an "available" employee in charge of TQM

- Making assumptions about customers' current or future needs

- Executiveness/arrogance/pompousness

    - "directing" implementation
    - maintaining distance from workers
    - pronouncing rather than listening

- Focus on the shop floor to the exclusion of other areas

- Not practicing what you preach

- Not adequately training and nurturing teams

- Pursuit of significant *short* term results

Organizations are like snow flakes. No two organizations have the same internal and external customers, the same inputs and the same desired outputs. If a consultant wants to provide you "his/her stuff," you should become an educated (world-class) customer, clearly define your desired outputs, and the measures you will use to ensure your satisfaction. Then you will be better able to determine which process is best for your organization. There are many "canned" TQM training programs available, and many TQM consultants. It is wise to expose yourself to a variety of approaches, and then choose and tailor a process to fit your organization. Insist on quality by asking for a satisfaction guarantee or you pay no fee. Ask total quality consultants to show you their process. If they don't have one, they may not be practicing what they preach.

DISCUSSION QUESTIONS

1. Why is learning more about total quality an essential pre-cursor to getting started?

2. Why is "visiting" your customers one of the first steps in taking the total quality journey?

3. Why should other companies already implementing total quality be visited?

4. Discuss how to get employees involved in starting total quality.

5. Why is strategic quality planning an important step in implementing TQM?

6. What criteria should you use to select your first process action teams?

7. What are the advantages and disadvantages of the two training strategies: train everyone first versus train as you form process action teams?

ADDENDUM 1

DEFINING YOUR TRANSFORMATION PROCESS

One approach to getting started is to try to view organizational transformation as a process, with customers, inputs and desired outputs. This may be difficult for you if you are new to total quality. A process based approach involves the following steps:

STEP 1: Identify and assess the internal and external customers of the transformation process.

STEP 2: Identify customers' desired outputs.

STEP 3: Identify customer satisfaction metrics.

STEP 4: Identify required inputs and activities necessary to produce their desired outputs.

Organizations that start implementing TQM without paying attention to customers, inputs, outputs and metrics are unlikely to transform successfully. They are trying to implement TQM using business-as-usual techniques, as one would implement a cost-savings program. A sample process model is presented in Figure 1. It would be wise for organizations starting the TQM journey to look at their customers, their desired outputs and their satisfaction measures in some detail, before they design inputs and activities to produce the desired outputs.

Whatever transformation process you design should contain these generic steps:

STEP 1: IDENTIFY THE INTERNAL AND EXTERNAL CUSTOMERS OF THE TRANSFORMATION PROCESS

Identifying customers sounds like it should be easy enough, but in practice can be quite difficult. Most organizations have many customers of the transformation process, sometimes with apparent competing and conflicting needs. Many times we attribute needs and requirements to our customers which are actually our own outdated assumptions about them. Total quality philosophy requires us to check out opinions and assumptions by measuring before we proceed with a course of action.

STEP 2: IDENTIFY CUSTOMERS' DESIRED OUTPUTS

Getting clear on why you are pursuing total quality is very important. If you are starting the TQM journey to improve internal and external customer satisfaction, you will have a much higher chance of succeeding than if you are doing it for the following reasons:

- Your Corporate/Headquarters office is "forcing" you.

- You want increased short term profits.

- You want to win a quality award to boost your business.

- Everyone else is doing it.

STEP 3: IDENTIFY CUSTOMER SATISFACTION METRICS

Organizations taking a business-as-usual approach to implementing TQM frequently use no metrics at all to measure how well their transformation process is working. Others use metrics that describe the occurrence of TQM-like activity:

Number of process action teams started
Number of hours/people trained
Number of times the steering committee met

These measures may or may not indicate effectiveness of your transformation. It is preferable to tie your metrics directly to what the customers of the transformation process (employees, suppliers, external customers) think are important. Some possibilities include:

Increase in effectiveness of meetings (meetings take less time, fewer meetings are necessary, and useable outputs of meetings increase)

Decreased competition and improved collaboration

Change in behavior of top management staff

Change in organization culture

% Reduction in cycle/span time of major processes

% Reduction in defects and errors

Dollars spent on TQM/dollars returned in improvement

Notice that some of these metrics are subjective. You should have a structured, disciplined, consistent method to gather these data.

STEP 4: IDENTIFY REQUIRED INPUTS AND ACTIVITIES NECESSARY TO PRODUCE DESIRED OUTPUTS

If you know what you want your transformation process to do for your internal and external customers, and know how to measure it, you are now ready to identify inputs and activities necessary to produce those outcomes. These are the activities listed in Phase 2 of Chapter 5.

A SAMPLE TRANSFORMATION PROCESS

SAMPLE CUSTOMERS:	SAMPLE POTENTIAL MEASURES:
External customers	Number defects/errors Time to market Delivery performance Responsiveness to change
Internal customers (Employees)	Job satisfaction Improved communication Increased trust Increased involvement in work activities Job security
Managers	Job satisfaction Job security
Shareholders	% increase in stock value
Community	Number of jobs provided Environmental care

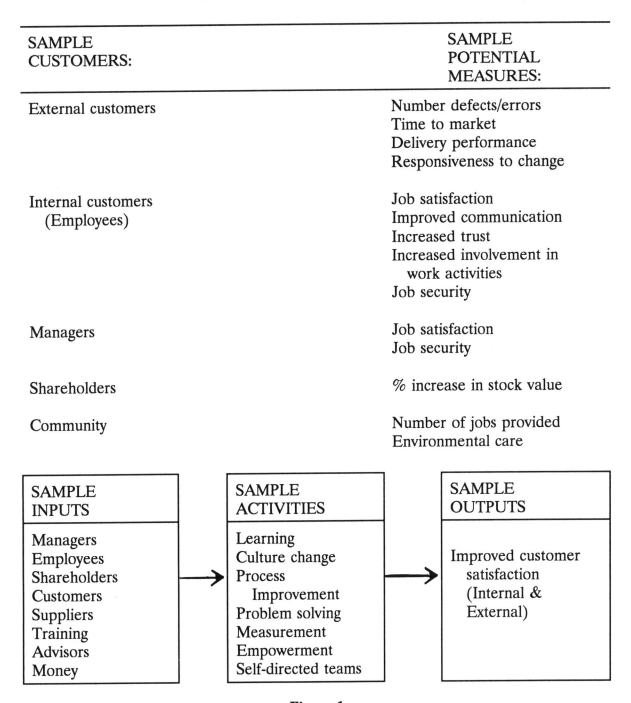

SAMPLE INPUTS	SAMPLE ACTIVITIES	SAMPLE OUTPUTS
Managers Employees Shareholders Customers Suppliers Training Advisors Money	Learning Culture change Process Improvement Problem solving Measurement Empowerment Self-directed teams	Improved customer satisfaction (Internal & External)

Figure 1

Chapter 6

ESSENTIALS OF TEAMWORK

WHY IS TEAMWORK CRITICAL TO ACHIEVING TOTAL QUALITY?

Total quality frequently requires multi-functional or multi- disciplined involvement to ensure effective process improvements which optimize achievement of organizational goals instead of individual functional objectives. However, the culture in many of our organizations has evolved to reward the individual contributor and problem solver, the "knight on a white horse". Today, our world is changing at such a rapid pace, no longer can we rely on any one individual's solution to be the best for complex inter-related organizational processes. We need the input, viewpoint and ideas of individuals across several functions to solve cross-functional problems and improve cross-functional processes. Teams with members from several functions in an organization are called "cross-functional teams". They can ensure solutions are not implemented to fit parochial interests at the expense of the overall system/organization. Total quality does promote a zealous pursuit of individual expertise. However, the expertise is applied by individuals working together as a team for mutual benefit toward a common goal.

Ownership of the results of teamwork is necessary for team effectiveness. Having individuals from several functions involved in process improvement or problem solving increases the potential that all team members buy-in to the solutions developed by the team. When a team works together using tools and techniques of total quality to improve processes, they not only achieve ownership of the outcomes of the team activity, but also are more motivated to implement the outcomes. Frequently, ideas, policies, solutions dictated from an individual are rejected or undermined by subordinates and/or co-workers—not because they aren't good ideas—but rather because the individuals feel no ownership for them. It is a type of intellectual "not-invented-here" phenomenon. People want to be involved in creating the processes, plans, policies, and methods that will affect them. Effective teamwork helps to achieve this end.

Working in teams can also help to promote good information flow horizontally throughout the organization. In organizations dealing with increasingly complex technologies, products, and services, it is essential for individuals to understand the functions and processes of their co-workers. Most organization functions are now inter-related and there are many, complex customer-supplier relationships across organizations. Teamwork can provide a forum for communication to better enable these internal customers and suppliers to satisfy each others' needs.

Having the opportunity to be part of a team working together to improve a process or solve a problem is a good feeling. It makes workers feel involved, important and "in-the-know". It is part of what makes employees of total quality organizations feel better about coming to work in the morning.

Teamwork promotes synergy, a well documented phenomenon. Synergy means the whole is greater than the sum of the individual parts. Properly selected individuals working in teams can frequently arrive at better solutions than those same individuals working alone.

Teamwork is also an effective tool to train and develop individuals for broader responsibilities. The exposure to other viewpoints, processes and issues obtained in cross-functional teams broadens individuals, and can make them a more valuable asset to the organization.

WHY DO SOME MANAGERS RESIST TEAMWORK?

Many individuals feel frustrated working in teams, especially if they are very aggressive, intelligent, independent, "Type-A" individuals. They want things to move faster, and don't understand why they have to involve others in problem solving to arrive at a solution they believe they already know. This type of individual typifies the aggressive American manager who just wants "to get on with it." It also typifies why many of the solutions developed by these smart managers tend to fail: 1) devoid of input of workers closer to the problem, their solutions are often not the best ones, and 2) their solutions may be stone-walled, sabotaged, undermined, or be given lip service by people have no ownership invested in them.

Other managers complain teams are ineffective committees who frequently invent camels. Many so-called "teams" *are* ineffective. It takes more than an assemblage of individuals to achieve teamwork. It is no accident the word "work" is part of the word "teamwork," as it *can* be quite a lot of work. It requires discipline, structure and a willingness to listen and share. It requires an open mind and an incredible amount of patience. It may require you to work closely with people different than you, whom you may dislike.

The more a manager has tendencies toward introversion, the more uncomfortable the manager may be working in teams. Some individuals' "batteries" are drained through interaction with groups of people. These managers generally prefer working alone and may be less than enthused about teamwork (Kiersey, 1978).

Does the necessity for teamwork mean there is no longer a place for individual contributions? Of course not. As a matter of fact, good teamwork depends on the zealous contributions of all the individuals on the team. However, individuals no longer go off in a room by themselves to solve a problem or improve a process which affects many people or multiple functions.

TYPES OF TEAMS

Organizational teams to solve problems or improve processes come in many sizes and shapes. Two types of teams are cross functional and functional:

Cross-functional — Members are comprised of individuals from several functions across the organization. For example, a cross functional team to improve an overhead expense budgeting process would have members not only from finance, but also engineering, marketing, manufacturing, purchasing, and contracts.

Functional — This team consists of members from one function. This type of team is best focused on processes wholly contained in that functional area, or involve technical focus or skill sharpening. For example, a functional team to improve the process used to track new business opportunities might consist of members exclusively from the business development or marketing departments. Engineers deciding on the best model for designing building trusses are another example of a functional team.

Effective teams must be comprised not only of properly skilled individuals, but must also be the right size. There are no set rules about team size, but one which is too small or too large may not be as effective as one having between 6 and 10 members. Teams smaller than 6 may not achieve the degree of synergy of larger teams. Teams larger than 10 start to inhibit synergy due to reduced opportunity for participation as the body count increases (Warrick and Zawacki, 1987).

Problem solving and process improvement teams go by many different names:

> Process action teams (PATs)
> Process improvement groups (PIGs)
> Process improvement teams (PITs)
> High performance teams (HPTs)
> Quality improvement teams (QITs)
> Critical action teams (CATs)
> Process effectiveness teams (PETs)
> Continuous improvement teams (CITs)
> Critical process teams (CPTs) and others.

Inventing a name for these teams is often a part of the process of giving total quality a unique identity for an organization.

WHAT ARE THE KEY INGREDIENTS OF EFFECTIVE TEAMS?

A Skilled Leader and/or Facilitator

A key ingredient is a skilled team leader, or facilitator. Some teams have both a leader and a facilitator, and some teams have neither, they are self-managed and self-facilitated. A leader can be thought of as responsible for the group as a whole, and the facilitator guides activities, acts as a consultant to the functioning of the group, and may also provide training to the group. There often is confusion about the role of the team leader. We have been trained in many of our business schools to believe the leader is "in charge," is the smartest one in the group, and is responsible for making all the decisions. This is not the concept of a total quality team leader. The total quality leader promotes high quality group interaction, i.e., ensures that the talent and expertise of all team members are used.

The role of the facilitator includes planning, selling, teaching, barrier busting, learning, coaching, cheerleading, coordinating, and reporting (Richey, 1987). This checklist developed by David Richey (Richey, 1987) is intended to aid in identifying individuals best suited to be facilitators:

1. Respected by management
2. Respected by employees
3. People oriented
4. Knowledgeable about the organization
5. Good speaker and teacher
6. Writing is clear
7. Has trust in people
8. Innovative/entrepreneurial/creative
9. Supportive and positive
10. Self-motivated
11. Willing listener
12. Knows how to lobby
13. Organized and systematic
14. Meets deadlines
15. Avid reader
16. Likes to coach, feels good when others win
17. Persistent, yet patient
18. Gets others to accept responsibility
19. Understands group dynamics
20. Understands steps to change

Shared Understanding and Support of the Team Purpose

One of the most important elements of good teamwork is a shared understanding of the purpose of the team. Individuals must not only understand the team's goals and objectives, but also believe in and support them. If team members have different perceptions of their purpose, individuals' efforts will not be effectively focused. Some "Process Action Teams" (PATs) are formed without adequate time devoted to achieving a common understanding of the purpose of the teams. This generally should be done through a dialogue of team members, rather than through team leader memorandum, fiat or proclamation.

Shared Responsibility for Outcomes

The team must share responsibility for outcomes. When individuals leave the team meeting, they must support the consensus of the team, even if they don't agree with it individually. This is the essence of consensus, all members get a chance to put forth and explain their ideas and ensure they are understood by all team members However, the course of action supported by the most team members will be the one pursued and then supported by all team members.

Collaboration

Collaboration is required for good teamwork. We are more used to competing with our colleagues at work. We need to transfer the teamwork feeling of a football squad to the playing field of work. A team whose members have win-win attitudes will be more effective than one whose members operate with win-lose attitudes. Win-win team members seek to optimize the system, not their own personal objective.

Adequate Resources

For a team to be effective it requires adequate resources. Teams need time, training, skilled members, skilled leaders, and may also need materials and equipment.

A "Safety Net"

Process improvement teams can benefit from having a "safety net." If you are on a process improvement team and identify a way to improve the process that eliminates your job, you need some pre-arranged assurance you won't be out of a job. A "safety net" is not a guarantee of life-time employment; rather, it is a commitment by the company to ensure your employability.

Focus on Improvement of Team Process

Effective teams focus on process and continuously try to improve their team process. Some teams apply total quality tools and techniques to their work processes, but fall short of applying principles/tools of total quality to the team process itself.

Ability to See Change as an Opportunity Versus a Threat

The best teams are made up of members who see change as an opportunity for growth. Resistance to change can be a significant impediment to effective teamwork (Buchholz & Roth, 1987).

Skilled and Aware Team Members

Team members can be thought of as "inputs" to the team process. Team members must have both the required technical skills and total quality problem-solving, data collection and analysis skills. It is helpful if team members have an awareness of themselves as process inputs and the strengths, weaknesses and behavioral preferences they bring to the team. Use of Myers-Briggs type indicator (1962) or Kiersey sorter (1978) may be helpful for this.

Management Support of Results

A key ingredient to the continued effectiveness of teams is management support of results. Team reward of results will help motivate continued success. Some organizations give rewards to the best individual on a team, the individual they believe contributed the most. Individual rewards can be destructive to effective teamwork as they may create competition between team members.

STAGES OF TEAM GROWTH

Because the inputs to teams are different, the team growth process is rarely the same. However, four common stages of team growth are identified in *The Team Handbook* (Scholtes, 1988):

Forming — Generally the first phase teams experience, where they are getting to know each other, and are trying to figure out what the task is and how team members will relate to one another. Everyone's expected to "be polite".

Storming — This is said to be the most difficult phase, and is likened to when the honeymoon is over. Team members lose their politeness and become more authentic. They may exhibit impatience, frustration, confusion, arguing, defensiveness, competition, disunity, resistance, depression, or pessimism (i.e., they "storm").

Norming — This phase is characterized by reconciliation, resolution of conflict, friendliness, cohesion, harmony, and acceptance of the team purpose and norms. This is also the stage during which unique individual roles may be given to different group members.

Performing — Teams in this phase have developed a satisfactory team process and can focus on performance of process problem solving and improvement.

The length and intensity a team experiences these phases depends on the team members and the skill of the facilitator. New members, new tasks and new information can all force a team to regress to previous stages.

HOW DO YOU FACILITATE EFFECTIVE TEAMWORK?

There are many ways to promote effective teamwork. The following are important requirements for both team leaders and facilitators:

- **Ensure the purpose of the team is understood.**

  This is accomplished through *two-way* communication. In other words, it is not enough for the leader to "tell" the group the purpose. The leader must involve the group members in a *dialogue* in which the team members' words will confirm their understanding of the purpose.

- **Ensure members are committed to the purpose.**

  Too frequently, leaders assume everyone shares their commitment to the purpose of the team. Taking time up-front to measure each individual's commitment to the purpose is an important step. It enables the leader to solve any problem of commitment before effort is wasted by members who attend meetings trying to stonewall or subvert team efforts.

- **Ensure group members agree on group norms.**

  There are many simple things to help teams function well which should be clarified and agreed to by the group. These are the "norms" of the group such as agreeing to start on time, end on time, having an agenda for each meeting, not interrupting when someone else is speaking, not carrying on side conversations, no smoking at team meetings, etc. These agreements should be developed and agreed to by the group.

- **Ensure the team is comprised of the right mix of people and members' roles are understood.**

Each team member has something to offer and a specific role to perform. Clarifying this early-on will help to ensure efforts are focused, the team is comprised of the right mix of individuals, and each member's talents are used.

- **Ensure team members have the right skills.**

Good problem solving skills are essential to effective teamwork. Without knowledge of the structured, disciplined problem solving tools of total quality (see Chapters 7, 8, and 9) team activity frequently degenerates into a power struggle of "endless-opinionating". It is essential training in problem solving techniques be delivered close in time to when the team will actually use the techniques.

- **Encourage risk-taking and creativity.**

Leaders must reinforce creative ideas, especially during brainstorming activities where creativity is essential. If "off-the-wall" ideas are discouraged by either the leader or the team members, the team's ability to innovate will be greatly diminished. You must "drive out fear."

- **Facilitate balanced participation.**

"Shallow brooks are frequently noisy." A good facilitator must draw out the more quiet members of the group, and ensure aggressive contributors do not dominate. This is sometimes difficult in groups where a very rigid pecking order exists, such as in some military groups. In those situations, the high ranking military members should be encouraged to establish a climate of balanced participation through soliciting input from lower ranking individuals.

- **Allow and manage conflict.**

Some people get the idea good teams always get along and never disagree. These teams seldom get beyond the forming stage. Disagreement is important to good team functioning, but should be managed by the team facilitator. Conflict should not be allowed to degenerate to the point personal attacks are made. The focus in resolving disagreements should be on using data and measurement, not opinions.

- **Focus on task accomplishment.**

  Team meetings are not social events nor opportunities to execute tangential agendas. A good team leader keeps the group focused on accomplishing the task. She/he has an agenda for the meeting and helps keep team members on track.

- **Ask open ended questions, not yes-no questions.**

  The role of the leader is not to be the omniscient fountain of knowledge. Rather, his/her role is to secure the involvement and the participation of the team members. Asking open ended questions rather than yes-no questions facilitates participation of the team members.

- **Pay close attention to eye contact.**

  We as human beings prefer to speak to those who we feel are important and who return our eye contact. Good team leaders are not seduced by the importance or eye contact of others, and actually try to involve seemingly disinterested group members by directing eye contact and speech to them.

- **Redirect questions to other members of the group.**

  Sometimes members will try to put the facilitator in the hot seat, or will look to the him/her for direction or confirmation. In this situation, good facilitators redirect the question or issue to another group member: "What do you think about that, Elizabeth?"

- **Let members ride their ambiguity.**

  Team members struggling with an issue sometimes reach the point of apparent stalemate. It seems as if no one wants to talk or move forward. This tends to occur on particularly sensitive issues. Often, the tendency of the leader is to jump in and save the group. Good team leaders have patience and let the group wrestle with the stalemate, and dissect the issue using TQM related tools and techniques (e.g., cause and effect analysis, brainstorming, force field analysis, etc.). A better solution will often result than if the team leader rescues the group with his/her answer.

- **Ensure members stay open to the ideas of others.**

  Team members frequently slip back into bad habits, one of which is to shut down others who they feel are not contributing worthwhile ideas to the group. Good facilitators ensure all team members ideas are respected and understood. Through the disciplined process of problem solving and reaching consensus, the group will discard ideas which do not have value.

- **Encourage members with verbal and non-verbal prompts.**

  We deliver powerful messages with our body language and voice. Facilitators must pay close attention to how they stand, what they do with their hands and arms, their facial expressions, and their voice intonation. The intent here is not to manipulate the group, but to be aware of body language messages we may be sending which can interfere with the group's effectiveness.

- **Use warm-ups, as appropriate, to stimulate involvement and promote team cohesion.**

  A "warm-up" is a short activity at the beginning of a team meeting to get all the team members involved, energized, and (frequently) smiling. They are sometimes described as "team building" activities. There are hundreds of these warm-up exercises published, and it is a good idea for facilitators to take advantage of these creative team building activities (Bianchi, 1990), especially if team members don't know each other.

- **Ensure meeting housekeeping tasks are taken care of.**

  Lack of attention to small details regarding the time, place, equipment requirements, note-taking, agendas, minutes, etc. can diminish team effectiveness. It is a good idea to develop a checklist of pre-and post-meeting requirements to ensure they are taken care of. Rotation of housekeeping duties (taking notes, getting coffee, distributing the agenda, etc.) is preferable to one individual getting stuck with them every time. It is a good idea not to assign housekeeping duties according to gender.

HOW DO YOU DEAL WITH PROBLEM TEAM BEHAVIOR?

Lots of things can, and frequently do, go wrong with teams. Most teams start out pretty well, but as the "work" element of teamwork sets in, team members frequently slip back into old behaviors. They may become so interested in the task they forget about their team process. Some of these disruptive behaviors include:

EXPERTS: Individuals who believe they know more than the others will tolerate team interaction for awhile, but may lose patience and try to bring the group to closure prematurely. They can be observed to very forcefully try to convince the group to do it their way, and frequently become loud and argumentative.

RULE BREAKERS: Although team members have signed the agreement on group norms, some members may forget or ignore them. These rule breakers can be observed arriving late, interrupting while others are speaking or having side conversations.

CHECKED OUT: Some people get tired of competing for air time with more powerful members of the group and just give up. They stop participating verbally and often mentally. You may observe them frequently arriving late and/or leaving early.

LOUDMOUTH: This individual has an obsessive need for air time to convince others and himself of his capability. He dominates the conversation, frequently interrupts others and rarely listens. Often this behavior masks serious personal insecurity and anxiety.

JOKERS: A little humor is vital to good teamwork. When it is overdone to the point the group cannot focus on the work it has to do, it can be very disruptive. These individuals waste the group's time with unnecessary stories and clowning around.

CHEERLEADER: This individual seems like a real asset to the group as his/her attitude is very positive. However, he commits to do things and doesn't follow through. He tends to gloss over real problems and the analysis required to solve them with a "Not to worry, we can do it" attitude.

WHINER: This individual is the opposite of the cheerleader. He believes nothing can be solved so why even try. He finds innumerable reasons to support his position, most of which involve blaming others. You may hear him say things like "Corporate/Headquarters will never buy it," or "Management will never change."

MULES: When you hear someone say "But we've always done it this way," or "That's not the way we do things here," you'll know you've encountered a mule. These individuals are not comfortable with change and display consistent opposition.

The facilitator has the primary role to manage these disruptive behaviors. However, he/she must be assisted and supported by the team members to keep team interaction focused and productive. Sometimes coaching these individuals off-line in a supportive, nurturing way will eliminate non-productive behaviors. Another approach is to invite the group to consider the team interaction as a process, and to problem-solve that process by brainstorming process problems. Without specifically discussing any individual, the group can develop metrics, and do a cause and effect diagram to identify root causes of teamwork problems. After reaching consensus on what is disrupting good team process, the group can suggest process improvements, test and measure whether process improvements are working.

DeMarco and Lister (1987) suggest that it may be helpful not only to look at the "how-to's" for effective teams, but the "how-not-to's." They describe seven sure-fire techniques to kill effective terms, i.e., to commit "Teamicide":

Defensive Management — not really letting go of control. This maneuver is engaged in by managers afraid of really trusting and empowering teams. This technique is fueled by fear that their people will make mistakes, or reluctance to give up power.

Bureaucracy — burying terms in mind-less paper pushing requirements.

Physical Separation — for effective teamwork, "absence may not make the team grow fonder."

Fragmentation of People's Time — it is difficult to be a member of multiple teams without sacrificing some effectiveness.

Quality Reduction of the Product — teams that are given the charge to reduce costs through reduction in quality will lose the sense of mission and esteem necessary to effective teamwork.

Phoney Deadline Spiels — teams given a task to do with an impossible deadline are being robbed of pride of workmanship from the start.

Clique Control — many managers feel the need to disband teams after "the job is done." Others simply miss opportunity to keep them together, and capitalize on a "jelled" team.

MEASURING TEAM PROCESS

Teamwork is a process which can be measured and improved. There are many ways of doing this, from the formal to the very informal. Team measures may be subjective, but some measures are usually better than no measures at all. In-process measures can be taken during team meetings, or after each session concludes. Measures can be taken on an overall effectiveness scale, or specific items addressed, such as balanced participation. Use of the gymnastic scoring card technique can be helpful here (see Chapter 3).

TRANSITIONING TO SELF-DIRECTED TEAMS

A self-managed or self-directed team is fully responsible for producing a well-defined segment of finished work, whether a product or service. Each member shares responsibility for the work done by the team. If the group has a leader at all, she/he fills that position for a week/month/year and all team members take turns sharing the leadership role (Sweny, 1991). Benefits include better satisfied customers, higher quality products and services, greater flexibility, increased commitment from employees and greater speed to market.

The transition from individual to team-based problem solving and process improvement is a difficult one for many managers. When starting to pursue total quality, some managers set up elaborate procedures for review of each and every process improvement suggested by teams. It makes them nervous that team members are off doing things in which they are not directly involved. They worry the team will come up with process improvements which may not be the way they would direct the team to do it. Managers excessively involved in "approving" every step taken by the team have not yet made the transition to believing the individuals closest to the work know best how to improve that work. They have not yet let go of the need to be "in charge." The function of the manager is to coach employees and to develop clear and useful policy which guides actions and sets boundaries for discretionary decision making by self-directed teams.

SUMMARY

A team is much more than a group of individuals assembled together to work on a problem. A team is characterized by team members' commitment to the good of the organization, not to sub-optimizing individual goals. To be effective, however, team members must pursue organizational goals with great individual zealotry. Teamwork does not mean no one is responsible for process outcomes; even cross-functional processes can have process owners. An effective team focused on total quality uses a structured, disciplined approach to problem solving, and relies on data and measurement, not opinions, to make decisions and resolve disagreements. The improvement process used by an effective total quality team is covered in detail in Chapter 7, and the tools and techniques used by teams are covered in Chapters 3, 7, 8 and 9.

DISCUSSION QUESTIONS

1.   Why is team work a critical concept to achieving total quality?

2.   What are the key ingredients of effective teams?

3.   Why is it initially difficult to work in teams?

4.   Who is responsible for the group process for a team?

5.   What is the goal in competition versus the goal in collaboration?

6.   What is a cross functional team and why is it important?

7.   What are the most important skills required of an effective facilitator?

8.   Why is ownership of outcomes an important ingredient of total quality problem solving?

9.   What are some sure-fire ways to inhibit the effective formation and functioning of teams?

REFERENCES

Bianchi, S., Butler, J., and Richey, D., *Warmups for Meeting Leaders*, University Associates, Inc.: San Diego, 1990.

Buchholz, S. and Roth, T., *Creating the High Performance Team*, John Wiley & Sons: New York, 1987.

DeMarco, Tom and Lister, Tim, *Peopleware: Productive Projects and Teams*, Dorset House Publishing: New York, NY, 1987.

Keirsey, D., & Bates, M., *Please Understand Me*, Prometheus Nemesis Books: Del Mar, CA, 1978.

Myers, I., *Manual: The Myers-Briggs Type Indicator*, Consulting Psychologists Press: Palo Alto, CA, 1962.

Richey, David, *Getting Results from Employee Participation*, Quality Group Publishing: Ventura, CA, 1987.

Scholtes, Peter R., *The Team Handbook*, Joiner Associates, Inc.: Madison, WI, 1988.

Sweny, Stephen, "Managing without Managers," *Information Week*, Nov 11, 1991, pp. 44-49.

Warrick, D.D., and Zawacki, R.A., *High Performance Management*, Eagle Publishing Company: Colorado Springs, CO, 1987.

Chapter 7

PROCESS IMPROVEMENT

WHAT IS A PROCESS?

If asked to describe what you do, you would probably respond by describing a number of responsibilities, activities and tasks. Total quality requires us to look at organizations as systems comprised of many interdependent activities which are called processes. "Process" is the term used to describe any activity which transforms identifiable inputs into desired outputs. Figure 7.1 is a simplified illustration of a process.

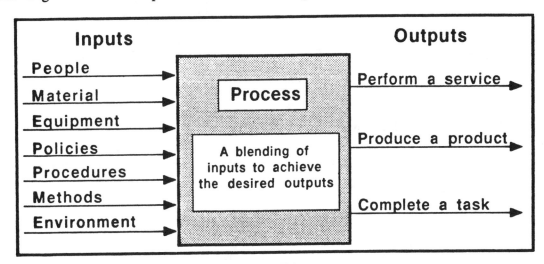

Figure 7.1

- **PROCESS** – ACTIVITIES WHICH TRANSFORM INPUTS INTO VALUE-ADDED OUTPUTS

Notice process inputs can include such things as people, material, equipment, policies, procedures, methods, and environment.

Breaking down organizational activities into processes, the steps required to perform activities, enables you to focus on and identify exactly how work gets done. It enables you to identify what inputs are required at each step and what outputs are produced at each step. The more clearly you identify desired outputs at each step, the better you will be able to ensure customer satisfaction with the output of each particular step. The more clearly process inputs, outputs and steps are described, the better you will be able to use measurement to monitor, control and improve activities.

Processes come in all sizes, and large processes are typically made up of many sub-processes or mini-processes which are linked together. To improve a process, it is important to have a clear definition of the process boundaries, that is, the step that starts the process and the step that ends the process. It is important to pick processes for improvement which are not too big, or else you'll trap yourself in endless analysis. It is best to select portions of large processes to work on, so team members don't get bogged down. Teams should have an opportunity to experience success. As you work to improve pieces of large processes, make sure teams working on different pieces of the process are coordinating and sharing data, process analyses and proposed improvements.

When selecting a project, you should ensure the project meets all or most of these criteria (Scholtes, 1988, and Juran, 1989):

1.   The process or project is related to important/urgent business or organization issues.

2.   The process targeted has potential for a large amount of improvement with direct impact on the company or organization's external customers. (Sometimes this can mean solving an internal customer problem which has a direct impact on external customers. For example, a Chinese restaurant had the reputation of good food but poor service. It turned out the owner was arrested for employee abuse. Solving the internal problem in this case was a precursor to improving service to the external customer.)

3.   The process is visible throughout the organization.

4.   The managers (at all levels) and the workers concerned with the process agree it is important to improve the process.

5.   Enough managers, supervisors and operators concerned with the project area or process will cooperate to make it a success. There are times when cooperation will be unanimous, but be prepared for some nay-sayers, especially where turf issues are concerned or there is a great deal of personal investment in the existing system.

6.   The process is not in the midst of change (except as it may be effected by the improvement project). This is necessary to give you a stable baseline from which to work. The project involves a product or service which has good potential for internal customer demand in the future.

7.   The project is one clearly defined process with easily identified start and end points. Without a bounded process, you may find yourself trying to improve problems such as "poor communications" or "poor morale." Efforts to improve these may be like trying to solve poverty or inflation. To get your arms around such problems, pick a process with a defined beginning and end, such as communications during weekly staff meetings.

8. The process is not being studied by any other group. This is to ensure you are not wasting resources re-inventing the wheel or competing with another group to create the "best" solution.

9. One cycle of the process is completed each day or two (this is most important for initial projects). This will enable you to go through one cycle of the improvement process and see results much faster.

10. The mission statement for the team describes a *problem* to be studied or an improvement opportunity, not a solution to be tried. Frequently problems are described as the "lack of" something (e.g., training, tools, time, information, etc.). Stating problems this way implies a solution before exploring potential problem causes.

11. The technology required for project solution exists.

PROCESS OWNERSHIP

With the emphasis in total quality on teamwork, many people get confused about who has the responsibility for improving a particular process. It appears many times to be the responsibility of the whole team, and therefore, it may appear as if no one is really responsible. Many organizations are using the concept of "process ownership." This means every process has an owner, an individual who has responsibility for the proper working of the process and the authority to make improvements to the process.

When processes cross many organizational boundaries, there may be several different process owners at the sub-process level, and one overall owner who orchestrates the entire process to ensure all internal and external customers are satisfied with the outputs of the process.

PROCESS PROBLEMS

There are generally six sources of problems in a process (Scholtes, 1988):

1. Lack of understanding of how a process *actually* works.

2. Lack of knowledge of how a process *should* work.

3. Errors and/or mistakes in executing process steps.

4. Practices which fail to recognize the need for preventative measures, such as maintenance or training.

5. Non-value added steps, activities which consume time and resources, but do not add value to the product or service.

6. Variation in inputs and outputs.

An effective process improvement process must be able to identify and eliminate these six types of problems.

SHEWHART AND DEMING CYCLES

One of the most significant distinguishing features of the total quality philosophy is its emphasis on *continuous* improvement. Thus, another key characteristic of an effective process improvement strategy is its iterative nature. Elimination of process problems must be a continuous cycle. Dr. Walter A. Shewhart advocated an approach to continuous improvement called the **"PLAN - DO - CHECK - ACT"** OR **"PDCA"** cycle, and is illustrated in Figure 7.2. Simply stated, first you **plan** the improvement, then you try it out or **do** it, next you **check** to ensure through measurement it worked, and finally you put it into **act**ion. It is very similar to what many have learned as the scientific method.

PLAN – Identify and select the process which will be improved. Bound the process using flow diagrams. Define the problem by clearly articulating what it is, where and when it occurs, and how customer satisfaction with the output of the process can be measured. Analyze the process to identify possible causes of the process problem and focus on the most likely cause(s). Propose process improvement(s). Develop a data collection strategy.

DO – Try out proposed improvement(s) on a small scale in a controlled environment.

CHECK – Collect and analyze data to determine if the proposed improvements result in improved customer satisfaction.

ACT – Implement effective process changes by integrating them into the existing system of processes.

A similar process often referred to as the "Deming cycle" is illustrated in Figure 7.3. Recognizing the opportunity is similar to the "Plan" step. You must define your process and determine your customer's needs (current and future). You may be faced with several opportunities, and may need to prioritize them by their importance, achievability and/or cost. The "test the theory" step is similar to the "Do" step above. A test must be designed which will tell you if your theory (relative to the process improvement) is supported by the data you collect. Observing test results is similar to the "Check" step and requires you gather data/measurements and compare them to the theory you proposed in the test step. Finally, you act on the opportunity, that is, implement it.

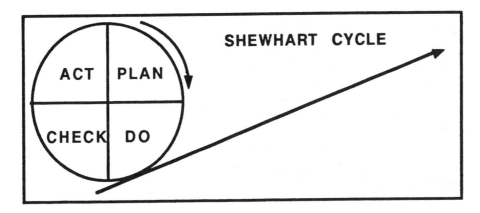

Figure 7.2 Shewhart Cycle

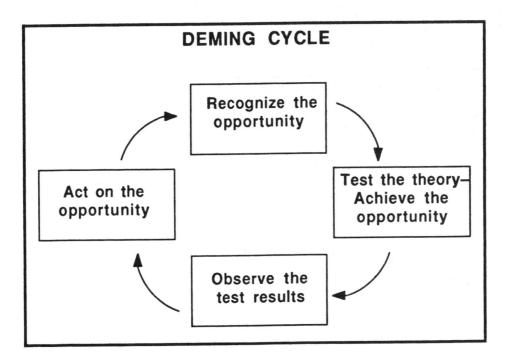

Figure 7.3 Deming Cycle

THE PROCESS IMPROVEMENT PROCESS

Both the Shewhart and Deming cycles have been used as a framework for step-by-step approaches to process improvement. Figure 7.4 illustrates such a process, developed by the Naval Personnel Research and Development Center (Chapter 9 explains common and special causes of variation).

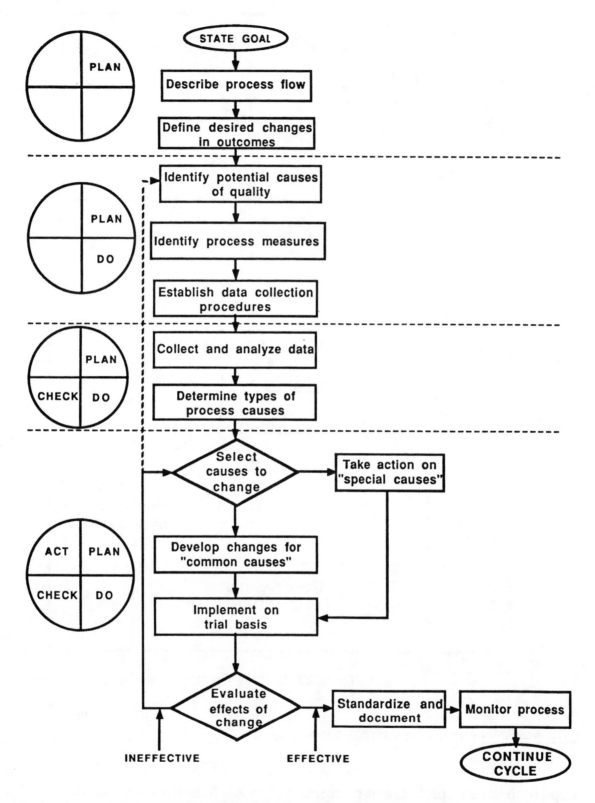

Figure 7.4 Flow Diagram for Process Improvement
(Houston and Dockstader, 1989)

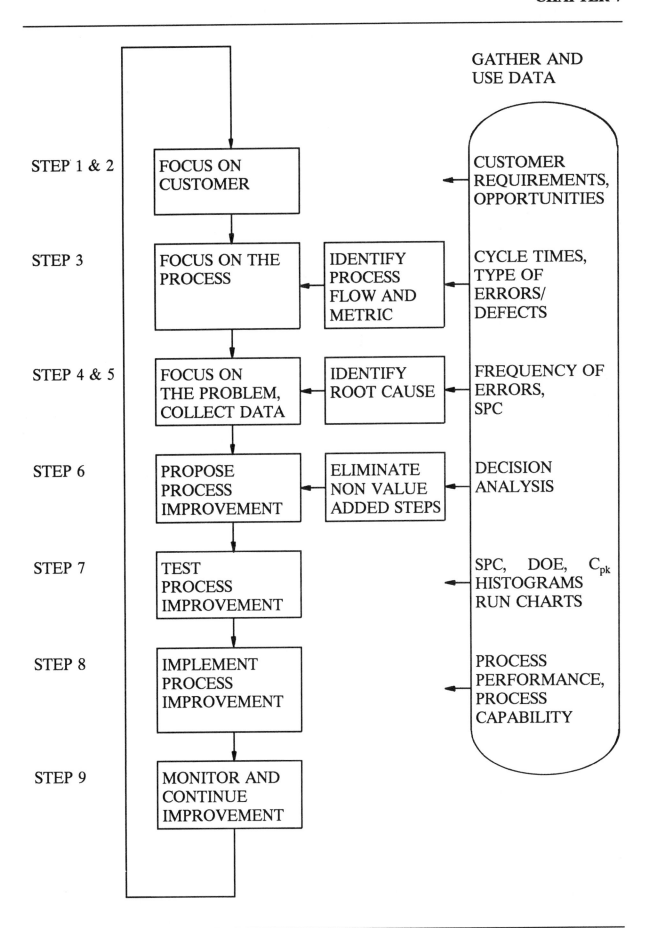

TQ Tool Kit

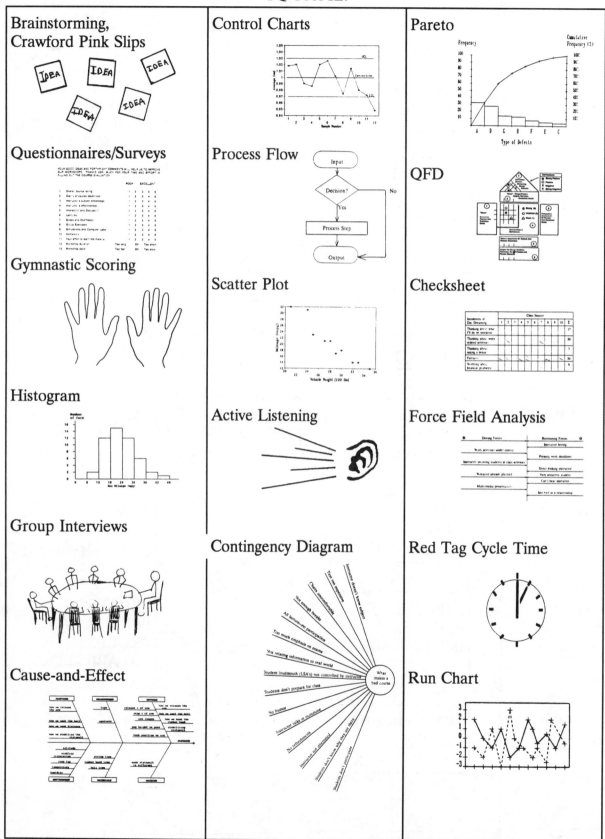

Brainstorming, Crawford Pink Slips

Questionnaires/Surveys

Gymnastic Scoring

Histogram

Group Interviews

Cause-and-Effect

Control Charts

Process Flow

Scatter Plot

Active Listening

Contingency Diagram

Pareto

QFD

Checksheet

Force Field Analysis

Red Tag Cycle Time

Run Chart

Another fairly simple generic model for beginners follows:

Step 1: **Identify opportunities for improving customer satisfaction (should be based on external/internal customer input or benchmarking).**

Output: A clear understanding of a brainstormed list of problems/opportunities based on customer needs and concerns. Should include a list of customers and what you provide them, for each of the problem areas.

Activities/Questions:

With what products/services are customers dissatisfied (be as specific as possible)?

What opportunities exist to increase customer satisfaction?

What areas seem to take too long or need a lot of inspection to "get it right?"

How is the process supposed to work?

What areas have high cost drivers in rework and repair?

What do the workers say needs improvement?

What do benchmarking activities show are areas in need of improvement?

What measures are available to substantiate suspected problem areas?

Step 2: **Decide which one to start with first.**

Output: A prioritized list of opportunities, with consensus reached on the most important opportunity to start on.

Activities/Questions:

What is the relative importance of the problems/opportunities in terms of criteria important to the company/organization (e.g., potential to increase customer satisfaction, potential savings, time to implement, ease of implementation, etc.)?

Use of Pareto charts may be helpful here, as you may be able to identify the 20% of the problems which are causing you 80% of the grief. Remember also the problem associated with the greatest number of defects or errors may not be the one which is costing the company/organization (and, therefore, its customers) the most.

It is important to achieve consensus on selected process improvements. Use of the Nominal Group Technique (NGT) and multi-voting may be helpful here. It takes more time than autocratic selection, however, it will pay great benefits in increasing the probability of success of the effort.

Step 3:   Bound and define the process.

Output: Process flow diagram, with key customers, inputs and outputs identified. Agreed to metrics which will be used to measure process improvement (for example, time to complete, number of errors, number of follow-up phone calls required, etc.).

Activities/Questions:

With what step does the process start and finish?

Who are the customers of the process?

What are the inputs and outputs?

What metrics could be used to measure customer satisfaction with this process?

Step 4:   Analyze process problems to identify causes and effects.

Output: Most likely potential root cause of process problem.

Activities/Questions:

What is there about people, machines, environment, materials, procedures, policies, methods, etc. which may be causing the process problem?

Use of an Ishikawa fishbone, cause and effect diagram, may be helpful here. It is important not to engage in solution-jumping at this point, but rather to focus on identifying the root cause.

Use analysis of past/historical data to guide, but not limit, your analysis.

It is sometimes helpful at this step to include someone in the cause and effect analysis who is not intimately familiar with the process. They ask great questions and are frequently able to see the trees and the forest.

Step 5:   **Collect data to determine baseline performance level.**

Output: Data/measures which establish a baseline of process performance, and also give you an improved basis from which to problem solve.

Activities/Questions:

Observe the process and collect performance measures. Use of check sheets and data stratification may be useful here, as well as histograms and scatter plots.

The data may give you insights into cause and effect which were not available at Step 4. Revisit your cause and effect analysis to ensure you are still on the right track. This is also an opportunity to "state your interest" in the process to the line workers and to enroll their involvement in potential improvements.

Step 6:   **Propose process improvements. Simplify process through elimination of non-value added steps. Decrease cycle and change-over times. Select process improvement to test.**

Output: Improvements which have been proposed by a cross-functional team using disciplined problem solving techniques.

Activities/Questions:

What steps consume resources but don't add value?

What inspection steps could be reduced/eliminated if the process were brought under control and made capable (see Chapter 9)?

What significant causes of variation exist which could be eliminated (see Chapter 9)?

Be creative at this point. Try to eliminate mental barriers to doing things differently using brainstorming or Crawford pink slips. The most immediate and obvious solution may not be the best one. Spend time generating a number of alternatives.

Re-visit process metrics identified in Step 3 to ensure they will enable you to identify the degree to which proposed improvements really work.

If you have identified a number of process inputs which may be affecting process outputs, it may be helpful to use a designed experiment (see Chapter 9) to test possible alternatives.

Step 7: **Select and test process improvements on a small scale.**

Output: Improvements which have been critically evaluated and selected by a cross-functional team using disciplined problem solving techniques. Process metric data which will reveal if proposed improvements really work.

Activities/Questions:

What is the relative desirability of the proposed process improvements in terms of criteria important to the company/organization (e.g., potential to increase customer satisfaction, potential savings, time to implement, ease of implementation, effectiveness, impact on other processes, etc.)?

It may be helpful here to do a force field analysis to identify the restraining and driving forces relative to the selected process improvement.

It may also be appropriate here to discuss potential changes with the customer. You may learn something which will help you select an improvement which will result increased customer satisfaction.

Put together a test plan which identifies "who, what, where, when, and how" for the test of the proposed process improvement.

Test the proposed improvement and gather data which will enable you to identify the degree to which the proposed improvement worked.

Remember process improvement generally proceeds in small iterative steps. Don't get discouraged with small gains.

Step 8: Implement process improvement.

Output: An implemented improvement, including necessary changes to procedures, training, or suppliers.

Activities/Questions:

Put together plan which identifies "who, what, where, when, and how" for the implementation of the process improvement.

Ensure process documentation, procedures and policies get changed in a manner in which everyone effected by the improvement can contribute to its success.

Are changes in training required?

Do changes affect suppliers?

Are there other areas in your organization/company which could benefit from the knowledge of this process improvement?

Is a written team report needed?

Step 9:   Monitor change and continue process improvement.

Output: Total quality is a never-ending journey. Continue to gather process data, and explore opportunities for improvement.

Activities/Questions:

Ensure responsibility for data monitoring is clear, including frequency and type of measures needed, etc.

Gather data to ensure process improvement is implemented.

Continue to monitor and problem solve the process to reduce variation and improve capability (see Chapter 9).

Until you get a lot of process improvement experience under your belt, it is good to follow the order of the steps, and to make sure you complete all the steps. A more detailed 14 strategy model of process improvement can be found in *The Team Handbook* (Scholtes 1988).

Which ever model you select, remember these important process improvement Do's and Don'ts:

- Don't improve a process based solely on what you think needs to be improved. Talk to the customer of the process to find out their needs and concerns.

- Don't leap to the solution without gathering data and analyzing the root cause of the process problem.

- Don't improve processes in a vacuum. Ensure all the right cross-functional players are involved.

- Document your process improvement and share results with other teams and functions who may be affected by or interested in your process.

- If your process improvement gets bogged down, step back and problem solve the process you are using to solve the problem.

- Sometimes process problems are caused by inputs generated by other processes "up stream" not under your control. Try to work with those up-stream process owners to assist them in improving the quality of your process inputs.

- Selection of initial candidate process improvements should be based on considering importance to the customer, achievability and cost. While you are learning the process improvement process, stick with processes that are not too complex and don't have long cycle times (weeks or months).

- Be patient. Total quality imposes a disciplined, structured problem-solving methodology which is not quick and dirty. To do it right requires time and patience.

- In analyzing processes, make use of historical data, such as formal policies and procedures, to ensure you are knowledgeable of requirements mandated by laws or regulations.

INTRODUCTION TO TOOLS AND TECHNIQUES

There are a number of tools and techniques which are useful to process improvement. The following tools and techniques have been described in detail in Chapter 3, Customer Focus.

- Active listening/Rogerian feedback
- Brainstorming/Crawford pink slips
- Group interviews/Focus groups
- Gymnastic scoring card technique
- Quality function deployment (QFD), see Chapter 8
- Questionnaires/surveys
- Requirements breakdown structure

The following tools and techniques, along with those described in Chapter 3, form the backbone of process improvement and problem solving. They are described in the pages following:

- Benchmarking
- Cause and Effect Diagrams/Ishikawa
- Check sheets and Stratification
- Control Charts/Run (Trend) Charts
- Cross-Functional Teams
- Force Field Analysis
- Histograms
- Nominal Group Technique
- Pareto Chart
- Process Flow Charting
- Red Tag Cycle Time
- Scatter Plots/Diagrams

A number of additional tools not described in this text are used in process improvement activities (Brassard, 1989):

- Affinity Diagram
- Arrow Diagram Method
- Contingency Diagram
- KJ Method
- Matrix Diagram Method
- Matrix Data Analysis Method
- Process Capability
- Process Decision Program Chart (PDPC) Method
- Relations Diagram
- Systematic Diagram Method

This section is intended as an introduction to these tools and techniques. Additional detail on tools used for statistical analysis (e.g., histograms, run charts, control charts, etc.) is provided in Chapter 9.

BENCHMARKING

==

PURPOSE:

- To identify opportunities to improve your performance based on the "best in class," that is, recognized leaders.

- To identify opportunities to improve customer value.

- To identify how you're doing relative to best-in-class, to help you with strategic market planning.

- To help you establish priorities for process improvement.

HOW USED:

1. Identify products, services or processes whose key characteristics you believe should be benchmarked. These should be based on characteristics which you know from customer contact are important to customer satisfaction, now or in the future.

2. Determine how to gather data on your organization and your competition (be sure to include a "best in class"). Possible data sources include:

> interviews
> professional journals/magazines
> surveys
> advertisements
> direct contact at trade shows, airports, bars
> market research studies
> consultants

3. Gather and compile data. Rank organizations with your own to determine your performance gap.

4. Decide which products, services, and/or processes to target, set goals, and implement process improvement.

5. Monitor progress, and periodically re-check benchmarks to update and recalibrate.

KEY SKILLS NEEDED TO USE THIS TOOL:

Research, brainstorming/NGT, listen well, surveys/questionnaires.

WHEN USED:

To identify a reference point against which you can measure which critical processes need to be improved to maintain or achieve industry leadership (Camp, 1989).

Tom Carter, of Alcoa, said that, to have a successful benchmarking process, people must feel comfortable with learning about others who are better than themselves. He indicated that those involved with benchmarking usually progress through four phases (Bemowski, 1991).

1. Don't want, don't ask. People are happy with the status quo.

2. Don't want, but ask. People become involved with benchmarking just because it's popular, but they don't listen.

3. Want and ask. People ask and listen, but are uncomfortable and a bit defensive. Initially, people might be embarrassed to find someone doing something better, so they defend their actions. They might even try to find people who aren't as good as they are because it is gratifying.

4. Seek, desire, listen, and use. People have matured and are not defensive; they take a progressive stance. They have enough self-confidence to seek companies with better processes. They view finding better processes as opportunities for improvement.

Helps you to base increasing the value of your products/services to your customer on what is known to be possible, rather than on arbitrary incremental goals.

CAUSE AND EFFECT DIAGRAMS
(also called FISHBONE or ISHIKAWA DIAGRAMS)

===

PURPOSE:

- To help focus on defining the problem and its root causes, rather than prematurely focusing on the solution.

- To analyze process improvement opportunities.

- To show the relationship between a set of possible process variables and a specific process result.

HOW USED:

The "fishbone" diagram is a graphic representation of potential causes of a problem, and their relationships.

1. Select problem (effect) to analyze (can be output of NGT). Ensure it is *what* is wrong rather than *why* it is wrong. Have people there who don't own the process, so they can ask "dumb questions."

2. Brainstorm specific causes and sub-causes in categories. Each category can be a bone, or you may have more than one bone for a particular category. Not all categories need be used, if they don't bear on the problem. Other categories can be used if they work better for you.

MANPOWER - Attributes of the people involved in the process, such as their training, level of experience, strength, personality, physical abilities

MATERIALS - The raw materials or resources used

METHODS - The policies, formal or informal procedures and/or information used

MACHINES - The tools or equipment used

ENVIRONMENT - Factors in the physical environment

OTHER - Anything else

ASK PROBING QUESTIONS TO STIMULATE CREATIVE THOUGHT:

What materials are involved? Where do they come from? How might they be defective?
What types of errors might the operators be making?
What are the process specifications and how might they be causing problems?
Are people adequately trained?
Are people experienced or new?
Are people and equipment located optimally?
What is the time factor and its effect?
Are operations occurring too fast or too slow?
Is area clean enough for quality process?
Do defects occur uniformly at all times of day?
Does time of day or weather have an effect on errors?
Are policies and procedures out of date?
Are there power struggles or personalities effecting quality?
Are people being rewarded for the right things?

3. Use NGT to reach consensus on most likely root cause. Use of Pareto charts can be helpful here.

4. Design an experiment to verify effect of the potential root cause on process performance. Gather data. Using data gathered verify problem cause or re-test with a new experiment. Typically other statistical tools can be helpful here, like histograms, run charts, Pareto charts, scatter plots, etc.

KEY SKILLS NEEDED TO USE THIS TOOL:

Brainstorming, creativity, NGT, measurement tools

WHEN USED: Used after high potential improvement opportunities have been identified.

ADVANTAGES:

Helps stimulate thinking about an issue, helps organize thoughts into a rational whole. Analysis not limited to lone ranger star problem solver. Analysis is data/measurement driven, not opinion driven. Focuses on the "pain."

DISADVANTAGES:

Can lead you down the wrong path, if you drink your own bath water. Group composition is key.

ILLUSTRATION: CAUSE AND EFFECT (FISHBONE) DIAGRAM - See Figure 9.18 on page 9-26.

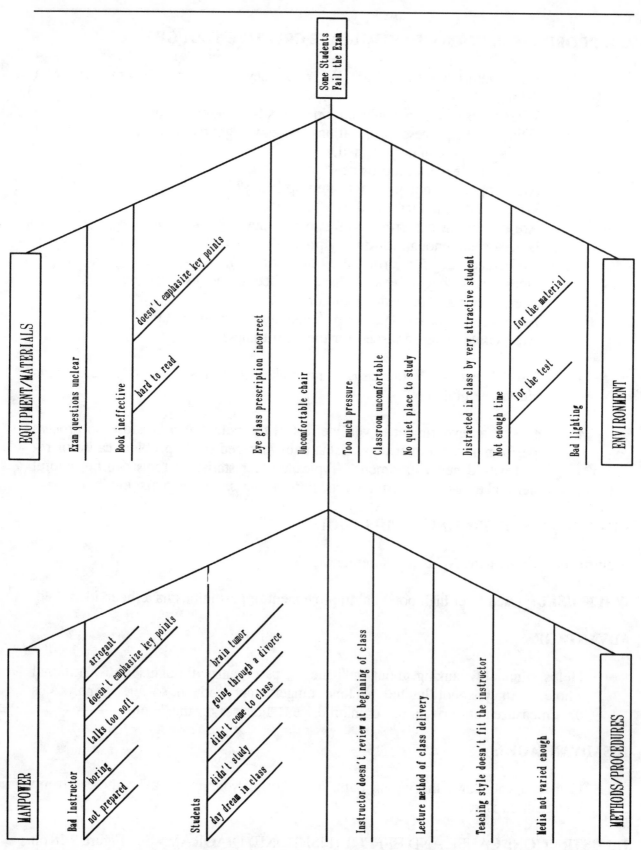

Example: Cause and Effect for Students Failing an Exam

CHECK SHEETS AND STRATIFICATION
==

PURPOSE:

- Check sheets provide a format with which to collect and tabulate data to facilitate analysis.

- Simplifies data collection and prevents data gathering errors.

- Standardizes data collection if you have more than one data gatherer.

HOW USED:

1. Identify the process to be studied and what data are needed about the process and/or product.

2. Decide how frequently data will be gathered and for how long.

3. Design a check sheet form that is easy to understand, easy to use, has adequate space for the data to be entered, and has space for required preliminary calculations.

4. If the form is to be used by others, prepare simple instructions, and dry run them to ensure they're comprehendible. If feasible, check sheets can be done on-line.

5. Gather and record data.

STRATIFICATION: (Also referred to as "BLOCKING.")

WHAT IS IT? Stratification is the process of collecting and recording data by factors which may affect the data.

PURPOSE: To identify factors affecting processes, differences among processes and to evaluate effects of process changes.

HOW USED: Frequent stratification categories include machine, batch or lot, day of the week, vendor, time of day, operator, etc.

Incidences of Day Dreaming	Class Session										
	1	2	3	4	5	6	7	8	9	10	Σ
Thinking about what I'll do on weekend	|	||	||	|||	||	|		||	|||	|	17
Thinking about work related activities	||||	THil	|	|||	||||	||	Til	|	||	|||	30
Thinking about taking a break	|		|	|		|		|	|	|	7
Fantasies	Hil	|| THil	|||| THil	| THil	THil THil	||	|||	THil	|||	Hil	50
Worrying about financial problems	|	|||	|		|		||		|		9

Example: Checksheet to Collect Data on Day Dreaming in Class

CONTROL CHARTS/RUN CHARTS

==

PURPOSE:

- A graphic representation of measured actual process performance relative to computed control limits, to enable you to evaluate the stability of a process.

- Enables you to distinguish between measurements that are predictably within the inherent capability of a process (common causes) and those which are unpredictable and attributable to special causes.

NOTE: Control charts are based on these concepts:

1. All processes fluctuate with time.

2. Individual points are unpredictable/predictable, only within limits.

3. A stable process fluctuates randomly, and groups of points from a stable process tend to fall within predictable limits.

4. An unstable process does not fluctuate randomly, and the non-random fluctuations are generally those that fall outside the upper and lower control limits of the control chart.

HOW USED:

1. You should not attempt to construct control charts without referring to a good introductory text on control charts (see pages 9-14) or a guide such as *The Memory Jogger* (1989).

2. You must start with a sample of process data from which you can prepare control limits. There are several control chart types and rules for sample sizes. You must select which type of chart and sample size to be used. Plot control chart, insuring that data show process is under control. If data are normally distributed, you can assume that 99.73% of the data should fall between $\pm$ 3 standard deviations of the mean.

3. Using these data, calculate the upper control limit (UCL) and lower control limit (LCL) and plot them on your chart.

4. Continue to collect and chart process data. Do not re-calculate the UCL and LCL. Identify points that are outside control limits or runs of points which indicate control problems.

5.   Determine causes of variation. Can use fishbone analysis here, combined with brainstorming and NGT techniques.

6.   Brainstorm and test ways to eliminate special causes and reduce variation of common causes.

7.   In testing ways to bring processes back into control, be sure to keep very accurate records to track what changes you have made to the process. Record these comments on the chart.

KEY SKILLS NEEDED TO USE THIS TOOL: Some statistics helpful

WHEN USED:

Control charts are used after you have described the process using a flow chart, identified sources of process problems, identified the adequacy of the process control system, and standardized the process. (Standardized means the process is done the same way–it may still have variation.)

To diagnose process variation problems and to help you reduce normal variation.

ADVANTAGES:

Allows corrective action to be based on data, not opinion.

DISADVANTAGES:

Requires some discipline in data gathering.

Control charts signal significant changes, but not always their reasons.

Control charts tell you if a process is in statistical control, not whether or not it is capable of satisfying customers.

ILLUSTRATION: Control charts - see pages 9-16, 9-25.
                         Run charts - see pages 9-10, 9-12.

See Chapter 9 for more detail on control charts and run charts.

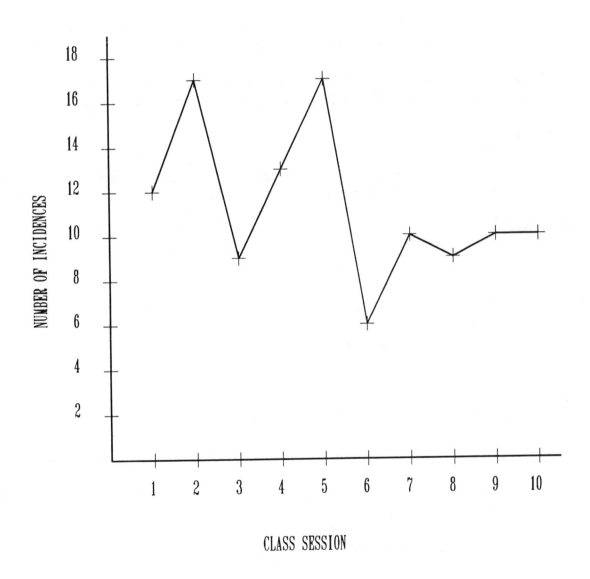

Run Chart: Incidences of Day Dreaming in Class

CROSS FUNCTIONAL TEAMS

==

PURPOSE:

- To problem-solve process problems.

- To accomplish process integration.

HOW USED:

The key characteristic of a cross functional team is its inclusion of representatives from more than one organizational function.

Teams should generally be between 6 and 10 members. Less than 6 participants and synergy is inhibited, more than 10 and the group becomes unwieldy.

WHEN USED:

When requirements, issues, and problems are multi-disciplined and cross functional. To gather data for a QFD analysis (see Chapter 8).

ADVANTAGES:

The interaction can lead to great synergy.

A relatively low cost technique.

Promotes ownership of solutions.

DISADVANTAGES:

Hard to be as objective and non-defensive as this forum requires.

If trust lacking, meeting can generate bad data - sometimes worse than no data.

Hard to get groups which are used to competing against each other, to work with each other.

Process is unstructured and requires a good facilitator.

Process feels like it takes more time than the usual way we do things, and will therefore frustrate aggressive, Type A problem solvers.

FORCE FIELD ANALYSIS

===

Force Field Analysis is based on the premise that driving forces facilitate change and restraining forces inhibit change.

PURPOSE:

- To help you identify things that may inhibit change or facilitate change.

- If you try to implement total quality without adequately assessing your environment and your stakeholders, you may experience difficulty in implementing change.

HOW USED:

1. First brainstorm "driving forces." Use of pink slip method or affinity diagrams can be especially helpful here.

2. Next brainstorm "restraining forces."

3. Prioritize forces, and develop action plans to diminish or eliminate the most significant restraining forces.

KEY SKILLS NEEDED TO USE THIS TOOL:

Creativity, systems thinking, brainstorming, NGT

WHEN USED:

To aid in formulating successful strategies for implementing change.

ADVANTAGES:

Assists in focusing on the non-technical aspects of change, which often tend to get ignored.

DISADVANTAGES:

If not done creatively or honestly, it can lead you to a false sense of security.

If not followed up with an action plan, analysis may have little value added.

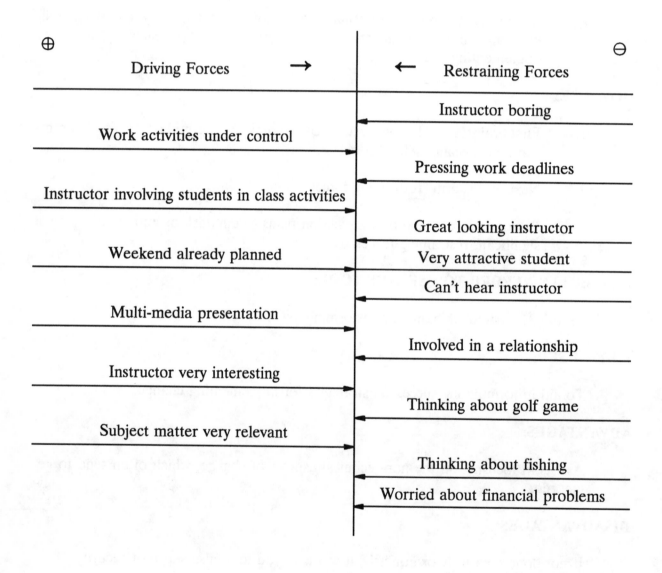

Example: Force Field Analysis—Reducing Day Dreaming in Class

HISTOGRAMS
==

Also called **Bar Graphs**: histograms are graphs that display relative frequency of occurrence.

PURPOSE:

- To depict variation in process performance or results.

- To show how the majority of process outputs compare with a target value, as well as with its specification limits.

- Can be a powerful communication tool to describe performance, support analyses and document improvement programs.

HOW USED:

1. Gather data. Calculate the range of the data by subtracting the smallest value from the largest value. Find an interval width which provides enough classes over the range of data so the number of classes is between 5 to 20.

2. Count the frequency of responses/data points in each category.

3. Plot the frequency for each class with a bar.

KEY SKILLS NEEDED TO USE THIS TOOL:

Basic math, information mapping

WHEN USED:

To show a large amount of data, very simply in a summarized format.

ADVANTAGES:

Easy to do.

DISADVANTAGES:

How you construct the categories can obfuscate the data; ensure data are properly stratified.

ILLUSTRATION: Histogram - See pages 9-13, 9-24

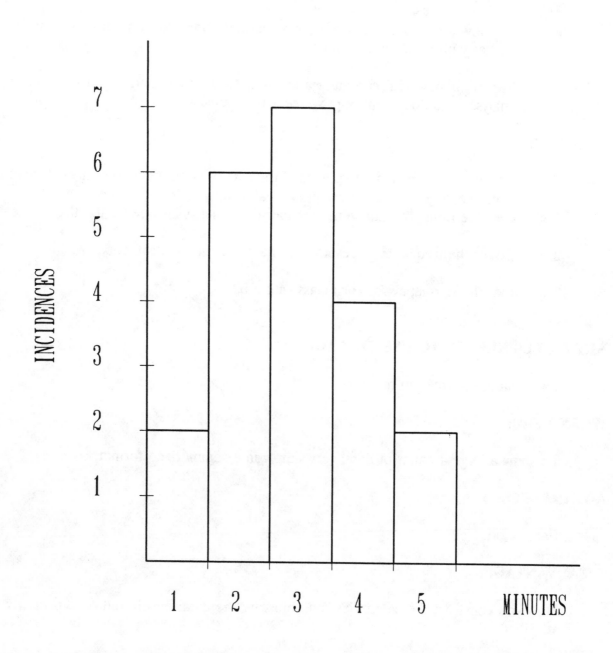

Example: Histogram of the Number of Minutes Spent Day Dreaming

NOMINAL GROUP TECHNIQUE/MULTI-VOTING
==

PURPOSE:

- To quickly and critically examine, evaluate, narrow down, and obtain consensus (an opinion held by all or most) on a list of brainstormed ideas.

HOW USED:

The key aspect of Nominal Group Technique is to get each person to make an independent individual commitment before he or she knows what the other ideas/votes of the group are. Every idea that gets a vote, gets an explanation.

1. NGT is used after brainstormed ideas have been clarified and combined (where possible). Members do a silent rank ordering of the top four or five. The facilitator tallies the votes to obtain a "most important" score. In multi-voting, each group member is given three to six votes (1/4 to 1/5 of the total number of ideas) to "spend" on those ideas which have the most to offer (or those items which are the most important/valid). Members decide their votes silently. Starting with the first idea, ask for how many have voted for that item, and continue around until all votes are spent or all items have been covered.

2. Be sure to multiply people times votes to determine how many total votes you should have at the end. This ensures no one votes more or less than they should.

3. Always allow time for discussion of the outcome to make sure it makes sense, to develop consensus, and to allow those people whose ideas have fallen by the wayside some time to speak their peace.

KEY SKILLS NEEDED TO USE THIS TOOL: Good facilitation skills

WHEN USED: After brainstorming, to prioritize and to achieve consensus and buy-in.

ADVANTAGES:

Easy effective way to give everyone an equal voice, ensures everyone gets a say in evaluating ideas, rather than the stronger ones dominating the weaker ones.

DISADVANTAGES:

Validity of the output only as good as the voting members: 5 Dummies + 1 brain surgeon = dummies overwhelm.

DAY DREAMING CAUSES:

A. Boring instructor

B. Thinking about weekend

C. Thinking about a relationship

D. Worried about financial problems

E. Boring subject

Problem	Person					Total	Priority
	1	2	3	4	5		
A	5	4	3	5	5	22	#1
B	3	3	4	4	4	18	#2
C	1	1	5	3	3	13	#4
D	2	2	1	1	1	7	#5
E	4	5	2	2	2	15	#3

Example: Nominal Group Technique

〟〟〟〟 | Boring instructor

〟〟 ||| Thinking about weekend

|||| Thinking about a relationship

|| Worried about financial problems

〟〟 | Boring subject

Example: Multi-voting

PARETO CHART
===

Named after Italian economist Vilfredo Pareto.

PURPOSE:

- To identify the 20% of the causes that are resulting in 80% of the problems.

- To display the relative contribution of each cause to the total problem.

- To identify the most costly of the most important problems (costly to the organization or costly to fix).

HOW USED:

1. List all possible problem problems/causes/elements (brainstorming may be helpful here). Ensure data are properly stratified.

2. Measure the elements for a specified time period, using the same unit of measure for each element.

3. Use the vertical axis as frequency and the horizontal axis to represent the causes/elements.

4. Order the elements from highest on the left of the horizontal axis to lowest on the right, and make a bar graph.

5. Create a cumulative distribution for the number of items and elements measured, and add a line graph.

KEY SKILLS NEEDED TO USE THIS TOOL: Ability to plot histograms.

WHEN USED: To identify which of the causes create most of the problems. This followed by an analysis of which are the most/least costly to improve can give you very valuable information about where to focus your improvement efforts.

ADVANTAGES: Simple and easy. Based on data not opinion.

DISADVANTAGES:

Data collection can be resource intensive.
If not properly stratified, data can obfuscate what is really going on.

ILLUSTRATION: PARETO CHART - See page 9-9.

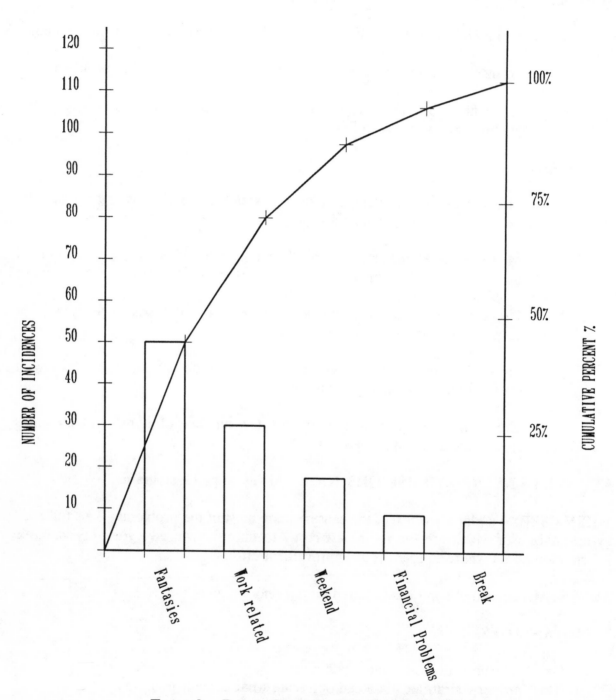

Example: Pareto Chart for Day Dreaming Data

PROCESS FLOW DIAGRAMS

PURPOSE:

- To visually show the operation of a given process, to examine and understand steps, relationships, inputs and outputs.

- To document formal and informal process sequence and activity, to give you a picture of the delta between your policies/procedures and the way work actually gets done.

- To give you visibility of value added and non-value added activities.

- To enable you to improve processes through simplification and problem solving.

- To make overuse of inspection visible.

- To identify decision points that will help you identify process problems.

HOW USED:

Use standard symbols, flow from top to bottom, left to right. There are three ways to lay out a process: 1) as it is occurs as documented in formal procedures, 2) how it actually occurs, and 3) how it should occur.

Formal and informal process flow are documented to identify how organization procedures must be changed. Diagramming the formal process may give you insight into some important historical data or regulatory reason why things may need to be done a certain way.

Updating procedures is an important collateral activity of process improvement. If you are going to have procedures, they should reflect process steps, as opposed to fiction.

Finally, using problem solving tools, design, test and implement an improved process.

STEPS FOR DIAGRAMMING PROCESS FLOW

1. Assemble a group of people both knowledgeable of and unfamiliar with the process. Including someone who is not familiar with the process is valuable to giving a fresh/unbiased look to how things might be done better. Include

representatives from all functional areas involved in the process. Decide on the beginning and end points, that is, the boundaries, of the process to be analyzed.

2.   Obtain formal policies and procedures relating to the process.

3.   Document using standard symbols, in the sequence in which steps occur. Using "Post-it" sticky notes on a large piece of flip chart paper is a convenient way to create process flow diagrams in a group. Boxes can be easily moved around, and the diagram is large enough for several people to see at once. Connect the boxes using arrows indicating the direction of flow of products, services or information. Identify customers and suppliers for key steps of the process.

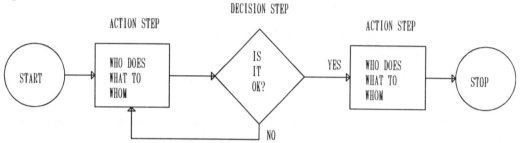

4.   If the group cannot reach agreement about how the process is performed, observe the process being performed. Have both experts and non-experts observe the process. Discuss until group reaches consensus on the steps in the informal process.

5.   If not possible to observe the process, gather a group both familiar with and peripheral to the process, to lay out the steps as they occur in the informal process.

      It is helpful to also identify inputs and outputs of key steps, to identify interdependence issues and clarify roles and responsibilities.

      Detailed process flow diagrams show every decision point, feedback loop and process step. Such detailed analysis is most useful at points in the process where problems are occurring or where improvement is likely.

6.   Simplify process by eliminating redundant, unnecessary and non-value added steps.

      Adding process and cycle time to the process flow diagram can be very helpful in this step.

7.   Problem solve process to identify how process can be improved to meet customer requirements (at benchmarked levels if possible).

KEY SKILLS NEEDED TO USE THIS TOOL:

Listen well, observe well, dissect steps well, clarity of documentation.

WHEN USED:

Processes are normally documented after someone has identified processes that have high potential as opportunities to improve customer satisfaction. Routinely documenting every single process would be fine if you had unlimited resources, but most companies focus on those processes causing their internal and/or external customers to be dissatisfied.

ADVANTAGES:

Highlights differences in how work actually gets done versus formal procedures.

Facilitates cross-functional communication.

Establishes a baseline based on consensus.

Helps you identify and eliminate non-value added activity.

Highlights bottlenecks.

Helps to clarify supplier and customer relationships.

DISADVANTAGES:

You can get bogged down in the detail.

Diagrams can get overly complex.

You can go down the wrong path if you only use people who are familiar with the process to diagram the process.

ILLUSTRATION: Process flow diagram - See page 9-21.

RED TAG CYCLE TIME

==

PURPOSE:

- To identify process time versus cycle time.

- To identify processes which have a high proportion of non-value added time.

- To identify opportunities to improve customer satisfaction where time is an important advantage.

HOW USED:

Frequently, the time it takes to complete a series of steps in a process of a series of processes is much greater than the sum of the time it takes for the individual processes added together. Quite often, steps such as inspections, approvals, sitting in stock, transit, etc. greatly inflate cycle time with no added value.

Red-tagging items allows you to measure process and cycle times so that you can identify opportunities for improvement. You should measure cycle time for a process for which you have developed a process flow diagram.

You can either literally tag an item (could be a report, a travel claim, a piece of hardware, etc.) at the beginning of a process or figuratively tag it by marking the date/time it started. Then mark the time of completion. This gives you the total cycle time. To gather process time, measure the start and stop time of each value added step in your process flow diagram.

KEY SKILLS NEEDED TO USE THIS TOOL:

A good stop watch, good rapport with process participants

WHEN USED:

To identify non-value added time in any process.

ADVANTAGES:

Based on measurement not opinion.

DISADVANTAGES:

When people know they're being measured they often don't perform the same as they normally would.

PROCESS IMPROVEMENT

SCATTER PLOTS

==

PURPOSE:

- To depict the degree of relationship between two factors.

- To help identify possible causes of problems through identification of correlation between factors.

HOW USED:

1. Develop hypothesis about the relationship between two factors. For example, a hypothesis could be that tire pressure is positively correlated to gas mileage.

2. Collect data to test hypothesis, insuring an adequate range of x values are used.

3. Summarize results by plotting each data point against an X-Y axis, for example, with tire pressure of 55 PSI, gas mileage was recorded to be 18 mpg.

4. After plotting ranges of values for your x variable, analyze results to see of a cause and effect relationship exists.

KEY SKILLS NEEDED TO USE THIS TOOL:

Knowledge of statistics helpful

WHEN USED:

To determine relationship between potential cause and effect.

ADVANTAGES:

Easy to construct and easy to understand.

DISADVANTAGES:

Need statistics to really determine if significant correlation exists.
Strong correlation does not guarantee that a cause-and-effect relation exists—this must be done with a designed experiment.

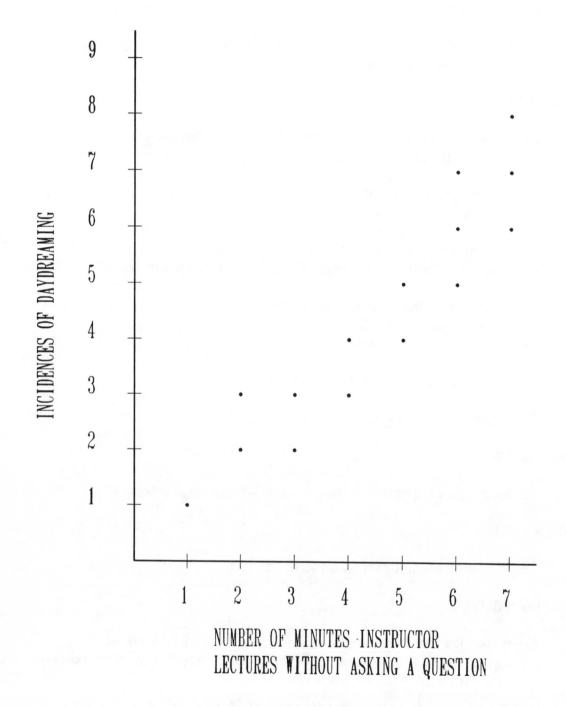

NUMBER OF MINUTES INSTRUCTOR
LECTURES WITHOUT ASKING A QUESTION

Example: Scatter Plot

DISCUSSION QUESTIONS

1. What is a process?

2. What is involved in recognizing an opportunity for improvement?

3. What is the purpose of brainstorming?

4. When would you use NGT?

5. What is the purpose of creating process flow diagrams?

6. Why would you construct a Pareto diagram?

7. What is the difference between a Pareto chart and a histogram?

8. What are the sources of benchmarking data?

9. Should you always comprise your team of process experts when doing a cause and effect analysis?

10. What is the difference between a run chart and a histogram?

REFERENCES

Bemowski, K., *Quality Progress*, January 1991, pp. 19-24.

Brassard, Michael, *The Memory Jogger Plus+*, GOAL/QPC, 1989.

Camp, Robert, *Benchmarking*, ASQC Press, 1989.

Houston, A., and Dockstader, S.L., *A Total Quality Management Process Improvement Model*, TR 89-3, Navy Personnel Research and Development Center, San Diego, CA 92152-6800.

Juran, *Juran on Leadership for Quality: An Executive Handbook*, Free Press, New York, NY, 1989.

Pryor, Lawrence S., "Benchmarking: A Self-Improvement Strategy," *The Journal of Business Strategy*, November/December 1989, pp. 28-32.

Scholtes, Peter, *The Team Handbook*, Joiner Associates: Madison, WI, 1988.

The Memory Jogger: A Pocket Guide for Continuous Improvement, 1988, GOAL/QPC, 13 Branch Street, Methuen, MA 01844, Phone (508) 685-3900.

Total Quality Contracting, Air Force Logistics Command, Wright-Patterson AFB, OH.

Chapter 8

QUALITY FUNCTION DEPLOYMENT[1]

Reams of paper have been consumed in recent years by various pundits, scholars and watchers of the American Business Scene in decrying the crises of quality, or rather lack thereof, in our products and services compared with our foreign competitors. American quality bashing has become so prevalent it is almost a cliche. But what some experts have failed to recognize is that in this ever-more-complicated world any attempt to explain the harsh reality that the United States is losing ground to foreign competition by saying that Americans are simply not quality conscious does not adequately explain the forces at work in today's international and domestic marketplace. While some Americans have been concerned with producing quality products, the complexity of modern technology has dulled our instinct in developing the methods of insuring quality.

As systems have become more complex, individuals have had to acquire specialized knowledge to support the new technologies. This increasing need for specialized knowledge results in problems translating technical and program knowledge across functional organizational boundaries. In addition to the degradation of organizational knowledge transfer, specialists tend to remain secluded in their areas of expertise causing significant differences in individual focus and emphasis during the development of a product or system. The result is a clouded view of the system characteristics and requirements which ultimately leads to excessive rework and program cost overruns. Often this is referred to as a "lack of quality".

The most compelling evidence of the need to integrate design knowledge can be found in analyzing cost drivers in major manufacturing firms. According to a special report published in Business Week (1987), the typical American factory spends 20 to 50% of its operating budget to find and fix mistakes. In addition, as many as one-quarter of all factory personnel do not produce end items, but rework things that weren't done correctly the first time. Finally, statistics indicate that as much as 80% of quality defects occur during the design phase of product development or as a result of purchasing policies that value low price over the quality.

These "quality" failures are not unique to American manufacturing. The Japanese were experiencing similar problems in integrating design knowledge in the 1970s. However, our overseas competitors moved more quickly to analyze the source of the problem. Thus, to prevent costly rework, a disciplined method was developed through Japan's Total Quality

---

[1]This chapter was written by Barbara Bicknell.

Control Program as a vehicle to force horizontal integration of design knowledge. The technique, now known as Quality Function Deployment (QFD), reflects our current system design process but offers advantages by using a format and language understood by customers as well as system design participants. QFD provides a mechanism for multifunctional teams to capture the knowledge of all segments of the organization to develop a full set of requirements and to fully integrate those requirements into their system designs.

The basic elements of QFD are not difficult to comprehend. However, application of QFD can be an exhaustive and tedious process. But when used correctly, QFD provides a powerful tool for consistently communicating and transferring information through highly technical processes. This leads to focused technology development in spite of conflicting system requirements and sometimes seemingly divergent customer needs. The use of QFD provides a structure for identifying those design characteristics that contribute most (and least) to customer requirements. It acts as a vehicle for incorporating manufacturing, test and inspection considerations early in the design phase through the identification of design targets and comparisons of process capabilities. The results of a QFD exercise can support cost benefit analysis between investments for technology improvements or maximizing the use of existing capabilities. Through the use of QFD, the quality defects attributed to product design can be substantially reduced resulting in major cost savings.

WHAT IS QFD?

The QFD process is accomplished by using a series of matrices and charts that guide the project team activities by providing easy, standard documentation during product and process development. Figure 8.1 illustrates the basic structure of the QFD matrices which is viewed as four major activities: product planning, product design, process planning, and process control planning. Customer needs and design characteristics that meet those needs are defined on the initial matrix. The traceability of design features and process needs to customer requirements is formed by taking the design characteristics from the top of the initial matrix and using them as the customer needs for the next matrix. This waterfall process continues until specific product and process specifications and manufacturing guidelines result. In this way the operator at the most detailed level of the process is able to trace how his job fits into the customer's needs. Although these top level matrices are illustrated as subordinate matrices providing requirements flowdown and traceability to the lowest levels of product and process elements, the segments are interdependent and should be developed simultaneously as an integrated activity.

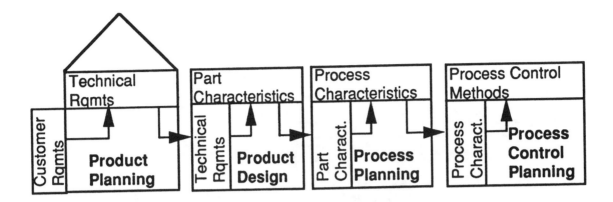

**Figure 8.1 Quality Function Deployment (QFD) Is A Structured Approach
For Capturing The User's Requirements And Mapping
Them Into Product And Process Parameters.**

Many articles written about QFD have focused on the QFD formats. However, what is most often overlooked in these articles is the use of QFD as a vehicle for assisting multifunctional teams to brainstorm and communicate in a structured way to achieve consensus. Using QFD matrices helps reverse segmentation among design functions and bring collective knowledge to identify alternatives for a successful product.

Applications

QFD matrices can be used for numerous applications including documenting customer needs and priorities and the constraints on meeting those needs. Because QFD is a flexible tool for virtually any type of product or process, it has been used for discrete manufacturing processes, construction, hotel service improvements, conceptual spacecraft design, administration process improvements, hospital improvements, training assessments and strategic planning. A few examples of the type of data that can be analyzed using QFD are illustrated in Figure 8.2. QFD is best applied to specific needs, products or processes in cutting-edge technologies or ones that require both needed or desired improvements or breakthroughs. Consequently, the QFD matrices are especially useful to proposal or development team leaders to manage the proposal-writing/development process by clarifying customer needs and identifying complete or unique methodologies to gain a competitive advantage.

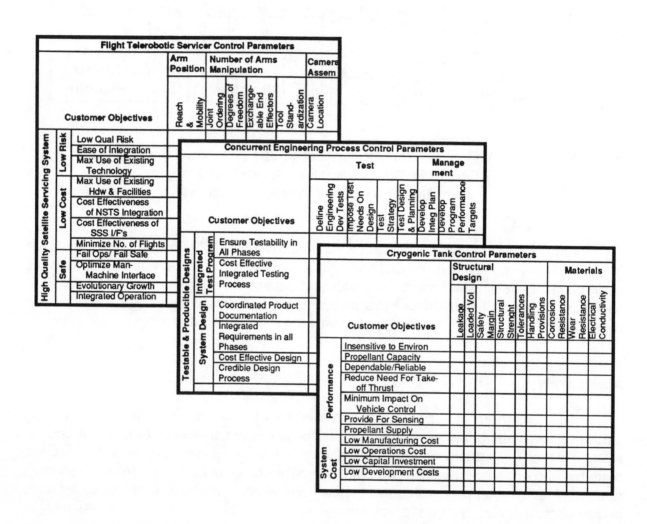

Figure 8.2 The Matrix Examples Illustrate that QFD Can Be Used to Evaluate Numerous Applications Including System and Subsystem Designs and System Processes

Background

Before venturing deeper into the actual application of the process it is helpful to understand the genesis of the approach. The term QFD is derived from six Chinese/Japanese characters that translate as follows: "hin shitsu" (qualities); "ki no" (function); and "ten kai" (deployment, development, or diffusion). The translation is not exact. Notice that "quality" is never mentioned, but the translation reflects our current system design process–identification of design qualities or performance requirements that deploy all of the necessary product functions.

The history of QFD can be traced to Dr. Akao's development of a series of matrices to improve quality for the Kobe Shipyard of Mitsubishi Heavy Industries Ltd. in 1972. Automotive use followed shortly thereafter; in 1977 Toyota implemented the system after four years of training and case study development. Introduced to the US in 1983 through an article in *Quality Progress*, a publication of the American Society of Quality Control (ASQC). The first US case studies emerged in 1986. Despite a slow start, interest is snowballing and QFD is currently being used by the major auto makers and their suppliers. Nonautomotive users include such diverse companies as AT&T, Bell Labs, Omark Industries, Martin Marietta, Digital Equipment, and Proctor & Gamble.

Potential Benefits

One of the first benefits to be realized by using QFD is improved communication. Because it acts as a vehicle for breaking down barriers between departments as well as with customers, it opens the lines of communication. The ultimate benefits of QFD are increased market share and larger profits. These benefits are realized because QFD plays a major role in creating products and processes with reduced costs, improved quality, features that satisfy customers, and significantly shorter development times. As a result, products are intrinsically more appealing to potential customers. In essence, it brings together all the specialized knowledge of many diverse program teams to analyze products and processes concurrently.

QFD has become an exciting investment for many companies because it is the cornerstone for implementing Concurrent Engineering and Total Quality Management (TQM) initiatives. As illustrated in Figure 8.3, the use of QFD acts as a method for implementing, integrating or enabling nearly all of the Concurrent Engineering and TQM initiatives. The final testimony for QFD benefits comes from those who have dared implementation. As presented in Table 8.1, the rewards are great.

Elements of Concurrent Engineering and TQM That are either Enhanced, Implemented, or Integrated with QFD Applications	
Programmatic Management Initiatives	Government Initiatives
●Education/Training ●Focus on Quality ●Multifunctional Teams ●Performance Based Progress Criteria and Risk Management ●Cost of Quality —Metrics System/Prevention/ Appraisal/Internal/External ●Operations Definitions	●Integrated Acquisition Strategy ●Risk Reduction Templates ●Best Practices (R&M 2000) ●RFP Instruction, Contract Requirements Source Selection Criteria Correlation ●Joint Cooperative-Based Relationship Between Government & Industry ●Revised Funding Profiles
Technical Management Initiatives	Recommended Tools
●Specs which Include Product and Manuf Efficiency Requirements ●Cost as a Design Criteria ●Enforced Rule Based Design Standards and Criteria ●Product Design/Manuf/Test/Process Optimization ●Value Analysis Engineering ●Rapid Product Prototyping ●Design for Manufacturing	●Design of Experiments ●Statistical Process Control ●Quality Loss Function ●Pugh Methods ●Ishikawa Seven Tools ●Brainstorming Techniques

Figure 8.3 Quality Function Deployment Is The Cornerstone For Implementing Concurrent Engineering And Total Quality Management Initiatives

The Benefits of QFD Implementation
• 30 to 50 % Reduction in Engineering Changes • 30 to 50 % Shorter Design Cycles • 20 to 60 % Lower Start-up Costs • Systematic Documentation of Engineering Knowledge • Competitive Pricing Resulting From Lower Development and Start-up Costs • More Satisfied Customers

Table 8.1 The Benefits of QFD Implementation Are Great By Those Companies Who Have Gambled Implementation

Types of QFD Approaches

There are generally two accepted QFD techniques: 1) the Four Phased Approach and 2) the Matrices of Matrices. Although the formats are slightly different they have common goals and elements as depicted in Figure 8.4.

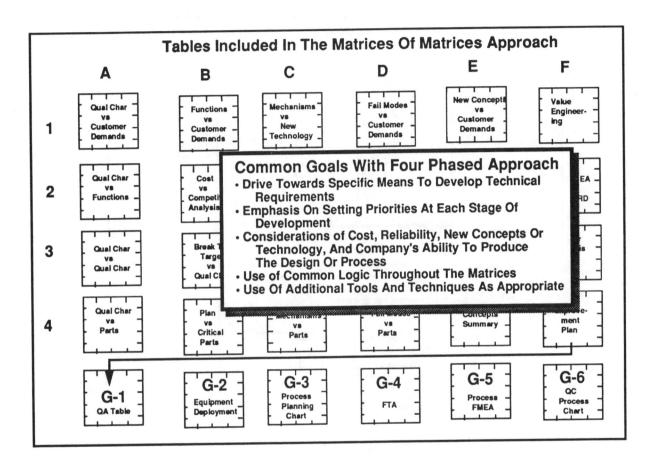

Figure 8.4 Quality Implementation In The Matrices of Matrices
Is Similar To The Four Phased Approach

BUILDING THE HOUSE OF QUALITY

The heart of QFD is the House of Quality Matrix. The House of Quality is a product planning matrix used to depict customer requirements, design requirements, target design goals and competitive product evaluations. At first glance the House of Quality matrix may seem very complex; however, when broken into individual elements it is fairly straight-forward. A summary of the house components is presented in Figure 8.5.

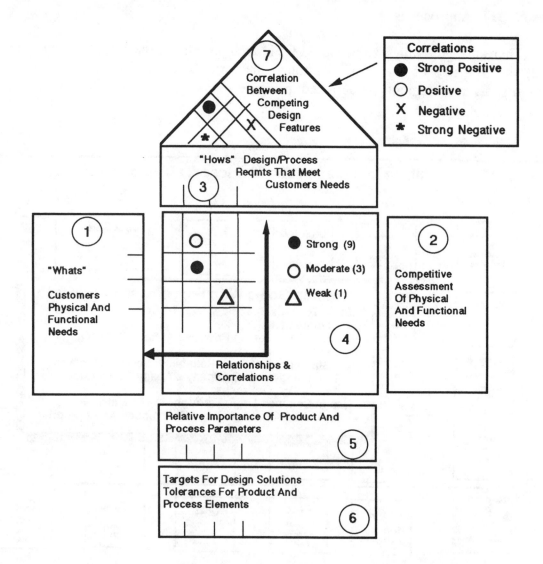

Figure 8.5 The House Of Quality Matrix Is The Heart Of The QFD Process

As illustrated, QFD begins with defining the customers' needs, sometimes termed as the "whats." The customers' needs are then prioritized based on marketing information of perceived customer importance and the need for company or product line improvements. Statements of "how" the contractor intends to meet the "whats" are generated and correlated to the customers' needs. In this way design features can be prioritized to meet the customers' needs. In addition, each of the how statements can be defined as a controllable target parameter and the desired goal of the product line or service can be put into an action.

As mentioned above, the basic approach used in QFD is conceptually similar to the practice followed by most American manufacturing companies. The process begins with customer requirements which are usually loosely stated qualitative characteristics such as "low risk," "affordable," "safe," and "easy to use." These then get converted into internal company requirements called design requirements, and are then translated into manufacturing and inspection requirements.

A detailed illustration and explanation of a completed House of Quality for a home video game is presented in Figure 8.6 and Table 8.2, respectively. Although the House of Quality is not particularly difficult to construct or understand, it does require some effort to get used to its conventions. Through experience the house becomes as easy to visualize as a roadmap.

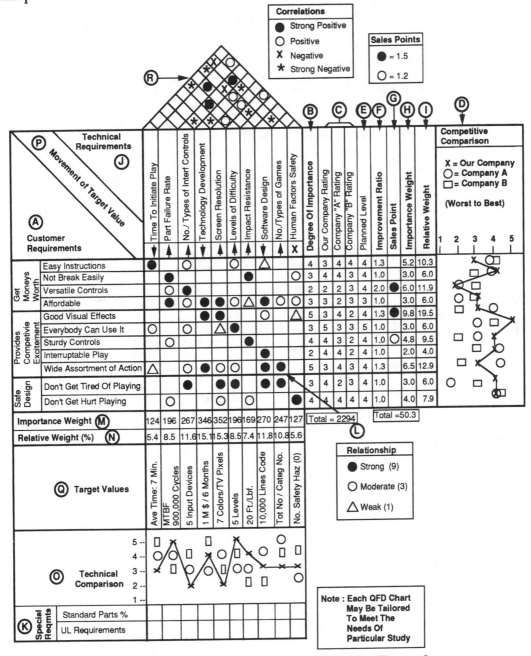

Figure 8.6 Video Game House Of Quality Example

	Instructions of Constructing the House of Quality
A	**Customer Requirements** • Identify all customer groups: internal and external. • Prepare plan for gathering and analyzing accurate information about the customer. Encourage customer participation. • Perform Brainstorming with multifunctional team to establish hierarchical tree of customer requirements. • Transfer requirements tree to House of Quality. • Establish a set of definitions for customer requirements.
B	**Degree of Importance** • Identify relative priority based on information and perception of customer. • 1 to 5 scale most often used: higher is better.
C **D**	**Competitive Comparison** • Identify current company and competitors capabilities to meet customers requirements based on marketing and research data. • Use scale 1 to 5: higher is better. • The use of symbols provides visual assistance in comparing company performance.
E	**Planned Level** • Set a time in future for planned improvement prior to submitting or implementing the product. • Use scale 1 to 5: higher is better.
F	**Improvement Ratio** • Equal to Planned Level (1 to 5) / Current company rating (1 to 5).
G	**Sales Point** • Attributes that may generate new business for additional products. • ● = 1.5 value O = 1.2 value
H	**Importance Weight** • Importance Weight = (Degree of Importance) × (Improvement Ratio) × (Sales Point value)
I	**Relative Weight (%)** • Normalize importance weightings.
J	**Technical Requirements** • Develop list internally to answer the following sentence: If I control __a__ then I am meeting my customers objectives to __b__. Where "a" is a possible technical requirement and "b" is a defined customer objective. • Develop requirements through a brainstorming session with the multifunctional team and create hierarchical diagrams to transfer to the matrix.

K	**Special Requirements**
	•Compliance requirements.
L	**Relationship Matrix**
	•Indicates strength of technical requirement to satisfy customer requirement as indicated by symbols.
M	**Importance Weight of Technical Requirements**
	•Importance Weight = column sum of (Value of Relationship) × (Relative Weight (%) of Customer Requirements).
N	**Relative Weight of Technical Requirements (%)**
	•Normalize row of importance weights.
O	**Technical Comparison**
	•Identify how well you and competitors are capable of meeting the technical requirements. •Use a scale of 1 to 5: higher is better. •Translate numerical values into symbols for visual comparisons.
P	**Movement of Target**
	•Use symbols to indicate desired direction for each corresponding technical requirement target value. ▲ = increase ▼ = decrease X = meet specified nominal value
Q	**Target Values**

	•Assign specific target values for as many requirements as possible.
	   –Define specific goals/ranges for designers and engineers.
	   –Establish targets for trade studies and analyses.
	•Use historical data where possible.
	•These are starting points that can be revised based on detailed analysis.

R	**Roof - Correlation Matrix**
	•Identify and compare the interaction of implementing technical requirements to the established target values. ● = strong positive O = positive X = negative ✳ = strong negative

Table 8.2 Instructions For Constructing the House of Quality

The following discusses some of the critical steps. The numerical labels correspond to the numbered activities in Figure 8.5.

Scope the Effort – The program manager of the multifunctional team should initially define the program objectives, expected outputs, use of data products and boundary conditions. It is not unusual for some time to be spent establishing the groundrules and scope of the project in terms that everyone understands.

1 - Identify Physical and Functional Needs of The Customer ("Whats") – The House of Quality begins by using the customers' physical and functional requirements (sometimes termed "attributes"). In the video game example these attributes are "get moneys worth" or "be user friendly."

The task of identifying physical and functional needs of the customer is often more difficult than it may initially appear. Customers can be either internal or external to the organization and their needs may be conflicting. Often focusing on the end user as the final customer can resolve conflicts and bring a team to resolution. There are several categories of customer needs. The first category consists of explicit customer expectations. A second category involves elements a customer expects without telling you, but are assumed to be part of the general requirements (e.g., tires on a newly purchased car). The last group includes expectations which are those items not specifically requested because the customer does not know of their possible existence. These are referred to as "excitement factors." When these features are not present people are not dissatisfied, but when they are present people are extremely pleased. Airbags and antilock brakes are good examples of excitement factors.

Usually formal methods are necessary to identify customer desires and may include marketing research, focus groups, indepth qualitative interviews, researching publications and other techniques engaged in by a multifunctional team. The resulting information is translated into customer requirements during a brainstorming session and categorically placed into hierarchical tree diagrams for the House of Quality.

2 - Competitive Assessment – Not all customer desires can be equally important. To bring the perspective and focus to team activities, the House of Quality measures the relative importance to the customer of all the defined requirements. Weightings based on the customers' perceptions are derived from the direct experience of team members with the customers or from surveys.

Companies which want to match or exceed their competition must first know where they stand relative to it. This is illustrated on the right side of the house where customer evaluations of competition are compared to in-house perceptions. Business development personnel will recognize this aspect of the house as a perceptual map to identify strategic positioning of a product which acts as a natural link between a product concept and a company's strategic vision.

3 - Product And Operations Solutions – "Hows" The next step involves brainstorming a list of quantifiable characteristics that will satisfy the customer desires. These should be controllable characteristics (e.g., "screen resolution" and "levels of difficulty" in the video game example). They can be described in measurable terms to provide targets for specifications and desired product improvements.

4 - Relationship Matrix – The "relationship matrix" indicates the impact of each engineering characteristic on the customer attribute. A project team should seek consensus on these evaluations basing them on expert engineering experience, customer responses and tabulated data from statistical studies or controlled experiments. The team uses numbers or symbols to establish the strength of these relationships as illustrated in Figures 8.5 and 8.6.

5 - Technical Assessment of Priorities – The relationship matrix can be translated into design priorities. The relational levels of importance not only define what is most important but also define what is least important. These results provide the basis for a technical plan as illustrated in Figure 8.7.

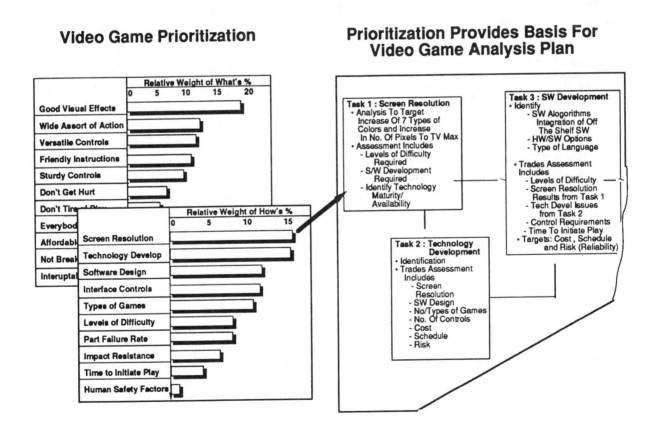

**Figure 8.7 The Results Of The House Of Quality Provides
The Basis For Developing A Program Plan**

6 - Set Target Values – At the bottom of the house targets are set for each corresponding characteristic ("900,000 cycles" or "10,000 lines of software code") to measure part failure rate and software design. If the characteristic is not measurable, then further definition is required. If a characteristic cannot be measured than there is no way to verify it has been adequately implemented into the design.

7 - The Roof or Correlation Matrix – Measurable does not necessarily mean achievable or conflict free. Very rarely does a system not have conflicting design elements. In a QFD matrix these correlations between the system characteristics are captured at the top of the matrix in what is traditionally referred to as the roof. The distinctive roof on the House of Quality assists engineers in specifying various characteristic features that need to be improved collaterally. Symbols are used to denote positive and negative relationships as illustrated in Figures 8.5 and 8.6. System characteristics exhibiting negative relationships are traded off to find the best compromise and strong positive relationships are studied to prevent duplication of effort. Sometimes one targeted feature impairs so many others that the team may decide to leave it alone.

Analyzing the House of Quality – A careful examination of the House of Quality should be performed to validate the results. Blank rows or columns indicate incomplete data. This can occur when requirements may not have been translated into technical requirements or a technical requirement is specified for which no customer requirement exists. If this happens the team should re-evaluate the data for missing customer and technical requirements, cross check the consistency of competitive data and analyze requirements with emphasis on discriminators between the competition.

Expected Results – Desired outcomes from the House of Quality include the prioritization of key customer requirements and design characteristics to satisfy those requirements. This effort should also yield which characteristics are targeted for improvements. As illustrated in Figure 8.7, such outputs provide the basis for defining a technical approach that includes trade study elements and a basis for allocating resources.

SATELLITE SERVICING SYSTEM CASE STUDY EXAMPLE

An excellent example of the power of QFD to focus a multifunctional team was demonstrated in support of a Satellite Servicing System Proposal effort performed at Martin Marietta Astronautics Group. A multifunctional team used the Quality Function Deployment methodology to identify all critical system and subsystem design characteristics of a Satellite Servicing System (SSS) to support the development of an integrated technical approach. Major functions of the SSS (pictorially illustrated in Figure 8.8) were to perform on-orbit autonomous rendezvous and docking, supervised autonomous orbital replacement unit exchange, and supervised autonomous fluid transfer with an experimental space vehicle. In addition, the SSS was required to simulate proximity operations for the future Space Station Freedom.

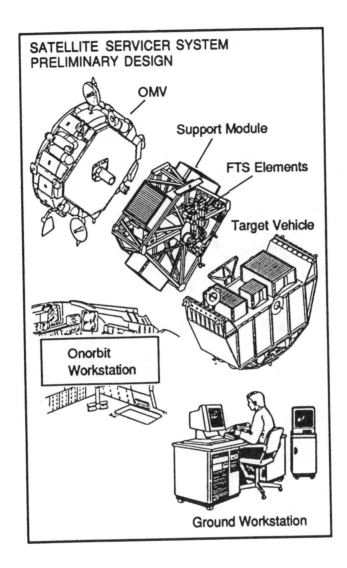

Figure 8.8 An Illustration Of The Satellite Servicing System

Training and completion of the House of Quality matrix was completed over a period of approximately 7 days. Over 140 design issues were identified and prioritized. These design issues were integrated into the technical approach. Not only did the use of QFD result in a strong proposal win, but the proposal was completed a week early with no questions prior to best and final awards. In retrospect, the team became empowered through the process and committed to the final product. Each member walked away with a thorough knowledge of how the program goals and mission objectives affected the design element and each of the system components.

Lessons Learned

The lessons learned from the Satellite Servicing program are similar to those experienced by many other successful teams. The following is only a partial list of those lessons:

1.   Expert facilitation is required and critical to the success of initial pilot projects. The facilitator must be able to assist the group in the definition of the problem, formulate the approach and guide the team in the right direction in an environment where the number of options is unlimited. The facilitator must keep the group from drifting in directions guided by personal biases.

2.   Each QFD matrix should be tailored to the needs of the work environment.

3.   In large-scale efforts, QFD matrices can quickly become too large to control. Identifying priorities is essential so that each matrix in a series can be scaled down by focusing on priorities only.

4.   Communication is more important than mathematical elegance.

5.   Program managers may find it difficult not to dominate, interfere or lead discussions.

6.   Time is needed to overcome a sense of vulnerability between team members.

7.   Success is directly proportional to the listening skills of group members.

8.   Differences in terminology will lead individuals to different end results. Provide definitions of terms as appropriate.

9.   Individuals have a tendency to leave the process, causing the group to rehash old discussions which result in the loss of valuable time. Set meeting schedules for full participation.

10. Observers cannot resist the temptation to participate, thinking they are being helpful. The group loses valuable time explaining the basis for their opinions or unknown information to the observer. Ultimately, the group can become resentful. Minimize interference for best team progress.

11. Large teams are difficult to focus. A team size of 10 to 15 is recommended.

12. Adequate time should be allowed for information preparation. Conceptual design by committee requires maturity of thought.

QFD AND ROBUST DESIGNS

One of QFD's major benefits is that it pinpoints where a company can efficiently use powerful tools such as Experimental Design and Statistical Process Control (SPC). The results of the QFD matrix (illustrated as elements 3, 5, and 6 in Figure 8.5) provide the data to describe the inputs and target parameters to perform an Experimental Design to optimize design performance. The roof or correlation matrix provides the interactions between competing design implementations that also need to be reviewed in the Experimental Design techniques. The targets identified in element 6 may be established from SPC data or historical data. In essence, the QFD matrices achieve the competitive edge for the user by identifying desired product goals and their interaction with process and product capabilities to allow focus on technical improvements.

QFD AND THE HOUSES BEYOND

The foundation of the House of Quality prepares the project for continued production and process planning through either the Four Phased or Matrices of Matrices approach. Matrices developed from the Toyota study presented in Figures 8.9 through 8.11, illustrate the type of information that can be obtained from the remaining three matrices of the Four Phased Approach. In Phase 2, the Product Design Matrix, technical requirements are translated from the House of Quality into specific part characteristics. "Parts" refers to items that eventually compose the product or service. The inputs include the highest priority technical requirements from Phase 1, target values and importance weights, product functions and required parts and mechanisms. The results of the Phase 2 matrix are the identification of key part characteristics and the selection of new or best designs.

Product Design Matrix

Quality Characteristics			Material				Water Drain		Sealer		
Design Requirements	Item Number / Degree Of Importance / Targets		Anti-Rust Steel	Resin	Body Sealer	Joint Adhesions	Hole Position	Hole Shape	Application Area		
			1	2	3	4	5	6	7	8	9
Weld Joint Rust	30 Cycl Corr	3	●			○	●	●	○		
Surface Rust	60 Cycl Scab	2	●	△	●		○	○	○		
Sketch							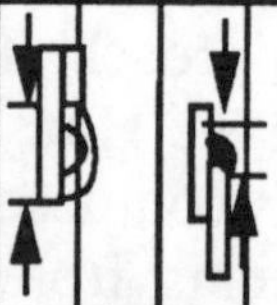				
Value Weights	Absolute		45	2	18	9	33	33	15		
	Relative (%)		29	1	12	6	21	21	10		
Target Values			85 u Zinc Coat	Tsk 1000	Tsk 751	Tsk 870	Lowest End	Bend 45	Sketch		

Figure 8.9 The Product Design Matrix Translates Technical Requirements Into Part Characteristics

The Process Planning Matrix of Phase 3 is the translation of design requirements into process parameters. Required inputs include the highest priority part characteristics from Phase 2, target values and importance weights, process steps to be used in the product and process failure modes and effects analysis (FMEA) results. The desired outcomes are the identification of critical process characteristics yielding controlled target values for process characteristics and the capability to develop operating instructions that preserve customers' intent.

Process Planning Matrix

Quality Characteristics		Key Process & Parameters		Receiving Inspection				Punch Press					Control Points
		Item Number		Carbon Content	Coating Adhesion	Coating Thickness	Formability	Cutter Hardness	Cutter Step	Clearance	Die Condition	Deflect/Thrust Brng	
		Degree Of Importance / Targets		1	2	3	4	5	6	7	8	9	
Anti-Rust Steel	Item 1		3	△									Chemical Cert
	Item 2		3		●		○						Bend Test
	Item 3	85 u Zinc Coat	3			●							Spot Test
	Item 4		3	△			○						Temper Color
	Hole Position	Lowest End	2				△			●	○	○	Visual Check
	Hole Shape	Bend Bk 45º	2				△	○	●	○		○	Visual Check

Sketch

Value Weights	Absolute	6	27	27	22	6	18	24	6	12
	Relative (%)	4	18	18	15	4	12	16	4	8
Target Values		Ink Test 80% Min	No Flake @180º B	15 Sec +/- 1	Limit Sampling	Rc 55 - 60	2mm +/- 0.5	6-8 % Plate Thick	Punch Aft Form	0.05 mm Max

Figure 8.10 The Process Planning Matrix Translates
Part Characteristics Into Process Characteristics

Finally, Phase 4 (Production Planning Matrix) is the implementation strategy for monitoring the process parameters. To minimize product variation, high priority items, process characteristics, target values and importance weights from Phase 3 along with process operations, FMEA results and key part characteristics are used to provide detailed plans for checking and controlling key part and process characteristics.

Process Control Planning Chart

Part Name/ Number	Part Characteristics Values	Process Name	Routing Sheet Number	Process Characteristics Values	Planning Reqmts			Control Methods				Inspection Methods				Test/ Measurement Tool		Persons Responsible		
					Training	Maintenance	Fail Safing	Location	Sample/ Freq	Standard	Data Evaluation	Inspect Item	Method/ Freq	Standards	Data Evaluation	Type	Calibration Reqmt	Measurement/ Inspection	Follow-up Actions	Remarks

Figure 8.11 The Process Control Planning Matrix Assigns Specific Control Methods To The Critical Process Characteristics

The Matrices of Matrices provides similar information. As illustrated in Figures 8.12 through 8.14, the information obtained in the matrices is complementary to the system design process and can be tailored to support a system requirements review, a system design review or a product design review. Although these charts are illustrated as a sequential flow, many of the activities can be performed simultaneously. For example, the development of test and manufacturing strategies can be done simultaneously with the development of the top level system product and process matrices. The sequential illustration of the charts provides system traceability and verification of design completeness.

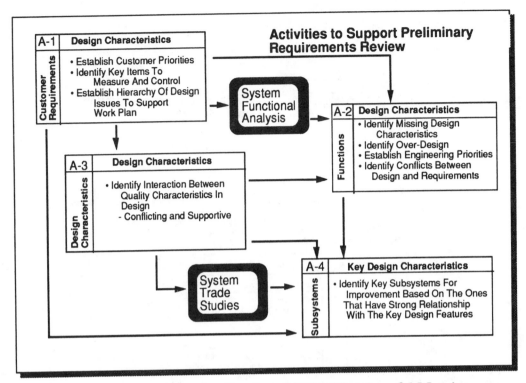

Figure 8.12 Example Application Of The Matrices Of Matrices Approach To The Development Of Preliminary System Requirements

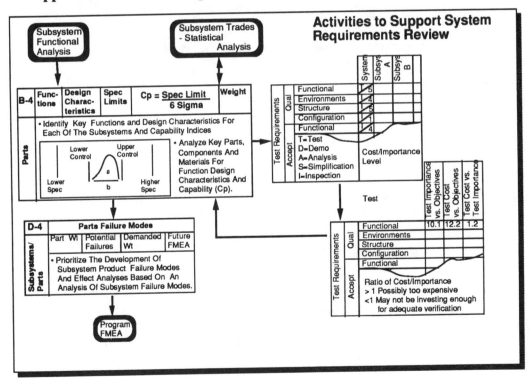

Figure 8.13 Example Application Of The Matrices Of Matrices Approach To The Development Of System And Subsystem Requirements

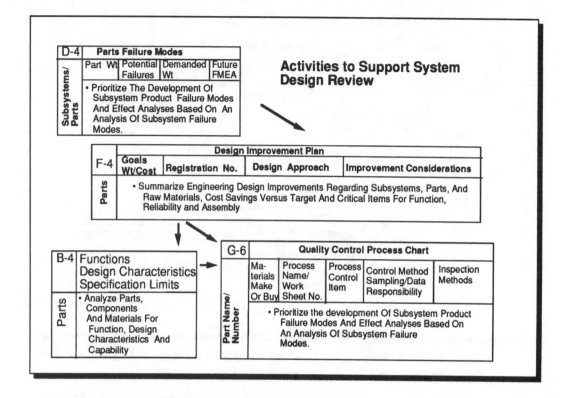

Figure 8.14 Example Application Of The Matrices Of Matrices Approach To The Development Of System Design

MANAGEMENT'S ROLE

The role of management is changing along with the implementation of QFD and other team building quality initiatives. Management's function is evolving from traditional responsibilities of planning, organizing, coordinating and controlling to three categories: interpersonal, informational, and decision roles. The interpersonal role requires the manager to act as a figure head, a leader and liaison. The informational role requires someone who will monitor and disseminate pertinent information and act as a spokesperson for the multifunctional teams. Finally, the decision role requires the manager to act as an entrepreneur, mediator and negotiator.

Given the new guiding principles for management, the tasks of management during a QFD pilot program include defining the purpose, expectations and boundaries of the QFD exercise. Management should also provide guidelines on schedules and team participation to the team facilitator. Although management participation is not mandatory during the QFD team sessions, occasional attendance will provide insight into team decisions. At a minimum the manager should review initial charts during the early stages to provide a validity check and understanding of team status. The most successful QFD programs demonstrate management commitment by providing adequate resources to do the job.

CONCLUDING REMARKS

In summary, QFD represents a method by which "quality" is the end result of an integrated system of prioritization. It is a powerful communications tool that assists the multifunctional teams to achieve their maximum potential by focusing and integrating their specialized knowledge and creative energy. QFD is the means by which quality becomes the natural by-product of a methodical approach to systems design. Ultimately, the risk of implementing a QFD approach in terms of investment is minor, but the rewards are great. Not only does the use of QFD help teams do things right, it makes them do the right things. In essence, the House of Quality is quality in-house.

REFERENCES

Business Week, "The Push for Quality", June 9, 1987.

Clausing, Don, "Quality Function Deployment" in *Taguchi Methods and QFD; How's and Whys for Management*, Nancy Ryan, Editor, ASI Press, Dearborn, MI.

Hauser, John R., and Don Clausing, "The House of Quality", *The Harvard Business Review*, May-June 1988.

Sullivan, L.P., "Quality Function Deployment The Latent Potential of Phases III &IV ", Presented at the AIAA/ADPA/NSIA First Total Quality Management Symposium, CO, 1-3, November, 1989.

King, Robert, "Better Designs in Half the Time - Implementing QFD in the USA," presented at the Growth Opportunity Alliance of Lawrence, MA, 1987.

BIBLIOGRAPHY

Ealy, Lance, "QFD - Bad Name for a Great System," *Automotive Industries*, July 1987, p. 21.

Eureka, William E., "Introduction to Quality Function Deployment," ASQC Automotive Sections Annual Quality and Reliability Conference, June 1987, Nov, MI (co-sponsored by ASQC's Greater Detroit Section and the American Supplier Institute).

Fortuna, Ronald M., "Quality Function Deployment; Taking Quality Upstream," Target, *Association for Manufacturing Excellence*, Winter 1987. pp11-16.

Ishikawa, Kaoru, *What is Total Quality Control? The Japanese Way* (Englewood Cliffs, NJ:Prentice Hall, Inc. 1985).

King, Robert, "Listening to the Voice of the Customer: Using the Quality Function Deployment System," *National Productivity Review*, Summer 1987, pp 277-281.

Kogure, Masao, and Yoji Akao, "Quality Function Deployment and CWQC in Japan," *Quality Progress*, October 1983, pp 25-29.

Sullivan, Lawrence P., "Quality Function Deployment," *Quality Progress*, June 1986, pp 39-50.

BOOKS

Quality Function Deployment: Integrating Customer Requirements Into Product Design. Yoji Akao, editor. Productivity Press, 2067 Massachusetts Ave., 4th Floor, P.O. Box 3007, Cambridge, MA 02140; (617) 497-5146.

Better Designs in Half the Time: Implementing QFD in America, by Bob King Goal/QPC, 13 Branch Street Methuen, MA 01844; (508) 685-3900.

The Customer Driven Company; Managerial Perspective on QFD, by William Eureka and Nancy Ryan. American Supplier Institute (ASI) Six Parklane Blvd. Ste 411, Dearborn, MI 48126

SOFTWARE

International TechneGroup Inc. (ITI) offer QFD/ Capture for PC's. Several companies have a strong preference for this package. ITI, 5303 DuPont Circle, Milford, Ohio 45150; (513) 576-3900. Or Rick Norman, (312)869-2963.

ASI offers QualitSoft Corp. called QFD/Designer, for PCs under Windows 3.0. ASI is listed under books above.

Chapter 9

TQM TOOLS AND TECHNIQUES: MEASUREMENT/STATISTICAL TOOLS

Before beginning a detailed discussion of statistical tools and techniques, it is important to point out that our purpose is not to make the reader a statistician; however, some knowledge of statistics is crucial for properly collecting, measuring and analyzing data. Statistics alone should never be used in making quality improvement decisions and thus statistics are not a substitute for experience, prior knowledge and common sense. On the other hand, failing to use statistical techniques as a supplemental tool during quality improvement will deny you the process information you need to compete in today's markets. Familiarity with basic statistical concepts is a necessity for anyone truly interested in quality.

STEPS TO TAKE BEFORE COLLECTING DATA

Prior to any data gathering exercise the following preparatory steps should be taken (Kiemele and Schmidt, 1990).

1. **Management must establish the proper environment to maximize the use of the data.**

   Any data gathering exercise will result in a non-value added activity unless management is prepared to be responsive to the information obtained from the data. Employees must be well trained in their jobs to insure the data are valid. In addition, employees should be trained to work in teams and feel free to provide candid remarks regarding the process. Most importantly, everyone should be evaluated on the basis of product (goods or service) quality and not quantity.

2. **Describe the process.**

   The process identified for improvement should be well defined through the use of previously described tools such as process flow diagrams, cause and effect diagrams, etc. It is also extremely important to identify all of the suppliers and customers associated with this process along with their needs and expectations.

3.   **Determine what is to be measured.**

What we measure is typically related to some predetermined problem statement and process improvement objective related to customer needs and expectations. Sometimes the quality characteristic of interest (Y) is expensive and/or difficult to measure and thus a surrogate characteristic (Z) which is highly correlated with Y might be a better choice.

4.   **Define the Measurement System.**

We must identify how to measure the quality characteristic and insure that the measurement system will be accurate, precise and stable. Without a good measurement system, our data will provide confusing and/or misleading results.

PROCESS DEFINITION

At this point, in our discussion, it is probably a good idea to review what is meant by a process. In general, a process is a blending of inputs which generate corresponding outputs. The outputs (often referred to as responses) are the quality characteristics related to producing a product, performing a service or completing a task. The actual quality characteristic selected for measurement could be numeric in nature (e.g., thickness, strength, cycle time, etc.) or it could be non-numeric (e.g., defective/non-defective, good/bad, or a subjective rating: unsatisfactory, poor, fair, good, excellent). If there exist only two categories of a non-numeric characteristic it is referred to as an "attribute" variable.

The inputs to a process consist of factors which typically fall into one of the following groups: materials, machines, methods, manpower, measurement, environment, policies, etc. These inputs can also be numeric (e.g., temperature, pressure, power, flow, time) or non-numeric (e.g., machine (A or B), method type, brand of tool, etc.). Measurement of the inputs is also crucial. To increase the likelihood of success in our quality improvement effort, variation of the inputs should be reduced and steps taken to hold them at fairly constant levels.

Variation and Its Impact on Quality (Schmidt and Launsby, 1991)

It should not be a surprise that even in well-controlled processes, measurements of quality characteristics will reveal that most products (goods or services) differ due to variations in the process. Too much variation degrades the quality of the product and causes a loss to the company. If large numbers of the product are produced outside specifications, and if products are not inspected to eliminate defects, then 1) customer complaints will increase, 2) repair or warranty costs will increase, and 3) eventually customers will become discouraged and seek a more quality oriented supplier. Historically, the approach to this problem has been to set up specification limits and perform inspections of finished products to ensure zero defects. This approach will dichotomize the quality aspect of any product into either acceptable (within spec) or unacceptable (out of spec). In this case, loss to the producing company is based on being out of spec as shown in Figure 9.1.

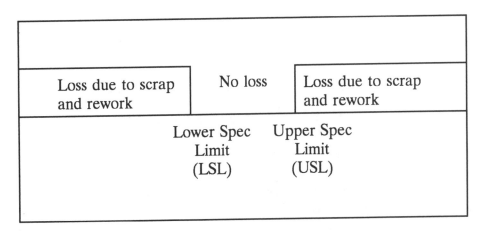

Figure 9.1 Old Philosophy of Quality

The optimal solution to this problem is not to increase inspections. According to Juran, these inspections are only 80% effective. Furthermore, inspection requires more manpower and results in rework and scrap costs that can become prohibitive. In addition, maintaining profits under these conditions requires sale prices to increase, resulting in a continued decrease in consumer satisfaction. It is also unreasonable to assume that a product just inside a specification limit results in no loss to the company. For example, consider building window glass and window frames. If the glass is at the lower limit and the frame is at the upper limit (or vice versa) the quality of the product is reduced. To develop a quality product at a reduced costs, quality must be designed into the process and focus must be on the target (nominal) value instead of just being "in spec" as depicted in Figure 9.2 (Taguchi, 1986). Deviations from the target result in loss to the producer in the form of scrap, rework, warranty cost, increased cycle time, tied up capital, increased inventories, etc. Losses to the purchaser are due to degraded performance and reliability, as well as increased maintenance costs. Eventually the purchaser (customer) will find a better producer (supplier) and, thus, the ultimate loss to the producer is reduced market share.

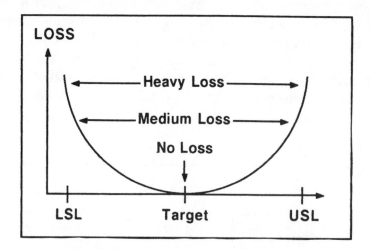

Figure 9.2 New Philosophy of Quality

To minimize the loss incurred due to deviation from the target, the variability of the product about the target must be reduced as shown in Figure 9.3. The shape of the curve for each product depicts the frequency of product measured at some quality characteristic value below the curve. *Notice* that both products have most of their product characteristic values centered around the target; however the spread in Product A values is much wider than those for Product B. Thus, Product B has a much higher proportion of measured values close to the target and will result in less overall loss to the producer and purchaser. Similar comparisons can be made for one-sided specifications where we try to minimize or maximize the quality characteristics.

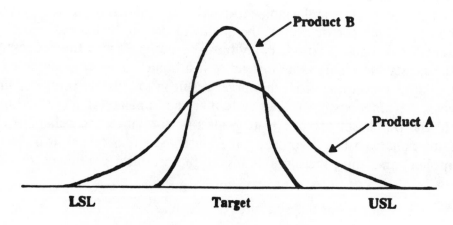

**Figure 9.3 Higher Quality Implies Variance
Reduction Around the Target**

Another way to describe the differences in Products A and B is based on the use of statistical measures of central tendency and dispersion. The average is a measure of the center of the distribution and would be labeled $\bar{y}$ (if we have labeled the output characteristic as x then the average is $\bar{x}$). To find the average, we would add up all the characteristic values and then divide that sum by the total number of values in the sum. The variance (s^2 or $\hat{\sigma}^2$; both symbols are used interchangeably) is a measure of the spread in the distribution of characteristic values. Obviously, the wider the distribution, the greater the variance. The square root of the variance is also used to represent the spread in the distribution and is referred to as the standard deviation (s or $\hat{\sigma}$).

Measurements of Quality

If a process average and standard deviation are fairly stable over time, the process is said to be in control and we can assess the capability of the process through the use of metrics such as the C_p or C_{pk} indices. The C_p index was designed to compare the variability of some quality characteristic (y) based upon the lower specification limit (LSL) and the upper specification limit (USL) while assuming the average of the characteristic (y) is equal to the desired target value (T). The formula for C_p is shown in Equation 9.1.

$$C_p = \frac{specification\ width}{process\ width} = \frac{USL - LSL}{6\hat{\sigma}}$$

$$where\ \hat{\sigma} = \sqrt{\frac{sample}{variance}} = \sqrt{\frac{\sum_{1}^{n} (y_i - \bar{y})^2}{n - 1}}\ and\ \bar{y} = \frac{\sum_{1}^{n} y_i}{n}$$

Throughout this text, the symbols $\hat{\sigma}$ and s are both used to represent standard deviation.

Equation 9.1 Computing the C_p Index

According to acceptable standards in industry, C_p values less than 1.00 are unacceptable, values between 1.0 and 1.33 are marginally acceptable, and values greater than 1.33 are desired. Many quality oriented companies such as Ford and Motorola are now requiring C_p values greater than 2.0.

Since the C_p index does not take into account deviations from the target, T, a preferred metric is the C_{pk} index computed as shown in Equation 9.2. Interpretation of C_{pk} values is similar to that described for C_p.

$$C_{pk} = minimum\ of\ \left(\frac{USL - \bar{y}}{3\hat{\sigma}}\right) or \left(\frac{\bar{y} - LSL}{3\hat{\sigma}}\right)$$

Equation 9.2 Computing the C_{pk} Index

A third measure of product quality is the number of defects per million (dpm). Obviously we need to minimize dpm in order to insure high levels of quality. For attribute (pass/no pass) type quality characteristics, one would simply count the number of defects per number of opportunities and multiply times 10^6 to obtain an estimate of dpm. For quality characteristics that are numeric (quantitative), we can estimate dpm from our previous capability index, C_{pk}. The relationship between C_{pk} and dpm is shown in Table 9.1.

C_{pk}	dpm
.50	133,600
.67	71,800
.80	16,400
.90	6,900
1.00	2,700
1.33	66
1.67	<1
2.00	.0018
3.00	<<1
4.00	<1 defect per billion

This information was obtained from an R&M 2000 Variability Reduction Process slide prepared by USAF/LE-RD.

Table 9.1 Relationship Between C_{pk} and dpm

Motorola's Six Sigma Process assumes that even processes under control continue to have up to 1.5 sigma shifts in the distribution average, $\bar{y}$. Thus, the Six Sigma Process has a slightly different C_{pk} to dpm conversion. See Figure 9.4 for an easy C_{pk} to dpm conversion as well as a dpm to sigma capability conversion.

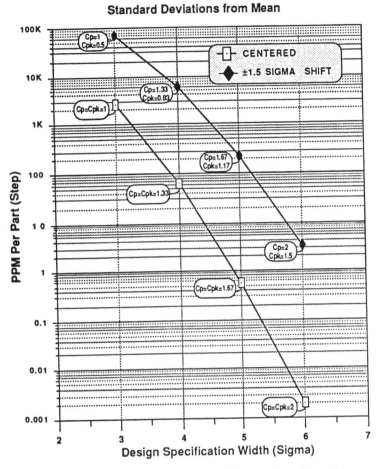

**Figure 9.4 Conversion Graph for C_{pk}, dpm
and Sigma Capability** (Harry, 1988)

Taguchi has developed a loss function which allows the researcher to associate a dollar value to the current state of process/product quality. This dollar amount can be used to identify key process/products to be improved and to evaluate the amount of improvement. The quadratic loss function shown in Figure 9.5 will, in many cases, approximate the true loss due to deviations from the target. Actual losses result from a combination of scrap, rework, poor performance, lack of customer satisfaction, increased cycle time, tied-up capital, inventories, loss of market share, etc.

The measured loss for a single product can be estimated using $L = k(y - T)^2$ where y is the response value, T is the target value, and k is the monetary constant. To determine k, we need to estimate the loss for any specific value of y. For example, if the estimated loss for y = 130 is $100.00, then k= $100 \div (130 - 120) = 1.0$. The loss function $L = 1.0(y - T)$ can now be used to estimate the loss associated with other y value products.

Another use of the loss function is the determination of average loss per product, $\bar{L}$. In *Understanding Industrial Designed Experiments*, the authors show that $\bar{L} = k(\hat{\sigma}^2 + (\bar{y} - T)^2)$

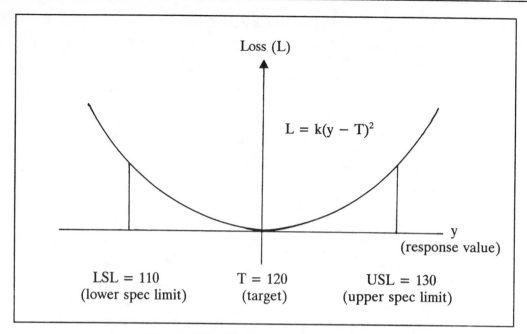

Figure 9.5 Taguchi Loss Function

(Schmidt and Launsby, 1991). Multiplying average loss times the total number of product produced (in a specific time period) we can estimate the total cost of our current state of quality. The route to improved C_{pk}, dpm, sigma level or average loss is the same. Improvements will occur as we reduce the response variation, $\hat{\sigma}^2$, and reduce the deviation of the response average from the desired target, that is, reduce $(\overline{y} - T)$. These improvements are primarily accomplished through the use of statistical tools that assist the engineer, researcher or analyst in understanding the process.

STATISTICAL TOOLS AND TECHNIQUES

Several statistical tools and techniques exist for turning data into valuable information. In this section we will discuss proportions, Pareto diagrams, run charts, histograms, control charts, experimental design, and robust design.

PROPORTIONS

For non-numeric outputs we would usually count the number of defects and/or the number of outputs in a specific category. This type of count data can also be converted to proportions for each category. For example, assume we counted defects from a process which produced 1000 parts. If 100 are defective, we can conclude that our defect rate is $100/1000 = 0.1$. Multiplying this rate by a million would provide us an estimate of the number of defects per million (dpm), that is, dpm = 100,000. From a Motorola Six Sigma standpoint (3.4 or less dpm) our example can use some improving.

To maximize information from non-numeric data, it is sometimes advisable to partition the categories. For example, defects can be further partitioned into the types of defects. Assume our 100 defects are a result of the following categories:

Types of Defects	Count (frequency)	Proportion
A	33	.33
B	12	.12
C	3	.03
D	27	.27
E	4	.04
F	8	.08
G	13	.13
	100	1.00

Table 9.2 Types of Defects and Frequency of Occurrence

The data from our process is now beginning to provide more information which can lead to good decisions for quality improvement.

PARETO CHARTS

Graphically, the type of defect data from Table 9.2 can be portrayed in a Pareto chart shown in Figure 9.6. Notice the obvious causes of the majority of our defects are from Type A and D defects.

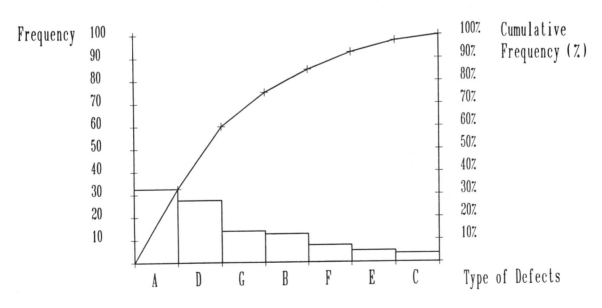

Figure 9.6 Pareto Diagram of Types of Defects

Using the process problem solving tools in Chapter 7, we can now brainstorm the most likely process input or set of inputs which are causing these type of defects.

RUN CHARTS

To monitor a process with non-numeric outputs, you could plot either the number of defects or the proportion of defects over time in a graph referred to as a run chart. (See Figure 9.7)

Consider the proportion of defects plotted over a one year period shown in Figure 9.7. The sample size for each month is 1000 products.

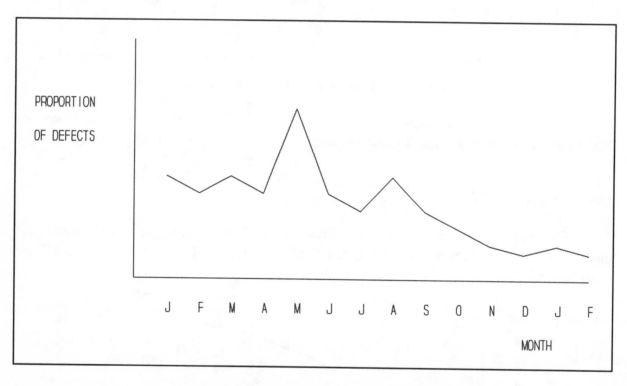

Figure 9.7 Run Chart of Proportion of Defects

Management can use run charts to investigate process performance, determine ways to improve, and monitor continuous process improvement efforts. In our example, management should be suspicious about the large jump in the proportion of defects during May. An investigation may indicate a change in one or more of the process inputs. For example, a substitute operator may have been used in May, indicating the need for more training of the substitute operator. Also notice the downward trend from September through the following February. If we changed vendors in September the graph would indicate the need to stay with the new vendor and/or work with the old one.

A similar set of Pareto charts and run charts can also be generated for number of customer complaints, or similar quality characteristics, in a non-manufacturing environment. Obviously, our intent is to present what these tools can do—you need to use your own creativity to visualize how these tools can work for you.

Some disadvantages with attribute type data (data based on counting the number of occurrences of one or two categories of a quality characteristic) are the following:

1.   When yields are reasonably high (greater than 90%, the sample size requirement on attribute data becomes extremely high.

Yield	Sample size
90%	50
95%	100
98%	250
99%	500
99.9%	5000

2.   Attribute data reflect the old philosophy of quality (i.e., quality is conformance to specification). (See Figure 9.1)

The new philosophy of quality is based on more than zero defects. Today's customers are requiring uniform defect-free products whose quality characteristic values comply as closely as possible to the desired target values. To focus on a target value and to quantify your state of quality requires the use of numeric quality characteristics. With numeric information from our process we can obtain more information with less data. For example, the following are a list of times (in hours) between unscheduled maintenance activities:

171, 156, 230, 147, 167, 183, 225, 190, 250, 245, 205, 210,
260, 270, 290

Plotting these times in chronological order produces the following run chart:

Data: 171, 156, 230, 147, 167, 183, 225,190,
250, 245, 205, 210, 260, 270,290

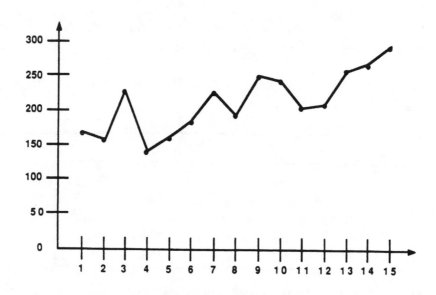

**Figure 9.8   Run Chart for Time Between
Unscheduled Maintenance Activities**

From the run chart, you can conclude a slight positive trend in time between unscheduled maintenance actions. This conclusion would indicate the quality of the maintenance program is improving. What is not provided by a simple run chart for numeric or non-numeric data is whether or not an apparent trend is real and/or meaningful. To address this question we could build a control chart. However, before discussing control charts, it is necessary to first take a look at histograms.

HISTOGRAMS

A histogram is a graphical tool for summarizing a large amount of information. Consider the following 50 data points for time (in minutes) to repair a system malfunction.

Time to Repair (in minutes)				
118	116	138	129	128
121	117	141	108	117
132	126	116	124	127
117	117	133	119	118
131	127	123	138	133
114	113	126	111	128
121	119	125	122	117
112	121	121	125	126
123	128	122	119	121
114	145	115	124	134

Table 9.3 Sample of time to Repair Data

Certainly the 50 values by themselves as shown in the table do not provide a feel for what is really here. Knowing that the data have an average of $\bar{y} = 123.2$ and a standard deviation of $\hat{\sigma} = 7.974$ provide some information. A histogram such as that shown in Figure 9.9 provides even more information about the process.

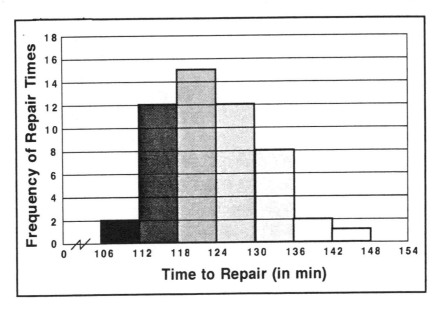

Figure 9.9 Histogram of Time to Repair Data

To construct a histogram, you would complete the following steps:

(1)   Find an interval width which provides enough classes over the range of data such that the number of classes is 5 to 20.

(2)   Count the frequency of data points within each class.

(3)   Plot the frequency for each class with a bar.

Since the histogram for repair times is somewhat bell shaped, it is reasonable to approximate its shape with a normal distribution curve. The normal distribution is useful to make statements about where future data points will occur. The graphic in Figure 9.10 shows a normal distribution and the percent of the data that appear between $\pm k\hat{\sigma}$ of the average, where k = 1, 2, 3, 4, 5, 6 and $\hat{\sigma}$ is the standard deviation of the data. If your data are not normally distributed, see *Introduction to Statistical Quality Control* (Montgomery, 1991).

CONTROL CHARTS

Using Figures 9.9 and 9.10, we can conclude that approximately 99.73% of the time to repair data should fall between $\pm 3\hat{\sigma}$ of the mean. For our 50 data points, the average is 123.2 and the standard deviation is 7.974. Therefore, 99.73% of the data should fall between 123.2 $\pm$ 3 (7.974) = [99.278, 147.122]. You can use the previous interval to form limits for a type of control chart which has a lower limit of 99.278 and an upper limit of 147.122 as shown in Figure 9.11. Since each dot in Figure 9.11 is based on a sample of size one, this type of chart is referred to as an individuals chart.

Control charts are used to: 1) determine if a process is in control (i.e., the mean and variance are stable); 2) establish boundaries for the natural variability of a process; and 3) determine if significant trends or shifts have occurred. Several different types of control charts exist such as $\overline{X}$, R, P, C, U, individuals and moving range. Good introductory references for control charts are found in *Basic Statistics: Tools for Continuous Improvement* (Kiemele and Schmidt, 1990) and *Introduction to Statistical Quality Control* (Montgomery, 1991). A simple example of a control chart application is presented in the section on a quality improvement example.

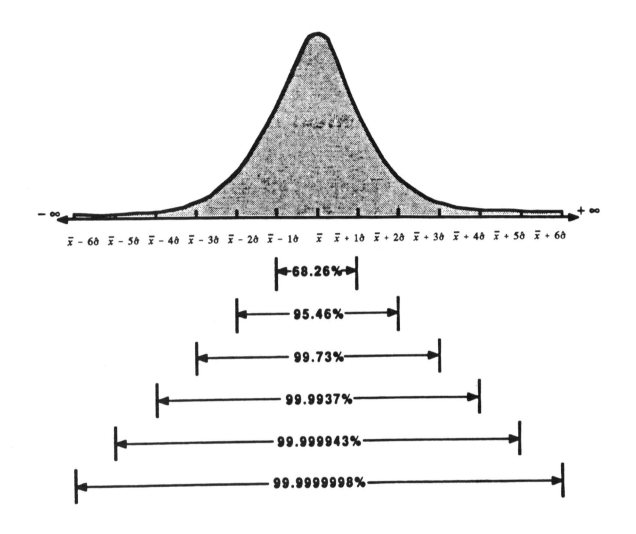

$\hat{\sigma}^2$ for sample data is found using $\quad \hat{\sigma}^2 = \dfrac{\displaystyle\sum_{1}^{n}(x_i - \bar{x})^2}{n-1}\quad$ where

$\bar{x}$ is the sample average and n is the sample size.

Figure 9.10 Empirical Rules of the Normal Distribution

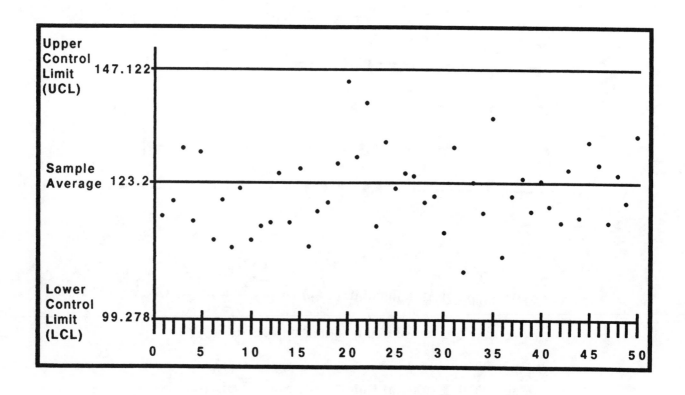

Figure 9.11 Control Chart for Time to Repair Data

Advantages of Control Charts

- Provides a systematic and efficient method of gathering data and transforming it into INFORMATION

- Allows us to make decisions on FACTS rather than intuition or memory

- Identifies non random impacts to a process

- Warns of system degradations prior to making defects

- Forms a basis for improving a process *within* the specifications

- Gets line workers involved

- Builds expert data base

- Shows evidence of process improvements

Disadvantages of Control Charts

- A state of control does not imply that your process is capable of satisfying the customers

- Problem identification takes time

- Control charts signal problems but not their reasons

- Analysis of past data that "happen to be available" may not provide a clear assessment of input and output relationships

Most of these disadvantages are overcome with the knowledge and application of designed experiments.

EXPERIMENTAL DESIGN [1]

The previous section on control charts indicated how we can "listen to a process" and turn the data into information. To overcome the disadvantages of control charts and instead proactively "interrogate" a process, we need to know something about designing experiments.

Experimental design consists of purposeful changes of the inputs (factors) to a process in order to observe the corresponding changes in the outputs (responses). The process is defined as some combination of machines, materials, methods, people, environment and measurement which, when used together, perform a service, produce a product, or complete a task. Thus experimental design is a scientific approach which enables you to better understand a process in a short period of time and to determine how the inputs affect the response(s).

The manager should be interested in experimental design to achieve the following:

(1)   improved performance characteristics
(2)   reduced costs
(3)   shortened product development and production time

Improved performance characteristics result from identifying the critical factor levels that optimize the average response and minimize response variability. This improved performance also leads to a reduction of scrap and rework, which greatly reduces costs. Understanding which factor levels are critical to improving performance allows for controlling the important factors while relaxing tolerances on benign factors or, when appropriate, selecting less expensive materials. Reducing the time to market can be accomplished by first understanding what the customer really wants and then using efficient testing procedures such as those used in experimental design to optimize the design of the product and/or process.

Historical use of one-factor-at-a-time experimentation and arbitrary selection of incomplete full factorial designs (experiments consisting of all possible testing combinations) have resulted in very inefficient and ineffective attempts to understand and optimize product designs and processes. No longer can these archaic methods be tolerated if a company intends to keep up in a highly competitive market.

---

[1]Most of this section is taken from *Understanding Industrial Designed Experiments*, Third Edition (1991), Schmidt, S.R. and Launsby, R.G., Air Academy Press, Co.

For the engineer who tests different design strategies of a new product or trouble shoots problems in an on-line process, experimental designs are used as:

(1)   efficient methods for gaining an understanding of the relationship between the input factors and the response(s).

(2)   a means of determining the settings of the input factors which optimize the response(s).

(3)   a method for building a mathematical model relating the response(s) to the input factors, which is referred to as process/product characterization.

The types of designs used in modern methods for experimentation include full factorials (only used when the number of factors tested is small), fractional factorials, Plackett-Burman, Latin Squares, Hadamard Matrices, Taguchi designs, central composite, Box-Behnken, and computer generated optimal designs. To effectively use the design of experiments tool, one should know about all these design types to include their objective, similarities/differences and advantages/disadvantages. Much controversy has developed over which approach to designed experiments is the best. Don't be confused by those who say one tool will solve all problems. Only by understanding the different approaches and their advantages/disadvantages can you optimize your process. See *Understanding Industrial Designed Experiments* for more information (Schmidt and Launsby, 1991).

Experimental Design Example for Improving Quality

A group of Air Force Academy cadets in an experimental design class were consulting Colorado Springs industry for a class project (Schmidt and Launsby, 1991). The company manufacturing a small bushing was experiencing variation problems with out-of-roundness on both ends of the bushing. The cadets led a brainstorming session with the appropriate operators, engineers and the local quality manager. The brainstorming produced 10 factors for experimentation at two levels (i.e., each factor was to be tested at a low and a high setting). The total number of combinations would have been $2^{10} = 1024$ tests, referred to as the full factorial. This was obviously an unsatisfactory number of tests for the company to consider. The final experimental design consisted of 16 tests, a fractional factorial. Because of the special nature of the tests contained in the fractional factorial design, the information from the 16 tests allowed the experimenters to predict all unexperimented combinations. The end result of the experiment was a set of new operating conditions which reduced the out-of-roundness standard deviation by 50%. Numerous applications of experimental design are found in *Understanding Industrial Designed Experiments* (Schmidt and Launsby, 1991).

Experimental Design Example for Improved Time to Market

Captain Burt Silich, an Air Force fighter pilot, indicated a need for a new type of advanced fighter aircraft with N-Dimensional capability. "The concept is based on an airframe with three primary lifting surfaces of equal size located at 120° intervals. This design should allow the aircraft to place its lift vector anywhere in 360° nearly instantaneously with minimum or no roll required. In other words, this aircraft will have the ability to dart unpredictably in any direction (up, down, left, or right) with a full load on the wings and with little or no roll required (Johnson, Rizwan, and Silich, 1990)."

The primary problem with the design is that little to no theory exists to provide sizing and performance calculations. The non-statistical approach to theoretical development could take years and millions of dollars. Today's competitive environment; however, necessitates that high quality and low cost products be developed more quickly. To accomplish a theoretical approximation of flight performance characteristics for a N-Dimensional fighter, a scaled prototype was built and placed in a wind tunnel. The inputs consisted of pitch, roll, and flap extension (for each of the 3 wings) while the outputs were the six aeronautical characteristics. The actual tests conducted were generated from an experimental design matrix (in this case a central composite design). After 30 different testing conditions (approximately one month of periodic wind tunnel usage) statistical analysis provided six Taylor Series models relating the outputs to the inputs. These equations are an approximation of the theoretical knowledge required for sizing and performance calculations. The confirmation of these models provided very acceptable results. Thus, blending engineering knowledge with experimental design will allow us to quickly obtain "profound knowledge" of our products/processes and gain a competitive edge.

Robustness

Through the use of experimental design the researcher can find process factor conditions which will make the end product or the process itself insensitive (robust) to difficult to control variations in the environment or in the process. This concept was popularized by a Japanese engineer and has become a key ingredient for developing higher quality at lower costs (Taguchi, 1986). A simple example is included in the example that follows.

A QUALITY IMPROVEMENT EXAMPLE

Suppose you are responsible for vehicle maintenance in a large organization. As an initial attempt to implement continuous process improvement (CPI), you would probably form a team to assist you in defining your mission and developing a process flow diagram for vehicle repair. The diagram, shown in Figure 9.12, can be used to improve quality by identifying non-value added steps to be modified or eliminated. An obvious CPI objective would be to ensure that "the right repairs are done right the first time." Just imagine how many steps could be eliminated from the process flow diagram if you could educate, train, and motivate your people to perform in this manner.

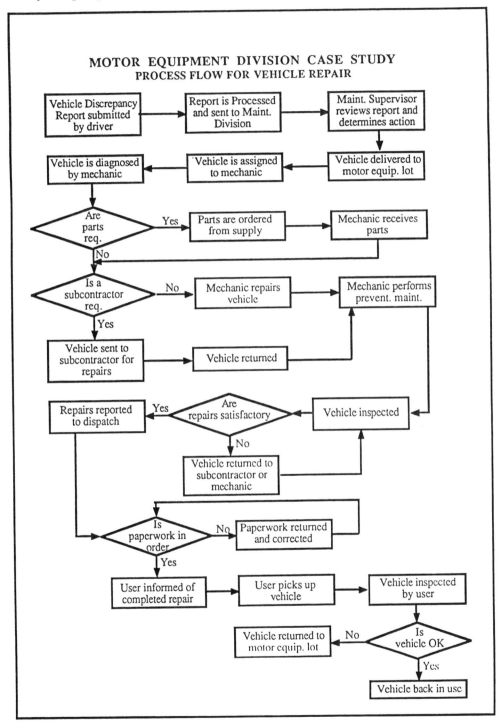

Figure 9.12 Process Flow Diagram for Vehicle Repair

After reviewing the process flow diagram, assume you decide to implement a gas mileage improvement strategy. To benchmark your current state of vehicle quality, you would probably direct that gas mileage data be recorded on each vehicle. The best way to display this data is shown in Figure 9.13.

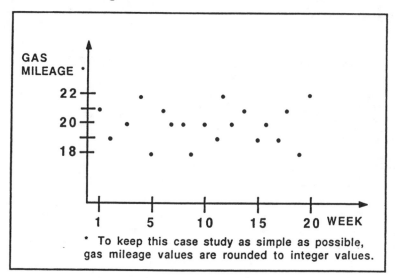

Figure 9.13 Graph of Weekly Gas Mileage

As you can see, gas mileage does vary from week to week. Your concern is whether this variability is natural or due to specific causes. The use of control charts can assist you in answering this question.

To present a simple overview of control charts, we will assume that the 20 weeks of data in Figure 9.13 are from a vehicle whose performance is currently known to be stable. Computing the average gas mileage over the 20 weeks will give us a feel for the vehicle's expected gas mileage. This average is found as shown below.

$$\bar{y} = \frac{\sum_{1}^{20} y_i}{20} = \frac{[21 + 19 + 20 + ... + 22]}{20} = \frac{400}{20} = 20$$

To obtain a measure of the variability in vehicle gas mileage, we can calculate the sample variance, $\hat{\sigma}^2$, of the 20 mileage values. The equation for $\hat{\sigma}^2$ is:

$$\hat{\sigma}^2 = \frac{\sum (y - \bar{y})^2}{n - 1}$$

which can be described as the sum of the squared deviations from the average, divided by $(n - 1)$. The deviations from the average and the variance calculations are displayed in Figure 9.14.

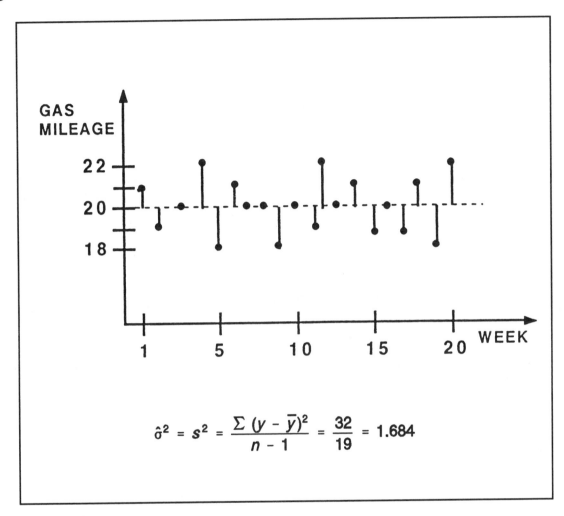

$$\hat{\sigma}^2 = s^2 = \frac{\Sigma \, (y - \bar{y})^2}{n - 1} = \frac{32}{19} = 1.684$$

Figure 9.14 Graph of Deviations from the Mean Gas Mileage

A common technique which is a simple, yet powerful, way to get a visual feel from the way data is distributed is to draw a histogram. A histogram is a graph which displays how frequently a given outcome occurs. The histogram for our data is shown in Figure 9.15. If a smooth curved line were used to outline the histogram, it would appear to be symmetric and bell shaped, much the same as a normal curve. Assuming, then, that our gas mileage values are approximately normally distributed allows us to make use of the empirical rule shown in Figure 9.16.

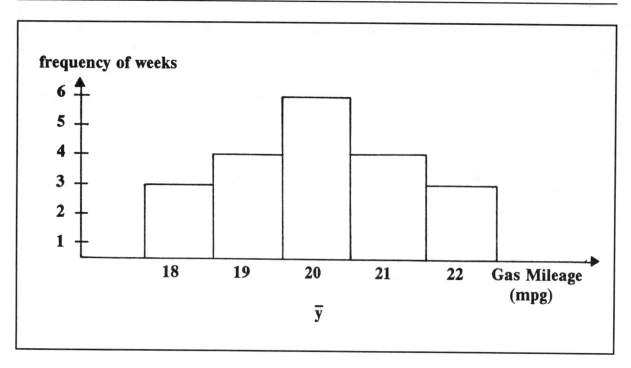

Figure 9.15 Histogram for Gas Mileage Data

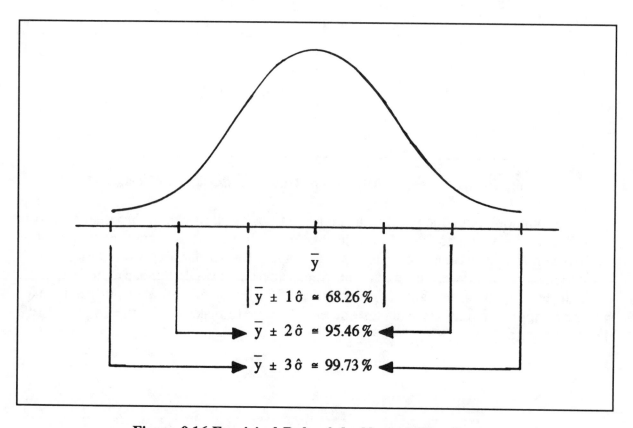

Figure 9.16 Empirical Rule of the Normal Distribution

The normal distribution of gas mileage values and randomness of the data in Figure 9.13 supports our assumption that the vehicle's performance is stable. We can now use the empirical rule to assist us in developing control charts. For example, $\bar{y} \pm 3\hat{\sigma}$ results in a lower control limit (LCL) of 16.1 and an upper control limit (UCL) of 23.9. (See Figure 9.17) The empirical rule states that approximately 99.73% of all future gas mileage values for this vehicle should fall within these limits. Therefore, we can use these limits to evaluate the future performance of this specific vehicle. For instance, if week 21 produced a gas mileage of 23, chances are that nothing specific has caused this value; however, a value of 16 is outside the control limits (i.e., outside the natural variability) and indicates that there is a 99.73% chance this value was caused by some specific change in the vehicle. Other control chart rules exist for determining out of control conditions due to trends or increases in variability (Kiemele and Schmidt, 1990) and (Montgomery, 1991).

Once an out of control condition is determined, the obvious next step is to determine its cause. To obtain this information, a brainstorming session with the appropriate members should be conducted. The results of such a session might resemble the cause and effect diagram displayed in Figure 9.18. After completing the brainstorming, the group should try to reduce the information to those inputs most likely to affect the gas mileage. You now have a set of input factors to the process which can be investigated each time the mileage control chart detects a change.

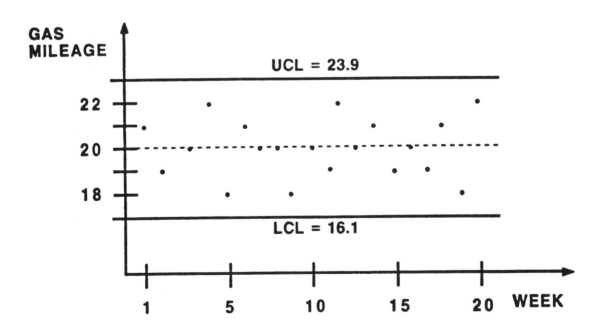

Figure 9.17 Control Chart Based on Gas Mileage Data

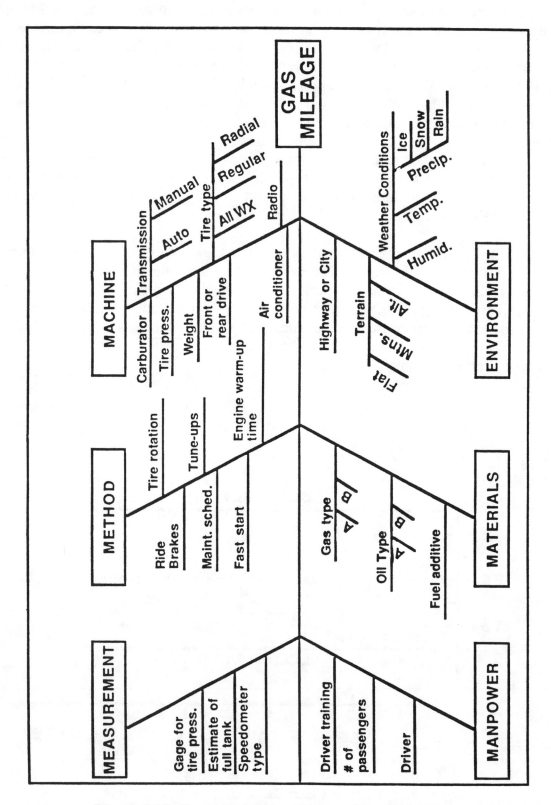

Figure 9.18 Cause and Effect Diagram for Gas Mileage

Assume your investigation revealed an extremely low tire pressure which you determine to be the cause of the out of control mileage value. You would obviously correct the low tire pressure problem and possibly begin to chart the tire pressure on a weekly basis. In this way, you are now controlling a critical input to the process instead of waiting for a substantial change in the process output. Thus, you have now entered a problem prevention mode versus detecting poor quality through inspection of output values.

Control charting is an excellent tool; however, engineers are not always sure which inputs are the important ones (vital few) and which ones are unimportant (trivial many). Furthermore, using control charting to gain an in-depth understanding of your process can be a long drawn out procedure. What is needed is a faster method for achieving "profound knowledge" of the gas mileage process. The statistical tool which provides this type of in-depth knowledge of a process in a timely manner is experimental design. The basic idea is to characterize the process by determining which inputs have a critical impact on the response. The design of experiments approach can be used effectively after control charts have been implemented; however, it is advantageous to characterize the process before production begins. This strategy allows for quality to be designed into the product from the beginning of the design engineering phase.

For our gas mileage problem, assume the brainstorming resulted in four input factors to be used in the experiment. To investigate all possible combinations of four factors at two levels would require the 16 runs shown in Table 9.4. The (−) values are shorthand for −1 and indicate a factor set at its low value. The (+) values are shorthand for +1 and represent a high factor setting. Notice that the design columns are all balanced vertically, i.e., there are an equal number of (+) and (−) values in each column. That is, the sum of all the numbers in each column is zero. Furthermore, these columns are also balanced horizontally for each level of each column. For example, when A is at a (−), the remaining columns have a balanced number of (+) and (−) values, the same balancing occurs for A at (+) and all other columns evaluated at their (+) or (−) settings. These balancing properties result in design orthogonality which allows us to estimate the effects of each factor independent of the others.

	FACTORS			
RUN	A	B	C	D
1	−	−	−	−
2	−	−	−	+
3	−	−	+	−
4	−	−	+	+
5	−	+	−	−
6	−	+	−	+
7	−	+	+	−
8	−	+	+	+
9	+	−	−	−
10	+	−	−	+
11	+	−	+	−
12	+	−	+	+
13	+	+	−	−
14	+	+	−	+
15	+	+	+	−
16	+	+	+	+

**Table 9.4 Full Factorial Low (−) and High (+) Settings
for a Four Factor Experiment**

The design in Table 9.4 is referred to as a full factorial design. It is capable of estimating the effect of all possible factor combinations on the response. In this case, there are 15 possible "effects." There are 4 "linear" or "main" effects (A,B,C,D); 6 "two-way" interactions (AB, AC, AD, BC, BD, CD); 4 "three-way" interactions (ABC, ABD, ACD, BCD); and only 1 "four-way" interaction (ABCD). Experimenters infrequently find interactions beyond two ways to be significant, and thus time and resources can be conserved by the use of a fraction of the full factorial design. For the gas mileage experiment, it was decided to use a fractional factorial design with eight runs or rows. Fractional factorial designs are discussed in depth in *Understanding Industrial Designed Experiments* (Schmidt and Launsby, 1991). The resulting design matrix for our fractional factorial is shown in Table 9.5. Notice that this eight-run design also has the balancing properties required for orthogonality. The column for factor D was formed by using the elements of the ABC interaction column, that is, multiplying the corresponding row values in columns A, B, and C together to get the value in column D. The result is that the settings for factor D are "aliased" (or identical) with the settings for the ABC interaction. This, in turn, will produce other "aliasings" as shown in Table 9.6. More will be said regarding aliasing once we have analyzed the data.

FACTORS				
RUN	A	B	C	D
1	−	−	−	−
2	−	−	+	+
3	−	+	−	+
4	−	+	+	−
5	+	−	−	+
6	+	−	+	−
7	+	+	−	−
8	+	+	+	+

**Table 9.5 Half Fraction Design Settings for Four Factors,
Each at 2 Levels (Low and High)**

ALIAS PATTERN	
effect	alias
A	BCD
B	ACD
C	ABD
D	ABC
AB	DC
AC	BD
AD	BC
BC	AD
BD	AC
CD	AB
ABC	D
ABD	C
ACD	B
BCD	A

**Table 9.6 Alias Pattern for the
Half Fraction Design in Table 9.5**

The four factors which were brainstormed to be used in the experiment and the low (−) and high (+) levels of each are shown in Table 9.7.

FACTOR	LEVELS
A: TIRE PRESSURE	28, 35
B: TIMING SETTING	LOW, HIGH
C: TYPE OF OIL	1, 2
D: TYPE OF GAS	1, 2

Table 9.7 Factors for the Gas Mileage Case Study

The completed experimental matrix with the response values (taken over three weeks for each run) are displayed in Table 9.8.

Run	A	B	AB	C	AC	BC	D	y_1	y_2	y_3	$\overline{Y}$	s
1	−	−	+	−	+	+	−	22.27	21.12	21.37	21.59	.60
2	−	−	+	+	−	−	+	14.22	15.40	10.46	13.36	2.58
3	−	+	−	−	+	−	+	22.49	23.15	22.08	22.57	.54
4	−	+	−	+	−	+	−	9.96	13.80	11.92	11.89	1.92
5	+	−	−	−	−	+	+	17.35	18.60	17.97	17.98	.62
6	+	−	−	+	+	−	−	27.08	24.54	24.57	25.40	1.46
7	+	+	+	−	−	−	−	18.36	17.63	17.04	17.68	.66
8	+	+	+	+	+	+	+	22.78	26.97	27.14	25.63	2.47

Table 9.8 Complete Experimental Matrix with Response Values for Gas Mileage Case Study

A graphical analysis for each effect in the design matrix is obtained by plotting the average response at the (−) and (+) settings and then connecting these two dots (see Figure 9.19). The * in Figure 9.19 was obtained by averaging the response values when factor A is set at its high (+), that is, the average response for runs 5, 6, 7, and 8. The other dots are found in a similar fashion. The steepness of the slope reflects the importance of each effect. From the graphical results in Figure 9.19, it is apparent that the most important effects are factor A and the AC or BD interaction. Since AC is aliased with BD, (see Table 9.6), we must go back to the factors to try and determine which interaction is most likely responsible for the steep slope in Figure 9.19.

Since it is highly unlikely to have a "tire pressure x type oil" interaction (AC), it is decided that the steep slope in Figure 9.19 is due to the BD, or "timing x type of gas" interaction. The BD interaction graph is shown in Figure 9.20 where the ★ was determined from the response average of the runs with B at (−) and D at (−).

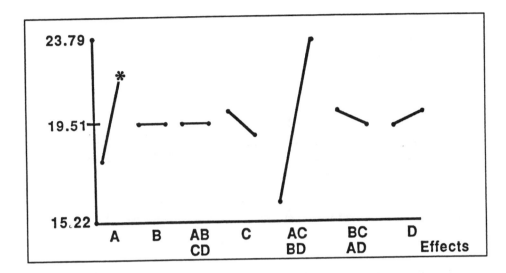

Figure 9.19 Marginal Mean Graphs for Gas Mileage Case Study

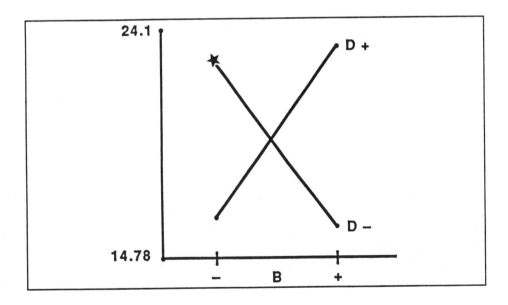

Figure 9.20 Interaction Graph for Factors B and D

Another graphical analysis can be used to determine if any of the factors shift the variability in the gas mileage. Figure 9.21 indicates that factor C has a big effect on variability.

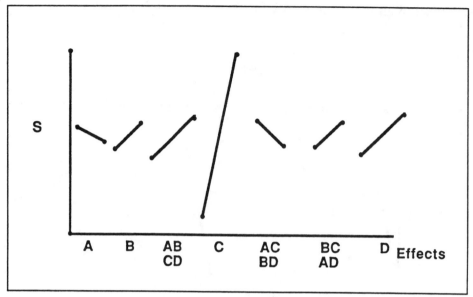

Figure 9.21 Marginal Average Graphs for Standard Deviation

To determine the best factor settings for maximizing gas mileage while minimizing variability, we must return to Figures 9.19, 9.20, and 9.21. Based on Figure 9.19, set factor A at (+). Figure 9.20 indicates that factors B and D should both be set at (+). Factor C is set at (−) to minimize variability. Thus, the final factor setting decision is as follows:

Factor	(−) or (+) Setting	True Setting
A	+	35 psi
B	+	high timing
C	−	type 1 oil
D	+	type 2 gas

At this point, one should feel pretty good about solving a quality problem and thus satisfying the customer. Be careful, though, because we made the assumption that the customer wanted high gas mileage. When a survey was conducted in Madison, Wisconsin as to what the customer (the motor pool driver and/or passenger) thought was important, the primary response was not mileage, but safety (Hunter, O'Neill, and Wallen, 1988). The point is that designing experiments to solve problems which the customer may not think important will not always be a productive strategy. One should first survey the customer through the use of a procedure such as Quality Function Deployment (QFD). It is not enough to simply determine customer needs and expectations. To satisfy the customer, processes should be designed to meet customer needs and expectations so that customers will purchase the process outputs (products or services). To accomplish this task, crossfunctional teams from marketing, purchasing, engineering and others must work closely together from the time the need is first conceived until the need is met. QFD provides a framework within which the crossfunctional teams can work. To review the concepts and techniques associated with QFD, see Chapter 8.

Taguchi Approach to Designed Experiments

The objective of parameter (Robust) design is to determine factor settings that achieve desired response targets (min., max., or specific value) while minimizing the variability due to uncontrolled or noise factors. To illustrate this concept in the gas mileage example, consider weather conditions which are outside the vehicle operator's control. It is desirable to find the best settings of factors A, B, C, and D that maximize gas mileage while also making mileage insensitive (as much as possible) to weather conditions. In this case, we would make specific replicates due to various weather conditions. In other words, the first replicate would all be obtained under rainy conditions (w_1), the second replicate obtained during snowy conditions (w_2), and the third replicate obtained under dry conditions (w_3). Thus, the test matrix would appear as shown in Table 9.9. The only difference between this strategy and that of previous sections

Run	A	B	AB	C	AC	BC	D	w_1	w_2	w_3	$\bar{w}$	s
				Factors & Interactions				Replicated Responses				
1	−1	−1	1	−1	1	1	−1					
2	−1	−1	1	1	−1	−1	1					
3	−1	1	−1	−1	1	−1	1					
4	−1	1	−1	1	−1	1	−1					
5	1	−1	−1	−1	−1	1	1					
6	1	−1	−1	1	1	−1	−1					
7	1	1	1	−1	−1	−1	−1					
8	1	1	1	1	1	1	1					

Table 9.9 Replicated Responses Based on Weather Conditions

is the specific condition of the replicated response. By minimizing the response variability over the noise factor levels we have found a condition for the process that makes it insensitive–or *robust*–to environmental conditions. Robustness can also be sought for process parameters which are difficult or expensive to control (Schmidt and Launsby, 1991).

DISCUSSION QUESTIONS

1.   What is a process? Give an example from your job.

2.   Describe what must be done before you initiate any data collecting on your process.

3.   What do we mean by numeric and non-numeric inputs/outputs?

4.   Discuss the difference between focusing on specs versus focusing on a target.

5.   What kind of loss is incurred for product within specifications but not on target?

6.   What must you do to improve your current state of quality?

7.   What is a run chart and what kind of information does it represent?

8.   What can a control chart do for you?

9.   Describe the benefits of a designed experiment.

10.   What do we mean by a robust product/process?

REFERENCES

Harry, M.J., *The Nature of Six Sigma Quality*, Motorola, Inc., 1988.

Hunter, W., O'Neill, and Wallen, C., *Doing More with Less in the Public Sector: A Progress Report from Madison, Wisconsin*, Center for Quality and Productivity Improvement, University of Wisconsin, 1988.

Johnson, L., Rizwan, R., and Silich, B., "The N-Dimensional Fighter", *AIAA Student Journal*, Volume 28 No. 3, Fall 1990.

Kiemele, M.J. and Schmidt, S.R., *Basic Statistics: Tools for Continuous Improvement*, Air Academy Press, Colorado Springs, CO, 1990.

Montgomery, D., *Introduction to Statistical Quality Control*, 2nd Edition, John Wiley and Sons, Inc., 1991.

Schmidt, S.R. and Launsby, R.G., *Understanding Industrial Designed Experiments*, 3rd Edition, Air Academy Press, Colorado Springs, CO, 1991.

Taguchi, G., *Introduction to Quality Engineering*, Asian Productivity Organization, 1986.

Chapter 10

TQM APPLIED TO SOFTWARE[1]

THE NEED

Whether you look at manufacturing companies, service organizations, government agencies, the military, academia or our personal lives, today's high-tech systems and fast-paced lifestyles often involve reliable, maintainable and user friendly software. According to Business Week, "US companies command nearly 60% of the world's $110 billion market for software and related services (Brandt, Schwartz, and Neil, 1991)." However, many of us can still remember when US companies held a commanding lead in automobiles and electronics. Unfortunately, unless managers in the software industry take heed, history may repeat itself. The signs are becoming clear; based on a report from MIT, Japanese software companies are already turning out programs with 50% fewer defects than US companies. Since there is a direct relationship between defect rates and cost, it will soon become hard for US companies to compete.

The article, "Reliability Engineering as Applied to Software", shows that the cost of software in military programs surpassed hardware costs before 1970 (Yates and Schaller, 1990). (See Figure 10.1) It is not surprising that the bulk of these high software costs were found to be associated with detecting and correcting errors, that is, poor quality.

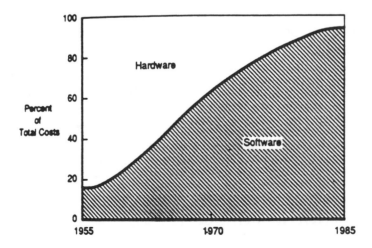

Figure 10.1 Hardware/Software Cost Trends (Yates and Schaller, 1990)

---

[1]Most of this chapter is taken with permission from "The Software Challenge: A Management Perspective" by Sue Hermanson, 1990.

Obviously, the US software industry has a sizeable problem, but exactly how do we begin to correct it? In software companies, most of the managers are intimidated by the software and the technocrats (people who understand it). Software seems to be something magic, something that is too complicated to understand and therefore too difficult to manage. The language of the software technocrats includes a long list of strange terms such as bits, bytes, bugs, worms, etc. and thus only adds to the confusion. Despite these and other problems in the software business, software development can and must be better managed. Years of management neglect led a 1987 Defense Science Board to conclude that software problems are typically not a technical problem; the root of the problem is poor management (Yates and Schaller, 1990).

The remainder of this chapter will provide a framework for managing software development and breaking down barriers. This framework consists of:

- defining software processes that are capable of producing software that meets customers' needs.

- continuously improving those processes to make them more effective.

- designing robust systems that are insensitive to causes of failure.

IMPORTANCE OF IDENTIFYING CUSTOMER NEEDS AND EXPECTATIONS

To determine what our customers need and expect requires that we ask them and then be willing to listen to their answer. It is also important to patiently assist the customer because often they do not fully understand their needs. The QFD method (see Chapter 8) might be appropriate to assist customer and supplier through this needs assessment process. The importance of correctly addressing customer needs is evident through the following finding of Yates and Schaller, "The requirement analysis phase is the biggest contributor to errors in the development cycle (Yates and Schaller, 1990)." (See Figure 10.2) The following graph indicates that the design phase is the second largest contributor to errors. With 72% of software development errors originating in requirements analysis and design, the obvious area to be emphasized for improved quality is at the beginning of the development cycle. A clear understanding of customer requirements will prevent numerous change proposals. Each change not only increases development time, it also increases the chance for new errors and increased costs. As you would expect, the cost for correcting errors will increase dramatically as the point of error detection moves downstream in the development cycle. Therefore, early error detection and prevention is of vital importance.

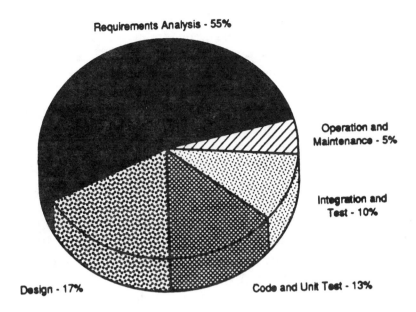

Figure 10.2 Percentage of Software Errors that Occur in Each Development Cycle (Yates and Schaller, 1990)

CAPABLE SOFTWARE PROCESSES

The first step to effectively managing software is to stop thinking about software as just code. Software is an integral part of a system; it is a very complex component that must be defined, designed, produced, tested and supported along with hardware components that comprise the system. These tasks (**defining**, **designing**, **producing**, **testing** and **supporting**) need to be defined and integrated into an overall development process capable of producing quality systems, software included, within cost and on schedule.

Capable processes, those that consistently meet customer needs and expectations, must include the following:

- a defined methodology that is implemented in organizational policies and practices.

- a disciplined commitment to the process and computer-aided tools that support the process.

- a mechanism for identifying and managing high risk items, and up-front planning in applying the process to a specific project.

Defined Methodology

From a developer viewpoint, whether military, in-house or contractor, a defined methodology means implementing software processes through established organizational policies and practices. The process needs to be written and must be in-place at the start of a project. This may seem obvious but when several companies that fared poorly in their software development efforts took a hard look at how they were doing business, they discovered that their employees' view of how to develop software varied considerably; they did not have a defined process. Each employee put emphasis on what he/she thought was important. Worse yet, when schedule was tight, important practices were short-circuited to save time. When these companies defined the process, and conducted training on the process, subsequent software development efforts had fewer problems.

For example in 1981, IBM examined its software development process. They revised and improved their in-house practices and standards. They established a program of early reviews and inspections of software development products (i.e., requirements specification, design, etc.) which included specific criteria to enter and to exit a review and pass to the next phase. They redefined the role of software quality assurance (SQA) so it wasn't just policemen, but an integral part of the process. They also enhanced SQA's role in improving the process. As a result they reduced the number of errors that reached the field (the user) from 28% to 5% as well as reduced the error rate (errors/KLOC, the number of errors per thousand lines of code) (IBM, 1986). This equates to dollars–big dollars–saved and more important, satisfied customers.

From a contractual standpoint, the development process, as it applies to a specific program, is defined in the Software Development Plan (SDP). The SDP should describe how the developer's policies and practices will be applied to the specific project. Mil-Std-2167A identifies the SDP to be delivered not later than system design review. Yet, many development efforts do not have an approved SDP until well past preliminary design review (PDR). That's too late! When the developer and the program manager can't define how the product should be built before the building process starts, the program is heading for disaster.

Disciplined, Repeatable Processes

Lack of discipline is one of the biggest reasons for downfalls in the software business. For too long programming has been looked at as an art–and artists are looked at as creative, not disciplined. Fortunately, the state-of-the-art has evolved to apply engineering discipline to software development. Unfortunately, few developers have made the commitment to practice it as an engineering discipline (D'ippolito, 1988 and Zahniser, 1988). This must change!

Discipline also means not short-circuiting the defined process to meet schedule. Software development is very much like the statement from an oil filter commercial "Pay me now or pay me later!" (and often it's pay me triple later). Would you want to buy a car from a company that is building it before the design is complete? Yet, when software runs behind schedule, management sometimes permits coding to start before software requirements are baselined or complete. This practice may generate lines of code, but often useless ones. Results: increased cost, frustrated people, and dilution of effort.

Tools

Software development and support tools do two things for a software activity: 1) they help enforce discipline and 2) they can track more data about the software product and the data relationships than the human brain. Used effectively, tools can improve the quality of the software and increase the productivity of software engineers and programmers. However, tools are not a panacea. Tools must be integrated into the defined software development process and should not be used as a replacement for defining the process. Tools should be selected that support the activity's already defined policies and practices. Some CASE (Computer Aided Software Engineering) tools can also be used for reverse engineering. The Air Force Standard Systems Center used one of these tools to capture the design of some of its more difficult to maintain programs and then restructured them. The result was an estimated savings of 200 maintenance man-hours per program (AFSSC, 1989).

Risk Management

The keys to managing and minimizing risk are understanding how to build a particular product and understanding what the process is capable of building successfully. Consequently, the high risk areas are those that: 1) have not been successfully developed using the process, 2) are new to the process, or 3) are historically tough to do. For information systems and command and control systems, the way software presents information to the user is the critical, but difficult ingredient in their success. For embedded systems, the challenges are meeting timing requirements and developing algorithms for functional performance. For both types of systems, integration of software with hardware and other software systems is high risk. These high risk areas need to be identified upfront and require extra care in developing. They need to be developed as a part of the normal process but special attention and techniques should be applied. Most importantly, risk areas need to be well-defined in terms of what is known, what needs to get done, and what is unknown (Boehm and Ross, 1989).

In many systems, requirements create risk. The system definition is so uncertain that requirements constantly change. It is often difficult for users to articulate what they want in the system. Consequently, they often change their minds. These requirement changes can be a direct change to the software requirements or they can be changes to the system hardware that have a domino effect on the software. Regardless of the source of change, instability of software requirements causes extensive risk. The later in the software development cycle the changes are identified, the more expensive the changes are to implement and the more they cause the schedule to slip (Boehm and Ross, 1989).

One way of avoiding requirements risk is to use interdisciplinary system design teams. Engaging software engineers, as well as production, reliability, supportability and other technical specialists, upfront enables addressing all aspects of a product early and reduces the need for change later in development. One defense contractor employed this concept on a recent project and reduced its cost per KLOC by 80%.

Planning

It is not enough to define a disciplined, development process. There must be a planning element that brings everything together–the process, people, resources, requirements, training, tools, constraints, schedule, etc. Planning needs to be done up-front as the initial steps of defining what to build and how to build it. As a part of the planning process, such things as the creation of resources (for example, reusable code) also need to be addressed. Planning is one of the most under-used tools in software development. Too often, developers charge into a new project without planning what they are going to do, how they are going to do it and who will do it (Boehm and Ross, 1989). For example, an acquisition strategy called evolutionary acquisition is often advocated for software development. This strategy is based on the philosophy "build a little, test a little, learn a lot." This approach is much more effective if the developer plans what portion of the system to build, how and what is to be tested to learn a lot and, most important, how that will be applied to the next build.

CONTINUOUS PROCESS IMPROVEMENT

It's not enough to just define a capable process. The process must be continually improved. Management can't do this alone; it must make employees partners in improving the process. The people who are performing various elements of the process are in the best position to see its effectiveness and suggest changes for improvement. In addition, a team which crosses the various software development functions should be tasked to oversee the entire process. Sometimes this is called a process group or process team.

METRICS

Software metrics are basically measures of performance, that is, defects per 1000 lines of code (KLOC), development time, number of changes, etc. Many developers fail to use software metrics because they view them as not accepted and not validated. However, software metrics have been validated and are mature in several different areas (reliability, efficiency, maintainability and cost). Developers collect data on their process and develop a statistically valid metric based on that data and that developer's process. What generally hasn't been done is that the metrics have not been calibrated for other developer's processes. Since each developer's process is slightly different, most metrics will need some tailoring to fit the individual process. Naturally, if the metric isn't tailored for that process, it won't be accepted.

In addition, since processes vary considerably from one developer and type of project to another, different metrics must be used to characterize the behavior of that process. Those metrics or characteristics are called the process critical parameters. When a metric is not a critical parameter, the metric is not very useful and will not be accepted.

PROCESS CONTROL

Before discussing how metrics are useful, let's look at one last reason some developers do not accept metrics. Although Figure 10.3 is a notional graph, it reflects the patterns I have observed for actual developers. Let's call our notional company Herm's Software, Inc or HSI. Through 1982, HSI looked at errors/KLOC as the report card at the end of a project and nothing more. Since the report card didn't look very good and profits and marketshare were dropping, they decided to employ the concepts discussed under the section on capable processes: defining the process, enforcing discipline, using tools, managing risk and planning the strategy. The result was their process stabilized; their results were repeatable. They could now reasonably expect that if they used the same process the errors/KLOC would be in the 1.5 to 2.5 range for the next project.

The difference between 1983 and 1985 was that HSI brought their process under control. Now metrics tell a story; they mean something because the process is repeatable. Before 1983, the metrics only said that the process was not under control. Having the process under control is the first step to continuous process improvement. Now when change is made to a process, the impact can be measured.

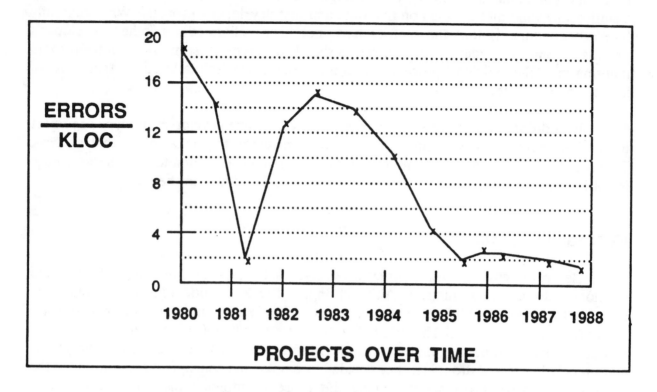

Figure 10.3 Process Maturity (Error Density)

BUSINESS STRATEGY

Metrics are also useful for determining business strategy; how are resources being used or consumed? For example, in producing hardware, management looks at a set of metrics for scrap and rework. From a software standpoint, management would want to see the same information—how much money, time, manpower did the process consume that did not contribute to the final product? One way a software project might consume too many resources is if defects made in the requirements phase are not being discovered and corrected until the coding phase. Not only does this create rework but the cost to correct a defect increases. According to a survey of IBM, TRW, GTE, and Bell Labs, the average cost to correct a defect during the coding phase is $953 (Boehm and Ross, 1989).

PROGRAM MANAGEMENT

Program management metrics follow the plans for a particular program. They are designed to show when the program is straying from the plan and to identify undesirable trends. Figure 10.4 is an indicator that can be used for monitoring program progress. Figure 10.4 tracks the actual design progression against both the original plan and revised plan. It also shows that CDR (Critical Design Review) was slipped two months and gives some insight that perhaps the slip was caused because seven CSUs (computer software units) had to be redesigned and five CSUs were added. Tracking this information gives insight into whether the program will meet its milestones. Also note that the information on the chart could be looked at from a business strategy standpoint; how much did the redesign cost? The redesign effort caused a slip in schedule of about one and one-half months. If this development has 50 software people at a cost to the developer of $120,000 per employee per year, then just the people cost of the rework is $750,000.

With metrics, management can determine where resources are wasted and where the process is breaking down. As a result management might make improvements to the process.

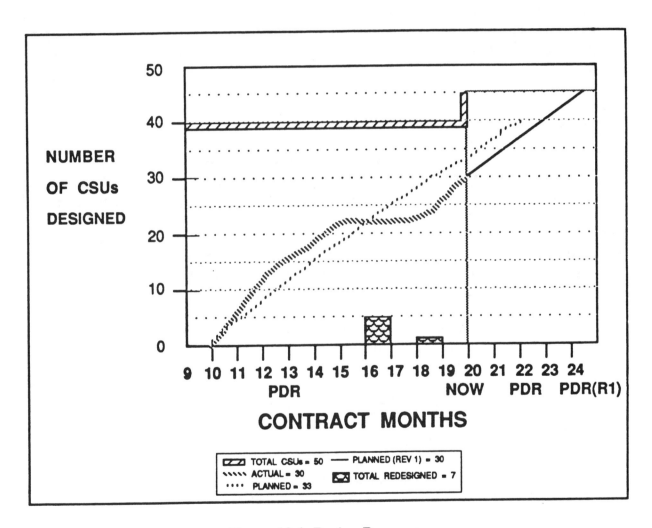

Figure 10.4 Design Progress

ROBUST DESIGNS

Robust software is software that is insensitive to errors regardless of the source–software, hardware, and people. In addition, robust software presents information to the user in a way that aids in the decision making process or makes information easier to comprehend. It is easy to use (the interface is designed to prevent human errors and their adverse effects) and accommodates different ways the user may elect to use the software. The software does not "lock-up" or abort except through a predefined termination procedure. Robust software should also be easy to modify; it should be structured, documented and written in a language that makes it easy to isolate and remove faults.

Robust designs start with well-defined requirements that emphasize meeting users' needs and employ a system engineering process that addresses the entire system. Robust software is designed using a modular structure that passes control and information only through well-defined interfaces. In addition, robustness is increased by using programming languages that limit variation in processing and data handling and make software easy to modify.

REQUIREMENTS

As pointed out earlier, defining requirements is an important aspect of developing the right product. Many say that software requirements cannot be defined completely upfront. Whether this is true or not, most will agree that defining software requirements is very difficult. Therefore, using special techniques and tools to define requirements can be very valuable. These tools and techniques provide a structured approach to requirements definition and reduce guess work. One of these techniques is prototyping. The purpose of prototyping is to model part of the software solution, such as the interfaces or a typical scenario, to help define and refine software requirements.

Prototyping enhances the ability to define critical interfaces–interfaces with the user, equipment or data bases. The importance of user interfaces is often underestimated. However, this is what the user sees and is the key to satisfying user needs. The user interface should be designed to minimize human errors in both data entry and interpretation of information. Data entry should be simple; data presentation should be easy to interpret. Under combat conditions or during an emergency this interface is critical.

For example, the original user interface for one of the Air Force's command and control systems was specified to "look like" another weapon system already in the inventory. However, this did not effectively exploit current graphics capabilities. As a result, the program office asked what could be done with state-of-the-art graphics equipment and software. Using existing data the contractor prototyped a user interface that significantly improved the presentation. Icons can be placed next to targets to permit visual identification. The fidelity of the presentation and use of color to emulate an elevation map permitted easy identification of areas where targets may be hidden, where communication links may lose line-of-sight and where an aircraft can ingress to a target and remain hidden by the terrain. These features will make the presentation easier for the operator to assimilate the information and make decisions.

However, developing a prototype also requires a disciplined process. The primary reason for this is that the better the model, the closer it will represent the intended product and consequently, the more likely it will be able to identify the difficult requirements. Also, the prototype may have to be modified to model different alternatives so it is desirable to make it easy to change and to be able to control those changes. And, finally, if the prototype is a high quality product, it might be transitioned into the final product.

SYSTEMS ENGINEERING

Despite the high cost and risk of software, many program managers continue to develop weapon systems using outdated acquisition strategies which center the design around the hardware and assume the software can be developed as an afterthought. As a result, poor hardware designs often compromise software maintainability by trying to "squeeze" the software onto a processor which is too "small" or "slow". Contractors are forced to develop new, unproven, faster algorithms which add to cost and schedule. In addition, memory and timing reserve disappear leaving no "room" for expansion or enhancement. To make matters worse, in order to make the software fit, the software design is abandoned and major portions of the code are written in assembly language. These actions make the software difficult to maintain and what might have been a minor change involves a major rewrite of the software system.

A better approach is to recognize the system for what it is—hardware, software, and people. Software does not exist unto itself, but as a part of the system. Therefore, it makes sense to develop a balanced hardware/software architecture which takes into consideration performance requirements, protocols, interfaces, language, and timing. In addition, timing margins and memory reserve should be allocated and retained for unplanned growth and software maintenance.

ARCHITECTURE

Software architecture is the structure and organization of the software just as the architecture of a building is its structure and organization. In software the architecture deals with structuring functional components or modules, designing the way data is used and defining interfaces (Fairley, 1985). This means structuring the software into groupings of simple, manageable units that logically belong together. Just as an architect for a building groups plumbing and wiring to give easy access for maintenance and modification, the software designer will group software for a single function into a single module. This practice makes the software easier to build and easier to modify. Structuring software also means passing information through a simple, controlled format. When this is not done well, a phenomenon called "spaghetti code" occurs. The flow of control among software components gets to be such a mess that it resembles cooked spaghetti. Trying to make changes to it is as difficult as untangling cooked spaghetti.

Another feature of software architecture that adds to robustness is independence. Software modules should be designed to be independent of other software modules and the hardware architecture. When software is independent, changes can be made in one module without impacting another module or changes can be made to the hardware without modification to the software. This makes maintenance easier to accomplish because it confines the maintainer's area of concern to a smaller section of code. In addition, it reduces the testing needed to be performed to ensure the modification is performing properly.

LANGUAGE

There are two aspects of language robustness. These are the preciseness of the language and the ease with which it can be modified.

Some languages allow the programmer to be very imprecise in the way information is handled; some languages are implemented differently on different processors. When using such a language the software maintainer must be aware of the areas of imprecision and look at them as a possible source of error. Unique machine implementations of a language make the software behave differently when the processor is changed. Imprecision and machine uniqueness are normally very subtle and add significantly to the level of knowledge required of the maintainer. The Ada programming language, on the other hand, was carefully defined to minimize imprecision and machine uniqueness. Therefore, it is easier to maintain software written in Ada.

Writing software is just that—writing. It should be written to communicate what it is doing. If it is easy to read the code, it is easier to determine what the code is supposed to do and, therefore, easier to change. Languages such as assembly languages or the C programming language require more experience to read. Ada, on the other hand, permits the use of more English-like statements making it easier to read.

An aspect of Ada that adds to its ease of maintenance is a mechanism that allows you to create black boxes of portions of the software. This eliminates the dependency of portions of the software on other portions so that changes in one area do not affect other sections of the software.

SUMMARY

Management of technically based processes is always a challenge. The further a manager is from the day-to-day details, the more he has to deal with issues from a conceptual standpoint. By emphasizing the concepts of capable processes, continuous improvement, and robust designs, software can be better managed. Software processes must be defined, disciplined and repeatable. These processes can be continuously improved through employee involvement and establishing metrics and measurements which provide insight into the process. The focus of the process is to produce robust software that performs as expected when needed.

DISCUSSION QUESTIONS

1. How healthy is the U.S. software industry?

2. What is the root of most software problems?

3. What is the biggest contributor to errors in a software development cycle?

4. List some commonly used software metrics.

5. Describe what is meant by robust software.

REFERENCES

Air Force Standard Systems Center, Presentation to M/Gen J.S. Cassity, 1989.

Boehm, B. and Ross, R., "Theory with Project Management: Principles and Examples", Transactions on Software Engineering, IEEE, July 1989.

Brandt, R., Schwartz, E.I. and Gross, N., "Can the U.S. Stay Ahead in Software?", *Business Week*, March 11, 1991.

D'Ippolito, R.S., "Who Killed Software Engineering?", Software Engineering Institute, Carnegie Mellon University, 1988.

Fairley, R., *Software Engineering Concepts*, McGraw-Hill, New York, NY, 1985.

Hermanson, S., "The Software Challenge: A Management Perspective", Headquarters USAF, Washington, D.C., 1990.

IBM, Presentation to B/Gen F.S. Goddell, Headquarters USAF, Washington, D.C., 1986.

Yates, W.D. III and Schaller, D.A., "Reliability Engineering as Applied to Software", *Reliability and Maintainability Symposium, 1990 Proceedings*.

Zahniser, R.A., "Computer Science vs. Software Engineering", SIGSOFT Software Engineering Notes, 1988.

Chapter 11

TOTAL QUALITY EDUCATION[1]

WHAT IS THE RELATIONSHIP BETWEEN TQM AND EDUCATION?

The relationship between TQM and education is symbiotic. Each influences the development and effectiveness of the other. Successful transitions to TQM generally have involved extensive education for everyone in the organization. The continued viability of TQM-oriented organizations also depends on continued education as well as skills training. Deming's first point, constancy of purpose, suggests that education links present operations to future opportunities: "to prepare for the future, a company must invest today. There can be no innovation without research, and no research without properly educated employees (Walton, 1991)." Conversely, many failures to institutionalize TQM concepts reflect inadequate efforts or ineffective methods of educating and orienting managers or workers toward quality.

The reciprocal effects also warrant consideration; widespread adoption of a quality orientation could affect educational institutions profoundly. Might many of the principles and procedures supporting TQM's successes in manufacturing and service industries also apply to educational systems? Could examples of the same faulty assumptions, dysfunctional influences and wasteful bureaucratic structures and procedures which led to the decline of traditional American corporations (Reich, 1988) be found in our educational institutions?

The similarity in the goals of education and TQM further strengthen their relationship. Over two decades ago, Postman and Weingartner (1969) suggested the essential function of schools should be to transform students into "shockproof crap-detectors". Substituting "waste" for "crap" in the following passage makes the similarity between their view of education and contemporary TQM efforts clear:

> ... the history of the human group ... has been a continuing struggle against the veneration of "crap." Our intellectual history is a chronicle of the anguish and suffering of those who have tried to help their contemporaries see that some part of their fondest beliefs were misconceptions, faulty assumptions, superstitions, and even outright lies (p. 3).

---

[1]This chapter was written and illustrated by David B. Porter.

Those familiar with Deming will have little trouble recognizing how well his experiences after WW II fit Postman and Weingartner's words.

HOW DOES EDUCATION DIFFER FROM OTHER INDUSTRIES?

In some ways, educational institutions are similar to any other company or corporation striving to remain viable in an increasingly complex and competitive world. The TQM principle of empowering workers (teachers) to continuously improve the quality of production or services (education) they provide to customers (students) by using relevant objective measures is appealing. Deming's definition of quality as "pride of workmanship (Aguayo, 1990, xi)" seems an appropriate academic goal for both teachers and students. Creating decentralized, supportive organizations might even cause collegial relations to develop spontaneously between faculty and students. No more time and energy need be wasted on counter-productive, adversarial relations between students and faculty or among students themselves. This seems so logical, one can't help but be surprised that the garden of American education has not already sprouted a hundred such successful academic nirvanas. Unfortunately, one does not have to look far to recognize that the quality storm sweeping through most other industries has barely moistened the fringes of most institutions of higher education. It is reasonable to ask: "why not?"

Education differs from other industries in several ways. Students are customers but they lack certain characteristics shared by consumers of other goods and services. The full "value" of education is unlikely to be immediately apparent to students and perhaps even the faculty (although the lack of educational quality is usually apparent to almost everyone). In many ways, students are less than informed and appreciative, "world class" customers. Many students could leap at the opportunity to enter the high paying jobs reserved for college graduates if they could be guaranteed the lack of a diploma would not restrict subsequent upward mobility. In this respect, college is likely to be seen by students as simply a punitive ritual which must be endured before they can get on with living the good life a college degree allows.

Admittedly, not all students are quite so negative; some actually, genuinely enjoy learning. As Lee Shulman suggests, however, these academic all-stars are the type of students who need teachers (and educational institutions) the least. It is precisely the students teachers are likely to refer to as "the wrong kind" who provide the surest measure of educational efficacy (Shulman, 1989). William Glasser makes a similar point when he defines an effective teacher as one who "convinces not half or three quarters but essentially all of his or her students to do quality work in school (Glasser, 1990)." Glasser goes on to explain why teaching may be the hardest job there is:

> As we are now inundated with students doing badly in school, more and more teachers ... are being blamed for what they do not know how to correct or ... cannot correct because they themselves are managed badly (Glasser, 1990).

In fact, competent, quality-oriented teachers often must face an academic Catch 22: if they teach conceptually and challenge students to think, their students will have a chance to learn something of value but might do poorly on fragmentary achievement tests or drop the course and the teacher will be labeled a troublemaker or failure. On the other hand, if she or he chooses to teach in the traditional way, most students will fail to learn anything worthwhile, but the teacher is likely to be praised as a team player and students will be blamed for their lack of effort, intelligence and progress (Glasser, 1990).

There is another issue which might confuse the application of quality principles to education. Variation in the "products" of education is desirable. Variation in products, however, is not the same as variance in quality. There are certain "qualities" educational institutions and potential employers expect college graduates to share. Inconsistent or underdeveloped analytical skills, partial or incorrect knowledge or bad attitudes would all reflect dysfunctional variance and thus diminish quality. However, separate disciplines and academic tracks have separate goals; this variation is desired by future employers. It may even be desirable for two graduates of exactly the same sequence of courses to vary from one another. The words of Robert Maynard Hutchins in his testimony before Senator McCarthy's Congressional Committee in 1952 add special emphasis:

> A university is a place that is established and will function for the benefit of society, provided it is a center for independent thought. It is a center of independent thought and criticism that is created in the interest of society, ... no totalitarian government is prepared to face the consequences of creating free universities (Seldes, 1983).

Henry Peter Broughman, the Scottish statesman of the 19th century observed "education makes people easy to lead but difficult to drive; easy to govern but impossible to enslave (Seldes, 1983)." Thus, graduates' capacity for "independent thought" is itself a characteristic needed by employers dedicated to developing quality-oriented organizations. It should also be recognized that such "independent thinkers" are likely to reek havoc within traditional, hierarchical (dare we say even "totalitarian?") institutions. To be effective, groups and organizations must be able to manage diversity. Another way of putting this is: groups need most that of which they have the least. The advantages of heterogeneous groups where a diversity of perspectives, opinions and alternatives are discussed freely, increase as the uncertainty of problems and the complexity of their solutions become greater (Shaw, 1981). The more initial disagreement, the greater the likelihood the optimal solution will be presented for consideration. Perhaps John Dewey foresaw the emergence of quality-oriented industries when he urged educators to create a capacity and tolerance for conflict in their students:

> Conflict is the gadfly of thought. It stirs us to observation and memory. It instigates to invention. It shocks us out of sheeplike passivity and sets us at noting and contriving ... conflict is the sine qua non of reflection and ingenuity (Seldes, 1983).

At its best, education empowers students to become free and independent thinkers. In this regard, it cannot avoid generating variation. Again, such variation, although not specifically planned, enhances rather than diminishes the quality of education's products (viz., graduates). It would be a shameful irony if in the zest to apply TQM to education, statistical process controls were used to restrict or even eliminate the intellectual variety generated by higher education. The result of such a shift would be a homogeneous and monotonous group of graduates, profoundly ill-prepared and totally unsuited to survive in (let alone contribute to) quality-oriented organizations. The only way to avoid such a catastrophe, is to first understand the educational process and then use TQM perspectives and methods to initiate a process of continuous quality improvement of education for students, for faculty and administrators and for society. The initial step is to understand the nature of education.

IS THERE A DIFFERENCE BETWEEN EDUCATION AND TRAINING?

While it is true effective transitions to TQM orientations usually require both education and training, it is important to recognize the two terms are not synonymous. (Wouldn't it have been wasteful for Deming to devote a separate point to each (i.e., #7 and #13) if he saw them as being identical?) Training and education differ from one another in several ways.

Training involves the acquisition of specific skills through instruction and practice. The goal of training is to reduce variance from "the one best way" to perform a task. Ideal training schedules and procedures have been derived from the results of experimental studies conducted by behaviorists over the last 60 years. This school of psychology sought to discover the most effective way to use rewards and punishments to "shape" behavior toward desired goals with maximum efficiency (Skinner, 1974). The application of this approach to work as well as education is as obvious as it is frightening. With simple tasks and simple subjects, behavioral approaches are very effective; in the short run, rats, students and workers all tend to do more of whatever earns a reward and less of whatever is punished.

However, as the time frame extends, tasks become more complex or uncertain, external controls become less constant or direct and subjects become more oriented toward growth rather than survival or security, exclusive reliance on "training" (or operant conditioning as behaviorists refer to it) becomes much less effective. By taking control of processes away from workers, the experimenters (or managers) deplete tasks of their intrinsic motivational qualities. The external consequences or "contingencies" constructed to shape behavior become barriers which can prevent the performer from taking any satisfaction or ownership for their accomplishments even when they are successful(cf., Deming's 12th point).

This seems to hold true whether the performer happens to be a subject in a laboratory, a worker in a factory or a student in the classroom. The introduction of external rewards and punishments designed to control behavior reduce intrinsic motivation considerably (Deci, 1975, 1980). On the other hand, feedback which merely "informs" and is not perceived as an attempt to "control" behavior is not likely to reduce intrinsic motivation. The extension of externally imposed contingencies to control and sustain performance frequently has effects just the opposite of those intended. In many situations, training is the most effective way to teach new skills or procedures but over application of training principles is likely to disrupt the development of a general orientation toward quality. Effective performance in a total quality environment also requires perspective and will; training, per se, is unlikely to develop either of these.

Using rewards and punishments effectively requires two things: 1) knowledge of "the ideal solution" and 2) objective measures of performance relevant to this ideal. Education does not meet either of these requirements. There is little evidence yesterday's solutions can be directly applied to today's problems. As Alfred North Whitehead (1929) argued:

> This whole tradition is warped by the vicious assumption that each generation will substantially live amid the conditions governing the lives of its fathers and transmit those conditions to mould with equal force the lives of its children. We are living in the first period of human history for which this assumption is false (p. 24).

Education shifts the emphasis from learning answers to learning how to ask questions. As Postman and Weingartner (1969) submit:

> Once you have learned how to ask questions—relevant and appropriate and substantial questions—you have learned how to learn and no one can keep you from learning whatever you need to know (p. 23).

Both educational psychology and organizational behavior have drawn more heavily on social, cognitive, humanistic and developmental psychology than classic behaviorism. From these perspectives, the work itself (learning in the case of students) is seen to be intrinsically motivating; given the opportunity to engage in challenging tasks, workers and students alike can be motivated by their natural desire to increase their effectiveness and their need to gain acceptance and social approval by contributing to shared goals. Education inherently has much broader goals than training; it seeks to instill certain qualities in students which will enable them to respond effectively in the future to diverse intellectual challenges. Education involves more than the memorization and regurgitation of facts; it also must incorporate students' development of critical thinking abilities and constructive attitudes about themselves, their work and society.

HOW MIGHT A TQM APPROACH ENHANCE EDUCATION?

It is disappointing to see slick TQM consultants touting Quality as though it were a new religion, offering salvation to all who have faith and simply accept the true word of one or more of the new quality gurus. Some even insist that to become a true convert, one must first believe; only then will success and eventually understanding follow. The irony of this approach is that it stands in direct opposition to the basic processes and principles of quality. As Alan Watts noted: "Irrevocable commitment to any religion is not only intellectual suicide; it is positive un-faith because it closes the mind to any new vision of the world. Faith is above all, openness—an act of trust in the unknown (Postman and Weingartner, 1969)."

Total quality can only be achieved by those who insist on understanding things before they "believe" in them. Success takes both insight and effort, no matter whose paradigm or formulation is adopted. Understanding is not sufficient to bring about a successful quality transformation, but it is absolutely essential. Deming's tenth point, eliminate slogans, exhortations and targets for the work force, reflects a similar concern for this all too prevalent misapplication of quality (Walton, 1986). Bumper stickers never tell the whole story and often foreclose opportunities for further discussion, exploration and real understanding.

Effective quality interventions must start with an understanding of process. Other chapters explain the ways and means of quality in general. To apply these principles effectively, however, demands an appreciation and awareness of how education works. There is no quicker way for quality consultants to embarrass themselves than by "premature evaluation." To prevent this, a tentative model which includes key factors and important processes will be presented. Constructing such a model helps to understand the fundamental concepts and relationships and also can suggest opportunities to increase quality. As Deming suggests:

> As you improve your process, you improve your knowledge of process at the same time. Improvement of product and process goes hand in hand with greater understanding and better theory (Aguayo, 1990).

WHAT IS "THE PROCESS" OF EDUCATION?

Philip Crosby (1984) suggested "All Work is Process." John Dewey certainly saw education from this perspective: "Education is a social process ... Education is growth ... Education is not preparation for life; education is life itself (Seldes, 1983)." Clearly, education is a process.

The process of education occurs at many different levels. Courses are derived from disciplines and put together by faculties and administrators to form curricula which support a variety of degrees. Likewise, any course can be broken down by blocks of material, assignments, class sessions, or even by brief episodes within each class session. The important thing is to start with a relatively simple general model then use it as a guide to increase understanding.

Initial models must be revised and elaborated as new information and new insights emerge. Actually, developing a useful theoretical process model is an essential part of the first step in the Shewhart (1986) Cycle of plan, do, check and act. A general educational model relevant to many quality principles shown in Figure 11.1 (Porter, 1988). Although the layout differs slightly from other input output models in this text the conversion is relatively simple. The focal process is "learning activities & experiences"; factors with arrows going into the process are inputs and those at the end of arrows coming from the process are outputs. The question of external customers and suppliers will be dealt with shortly.

GENERAL EDUCATION MODEL

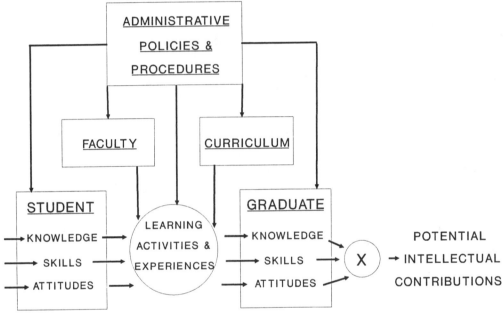

Figure 11.1

Several aspects of this model deserve comment. The first is an implicit assumption that causation flows downhill; administration's policies and procedures are at the top. Institutions often create academic games by establishing rules and procedures without due consideration for their potential impact on the process of education. While certain, political, fiscal, legal and even administrative issues can be important, they cannot be allowed to overwhelm the university's primary reason for being: to provide quality education to students. Unfortunately, once institutions have formulated the "academic game," they display a disturbing propensity to blame both faculty and students for playing it.

Unlike power and influence, the real work of the institution (i.e., educating students) takes place in the trenches at the bottom of the model. "Learning activities and experiences" appears at the center bottom of Figure 11.1. Although the classroom is often a central, common focus for courses, other activities also influence students' learning. Research supports the simple proposition that students who study outside the classroom, learn more than students who don't. However, what happens in the classroom frequently determines both the quantity and quality of students' activities outside the classroom. The preparation of both the students and teachers is likely to be manifest in the classroom. If you want to know something about the quality of education at an institution, visit a classroom; not the president's office.

A third point is the special position and representation of students. Students are at the bottom of the model and traditionally have had the least power to change the system or influence any of the other factors. Many traditional, didactic approaches to education practically ignore students and focus on what the teacher needs to know about the subject and needs to be able to do to present the material effectively. This ignores the fact that students are customers of both faculties and educational systems. If they don't "buy" what the teacher is "selling," education simply doesn't occur and all the teacher's brilliance is "waste." The work that was supposed to be done in the classroom will have to be redone later or the quality of the product will be diminished. The customer role is not the only one students play, however.

Students may also be viewed as both the raw materials and finished products of the educational process. Isn't it the quality of an institution's graduates that best reflects its worth? From still another perspective, students (whose active participation in education is essential) could be viewed as the real "workers" in the educational system. Whether we label students as supplies or products, workers or customers, it is important to recognize these diverse and sometimes conflicting roles make the task of enhancing the quality of education very difficult.

Students not only fill several different roles, they themselves are multidimensional (Figure 11.1). Their explicit knowledge of the subject is only one of several characteristics affected by education. (The ascendent role students' knowledge has gained in educational assessment may reflect its ease of measurement rather than its real importance but this will be covered later.) Students' ability to actually do something with the knowledge they acquire is also a relevant quality criterion. If the system hopes for students to take pride in their own learning then it must learn to see them as more than passive, reusable receptacles of knowledge as shown in Figure 11.2. Perhaps the most important student channel is the one labeled "attitude." This reflects students' values, beliefs and feelings. The value of any educational system is the net effect it has had on the potential intellectual contributions of its graduates. The model suggests that the quality product is also a mathematical product of the value added to each student's knowledge, skills, and attitudes.

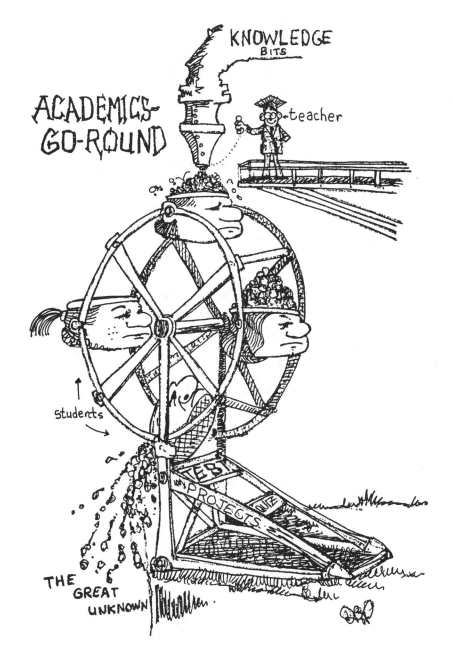

Figure 11.2

Suggesting the outcome is a product rather than a sum in Figure 11.1 has several implications which may not be immediately obvious. Which of the three student channels is most important depends on the state of the system (i.e., the current value of each of the three channels). For example, if the value in each channel is 3 standard units, then their product will be 27. Adding one unit to either knowledge, skills or attitudes would increase the outcome by 9 (33%) to a total of 36.

However, consider another case where the original 9 units are distributed differently; for example: 6 to knowledge, 2 to skill, and 1 to attitude (for the moment, we'll ignore the sobering possibilities that student attitudes could actually be "0" or even negative). The value of the output in this initial state would be 12 (less than half the initial value of the previous system with the 9 units distributed equally). In this case, adding one unit to knowledge would increase the output value by only 2 (17%). However, adding one unit to attitude would increase the total product value by 12 (100% or double the present value).

The general educational model suggests the relative emphasis on students' knowledge, skills and attitudes is a direct reflection of the institutional policies and procedures (i.e., the academic game that has been created "at the top"). If there is a distortion or imbalance in the educational system, simply exhorting students and faculty to work harder or even selecting brighter and brighter faculty and students is unlikely to increase the total quality of the products of the educational system. The only way to improve quality of an unbalanced system is to change the system not to blame the workers.

Unfortunately, even a brief exploration of the individual components within the system is beyond the scope of this chapter. "Profound knowledge" of the educational system is, however, necessary. There are literally thousands of books and published articles on the educational process and how it works. This existing knowledge can be used to "elaborate" (both expand and fill-in) the general model. Relying on the information gained by others is a very efficient way to develop an initial understanding of the education process.

The next three sections contain examples of how existing knowledge might be used to enhance system understanding. Each topic is particularly relevant to quality. The first section introduces human development as a context for education. Understanding what happens before and after college (our focal process) helps to better understand the changes occurring during college. Quality often involves expanding the boundaries to get a view of "the big picture." The second example discusses some ideas about cooperative student groups and their potential role in education. Cooperation is a well-established component of quality transformations; it could become an equally important factor in education. The quality approach also suggests that although most relevant processes occur at the bottom of a system (i.e., among students and teachers) most of the waste is generated (and thus can only be eradicated) at the top of the system (i.e., the administration). Focussing on the administration or management of educational systems, thus seems appropriate.

WHAT IS THE RELATIONSHIP BETWEEN EDUCATION AND DEVELOPMENT?

Life is full of change. Development is directional change. Change can occur in either positive or negative directions. We refer to positive changes as growth and negative changes as decline. Along some of life's dimensions, change is gradual and relatively continuous. Along other dimensions, changes occur less evenly (Figure 11.3). During some periods, change is rapid; these are periods where the individual is actively "accommodating" to environmental demands. At other times, individuals appear to change little; during these times individuals are "assimilating" by developing their existing skills. These periods of relatively little change are known as "stages." Abilities and behaviors at one stage differ qualitatively (i.e., in kind not just amount) from the abilities and behaviors at other stages. The French psychologist, Jean Piaget (1929) is generally acknowledged for introducing the "developmental" perspective, especially as it applies to the systematic changes in children's thinking abilities and sense of right and wrong.

DEVELOPMENTAL MODELS

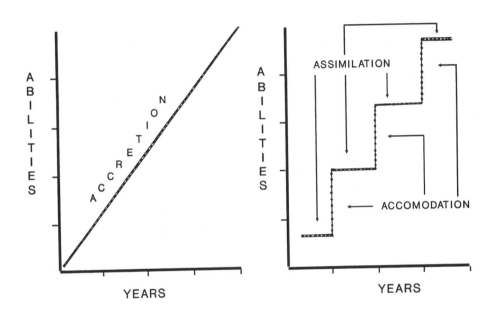

Figure 11.3

Development occurs before, during and after the time students spend in school. Their level of functioning determines which method of instruction and curriculum will be most effective. As every good farmer knows the fodder must be put where the calves can get at it. Education is a cumulative process and institutions increasingly recognize some students' need for supplemental skill development. Receiving under-prepared students from high-school or previous college courses limits subsequent instruction. Attitudinal deficiencies are even worse. J. B. S. Haldane, the English geneticist, illuminates this problem:

> ... children are taught it is a virtue to accept statements without adequate evidence, which leaves them prey to quacks of every kind in later life, and makes it very difficult for them to accept the methods ... thought successful in science (Seldes, 1983).

Students' attitudes about themselves and their relations to others as well as their attitudes toward knowledge and thinking are extremely important (Dweck, 1988; Greeno, 1989; Glasser, 1990). Nowhere is this more apparent than in issues concerning collaboration with peers. The following excerpt from Albert Einstein's comments in Monthly Review (May, 1949) reflects this concern:

> the crippling of individuals I consider the worst evil of ... our whole educational system ... An exaggerated competitive attitude is inculcated into the student, who is trained to worship acquisitive success ... (Seldes, 1983).

The consideration of student attitudes must begin with an appreciation of not only what these attitudes are but where they've come from and why they're maintained. Understanding is unlikely to develop unless high levels of trust and mutual respect are established between teachers and students. Perhaps Deming's eighth point (drive out fear) was derived from experience around these issues of power and attitude change. A brief examination of how these ideas about development apply to each of the student channels proposed earlier (i.e., knowledge, skills and attitudes) shows the value of a developmental perspective.

Change in knowledge usually occurs gradually. Knowledge is gleaned from exposure and experience and these happen continuously. Each new bit of information is fit into existing knowledge structures. People may study a little more at one time than at others (e.g., right before a scheduled test) but basically the processes involved seem to remain constant. What a person already knows has a great effect on what they experience. One exception to this slow accretion of knowledge is when the individual encounters a significant emotional event or when a paradigm shift occurs (which can also be pretty emotional). During such times, everything an individual knows is reorganized into different structures and categories. Things assumed to be true and eternal appear obviously false and even fraudulent in retrospect; things previously considered repugnant may become acceptable (Kuhn, 1970). Paradigm shifts are dramatic but relatively infrequent. Aguayo (1990), however, argues that many traditional managers must go through just such a shift to really understand "quality".

Changes in the process of thinking (i.e., skill) seem to occur more unevenly. Piaget (1929) proposed distinctly different stages of early childhood development and others have extended this work considerably. His theory suggested children don't just think more as they grow older, they think differently. The way a seven-year-old looks at a problem is unlike the way an eleven-year-old looks at the same problem.

William Perry (1981) has proposed one of the most widely-used schemes of later cognitive development. At the heart of Perry's scheme lie nine levels of cognitive and moral development which reflect different ways individuals "make meaning" of the world around them. The first five of these deal directly with changes in cognitive complexity while the final four focus on issues relating more closely to morality and values. Perry suggests many students enter college with an initial view that the world is comprised of strictly black and white components (stage 2 - dualism). Through educational experiences, students learn to see more and more shades of gray until they reach a point where they see everything as being equally gray (stage 4 - late multiplicity). Perry proposes that eventually students realize that although life may provide nothing but shades of gray, one can make meaning by making judgements (stage 5 - contextual relativism). Perry's scheme is directly applicable to many institutions' goals of enhancing cognitive development. Unfortunately, attempts to operationalize and apply this scheme to student development have met with only limited success.

Another psychologist, Erik Erikson, focussed more directly on the developmental aspects of individual's beliefs, feelings and attitudes. His model of development is especially relevant to attitudes, productivity and orientations toward institutions and values. Erikson (1968) observed that, as they grow, individuals frequently come into conflict with their physical or social environments. Such conflicts tend to be resolved during brief but memorable episodes (i.e., "interactional crises (Erickson, 1968)"). Individuals' values and attitudes reflect the way past crises were resolved. Conversely, individuals' attitudes and values influence the way they resolve future conflicts. To the extent crises are resolved in favor of "trust, autonomy, initiative, industry and identity," individuals are likely to develop positive orientations toward society and its institutions. To the extent the opposite occurs, individuals are likely to withdraw either physically or psychologically and limit the number and quality of future interactions. Deming's eighth point (drive out fear) reflects his recognition of the implications of Erikson's perspective to the work place. Fear inhibits trust.

CAN EDUCATION EVER BECOME A TEAM SPORT?

An exploration of the educational process should include not only factors of importance in the present system but also the potential factors in an ideal system. The formation and development of student groups could provide an extremely important adjunct to students' learning. Not only should groups be tolerated, they should be encouraged. Informal social groups of students have always characterized college environs, but their inclusion as part of a course's pedagogy is relatively recent. The assignment of group projects, papers or presentations where one grade (if any) is given to all is becoming increasingly common. Less frequently, students are assigned (or allowed to self-select) study groups. The collective individual performances of group members on examinations then becomes part of each student's individual grade (Porter, 1989).

There are many reasons why student groups might facilitate education. Groups are good for people; they directly satisfy human needs for affiliation and esteem and can provide essential emotional support. Groups also provide a forum where students actively engage each other as well as the material. Groups can produce better quality work than any individual student. Groups provide focus and control as well as generate energy and enthusiasm. Groups are also usually much more adept than the individual instructor at using "just enough" pressure to gain compliance from recalcitrant students.

Concern for quality provides a final and compelling reason for incorporating student groups in an institution's educational plan. Groups are the place for students to acquire the interactional skills necessary to contribute to future organizations (especially if these organizations are oriented toward TQM). Joe Pettit, a vice president at Georgetown, has been analyzing alumni's assessments of their college experience for three dozen colleges and universities. He asked 20-year alumni two basic questions about a long list of general skills: 1) "Is this skill important to you now?" and 2) "How well did your college experience prepare you to do this?" The biggest gap between what alumni now value and how they rated their college preparation was: "can work effectively in groups to accomplish goals." Over 80 percent said working in groups is an important current skill, but only 20 percent said college had helped them learn it (Marchese, 1990).

There is ample evidence student groups can facilitate learning (Johnson & Johnson, 1983; Kohn, 1986; Bruffee, 1987; Porter, 1989; Light, 1990). Many separate factors interact to contribute to the success of groups. Greeno (1989) suggests that diagnostic judgement and other "higher order thinking skills" are as much social as they are cognitive processes. Bruffee (1987) observed that students "learn judgement well in groups because (they) tend to talk each other out of (their) unshared biases and presumptions (p. 45)." (Similar to the statistical phenomenon of measurement errors canceling one another out as sample size increases.) One very clear finding of several recent studies at Harvard was that small student groups improved academic performance (Light, 1990). Kohn (1986) cites research which shows peer tutoring in cooperative classrooms benefits both helper and helped. An interesting subsidiary finding from the Harvard studies was that although women were more likely to benefit from participating in such groups (especially in science and mathematics), they were less likely to form or join study groups spontaneously.

A study at the Air Force Academy compared the performance and satisfaction of students enrolled in classes employing group-oriented projects and grades to those receiving traditional instruction. The 53 students in the group-oriented classes (in sections taught by four different instructors) performed significantly better on four different, common, objective tests than students in the control group. Students' self reports of participation and effort were also significantly higher. The most interesting finding, however, was the extent to which students in the experimental sections attributed their learning to one another rather than to their teacher. Student "testimonials" from previous similar experiments illustrate this: "I noticed an attitude developing in the class I'd never seen anywhere else. Everyone had prepared for the quiz but not just for themselves ... for each other." Another student suggests why collaborative learning might provide such potent pedagogy: "Your classmates are a very important source of information for one main reason: they are the same age as you and have more similar thoughts and values than the teacher or the author of the text (Porter, 1989)."

Groups may be natural phenomena but the skills necessary to keep them individually satisfying and academically effective require education and training, relevant experience, systematic feedback and sustained institutional commitment. Collaborative learning may well represent one of the best opportunities for enhancing the general quality of education across the curriculum. Unfortunately, decisions concerning this and practically every other aspect of educational systems tend to be made in buildings and minds that are often separated from the fundamental processes of education in the classroom.

ADMINISTRATION: WHAT? WHO? AND HOW?

Sometimes a word's etymology gives a hint of its original purpose even when time and tradition have so convoluted it's function, it's essence has become obscure. The Latin root of administration is "ministare," to serve or provide support. Current definitions of the word, "administer", however, show a shift toward activity and away from purpose; "to manage or execute," "to mete out or dispense," and "to give ritually or remedially" are all common synonyms. Unfortunately, this is more than a quaint etymological detour; in the minds of many, "administrative support" has become a disappointing oxymoron. Administration manages education. Most quality experts suggest 85 to 95 percent of the responsibility for waste and low quality lie with management; is there any reason to believe a similarly high portion education's inadequacies do not emanate from "administration?"

Perhaps President Garfield was right when he suggested quality education required only a pine log with a student on one end and a good teacher on the other (Seldes, 1983). Unfortunately, even if this formula would have worked a hundred years ago, it won't work today. Technology may have affected education more than any other industry. Many educational institutions today are larger than small cities. Communication and coordination requirements are greater and more complicated than ever.

There's a term familiar to physical scientists that also has interesting social implications. The term is "entropy." Entropy is a tendency toward chaos, the degradation of matter, energy or information toward a state of inert uniformity. Entropy applies to institutions as well as rocket engines. The more complex the system, the greater the rate of entropy. The purpose of administration is to stave off entropy by providing support. Unfortunately, all to often, the effect is just the opposite of the intention. This begs the question "why?"

Administrators, whether in education or elsewhere, don't intend to diminish quality or accelerate entropy. They often speak of bottom lines, trade-offs and standard procedures, cite complex regulations and decry the fact that their hands are tied by ubiquitous red tape but few (if any) want to harm the system. (Some administrators may confess to wanting to harm students or faculty in the interest of preserving the system, but they view this as being an altogether different matter.)

Do those attracted to the job of administration possess distinctive personalities? Do these differences make communication with others more difficult and thus create or amplify problems? This isn't necessarily anyone's "fault" but if there are distinctive traits among those drawn to the business of administration, this might provide a toehold from which to begin to understand how an institution full of people who want to go in one direction end up getting nowhere.

According to Myers and McCaulley (1985): "At all levels, educational administrators have large numbers of tough-minded TJ (Thinking-Judging) types found in samples of executives in nearly all business organizations (p. 136)." These authors suggest TJs' greatest strengths are "organizing, planning, and analysis." However, many students and teachers are feeling types (Fs) who are most likely to respond to appreciation and opportunities to serve others. By their nature, TJ administrators are likely to overlook the need for teamwork or communication; in their pursuit of expediency. Another potential conflict is that many administrators are "reality-based" sensors (Ss), but most faculty members are "opportunity-based" intuitors (Ns). These two types simply see things differently.

Not all administrators have the same personality but the tendency of the job to attract and retain a group of people who view the world in a particular way can create problems. Extra efforts must be made not only to capitalize on administrator's common strengths but also to compensate for their common blind spots. As inefficient as it may seem to administrators, others (viz., teachers, students and even outside experts) need to be included in important decisional processes. Unfortunately, personal involvement, developing teamwork, inclusive structures and emergent processes are phrases that sound a lot like "creating chaos," "askinfotrouble" and "wasteomypreshustime" to many administrators. TJs need to be both fair and efficient is great; so, for them, the best solution is to build a system that treats everyone the same. "Mom and pop" style organizations that provide special consideration and show appreciation are not only inefficient, they can also be vindictive and cruel. Bureaucracies are the administrative solution to inefficiency and favoritism. In the eyes of many administrators, maintaining order by systematically and impersonally holding others accountable is the way they show they care. Regulations provide answers before people even come up with questions (you can't get much more efficient than that!).

Bureaucracies are, by nature, resistant to change; there is often a mindless as well as heartless quality about them which can cause them to accelerate rather than impede entropy. Bureaucracies are natural repositories for "conventional assumptions" and "standard practices"–two common accelerators of entropy. It is unusual to find an institution of higher education whose administration has not established extensive rules and regulations which specify almost every aspect of the college experience. Often the actual effects of these rules differ considerably from their intent. The good news is that the recent attention "quality in higher education" has received has energized many administrators to begin to take action; the bad news is that such action without understanding is likely to accelerate entropy more than ever.

Several slogans have emerged from quality "experts" despite Deming's warnings to the contrary (viz., his tenth point). One of these is "if it ain't broke, improve it!" Unfortunately, a subtle but significant point of statistical process control is that one must first understand the process before initiating changes. There is a key distinction between processes that are in equilibrium or "under statistical control" and those that are not. If a system is "stable," changes can do one of four things: they can make it better; they can have no effect; they can make it worse; or they can destabilize the system which will make it both worse and unstable, thus uncontrollable.

Lloyd Nelson, the 1987 Deming Prize winner, developed a demonstration to illustrate this important point (Aguayo, 1990). A funnel and stand, a marble small enough to pass through the funnel and several square feet of carpet are needed. The first phase is simple measurement and documentation. The procedures for this stage are to 1) mark a small target on the carpet, 2) position the stand to hold the funnel about six inches above the target, 3) drop the marble through the funnel, 4) record its position and 5) repeat steps 3 and 4 about 500 times. The plot of the landing points should resemble a donut (about 4 inches in diameter), with the "hole" directly under the funnel. This is a stable system but there might be ways to reduce variance (i.e., decease the average distance between the target and marble position).

One way to improve the system might be to move the funnel a small amount in the opposite direction after each miss (method of modest adjustments). (This is the same as the standard practice of firing a gun once for sighting then making an adjustment to compensate for any error.) During the second phase of the demonstration, the five steps listed above are repeated exactly as before except the funnel is moved if and as required after each drop. Most people suspect this procedure will help close the hole in the "donut" and thus reduce variation. Although the "hole" does disappear, the outer circumference of the circle extends so far it nearly doubles total variance. The system is still "in statistical control" but the result (increased variance) is just the opposite of what was intended (reduced variance).

If the adjustment strategy is based on the relative position of the target rather than the previous drop (i.e., an adjustment for a drop that landed three inches south of the target would now be to move the funnel to a position three inches north of the target instead of three inches north of its own previous position) the system will destabilize and the pattern is likely to "blow-out" across the carpet. This is the method of "extreme adjustments." Similarly bizarre "out of control" patterns will occur if a "just like the last" adjustment strategy is adopted (i.e., the funnel is aimed at the resting position from the previous drop). Aguayo (1990) offers many convincing examples of ill-informed mangers and administrators adopting functionally equivalent strategies in efforts to reduce variance in systems they don't understand.

Is it possible to improve a stable system? Of course it is but understanding the system is essential. Moving the stand around in the above example simply increases variance. Unfortunately, this is the kind of obvious adjustment that managers might point to with pride as an example of how well they're "managing." Once the data start accumulating, however, effective managers or administrators will rethink their assumptions and realize their errors. Poor managers are likely to simply quit measuring or create arguments as to why the position criterion is irrelevant. By the way, how would you improve the performance of Nelson's funnel? How about lowering the funnel to only three inches above the carpet?

Better yet, how about smearing honey or syrup over the carpet? (Sometimes a little sweetness can improve quality considerably.)

Educational processes need more service, support and sustenance today than ever. Students need to be prepared to get the most out of their college experience. Teachers, selected principally for their knowledge of a particular subject need to be given the opportunity, education, training and support they need to develop professional skills. Teaching is a very ego-threatening occupation. The way teachers are treated by the administration affects the way they treat students. As Parker Palmer notes: "When our fears as teachers mingle and multiply with the fears inside our students, teaching and learning become mechanical, manipulative, lifeless (Palmer, 1990)."

New perspectives or paradigms developing outside the hallowed halls of academe must be allowed to enhance education. Education cannot occur in a vacuum. As John Gardner, former Secretary of Health, Education and Welfare once put it:

> The problem is not a shortage of good new ideas but getting a hearing for them. And that means breaking through the crusty rigidity and stubborn complacency of the status quo. The aging society develops elaborate defenses against new ideas ... As a society (or institution) becomes more concerned with precedent and custom, ... the person who wins acclaim is not the one who 'get's things done' but the one who has an ingrained knowledge of the rules and accepted practices. Whether they accomplish anything is less important than whether they conduct themselves in an 'appropriate' manner (Postman and Weingartner, 1969).

A commitment to Total Quality Education offers academic institutions the opportunity to become vital, self-renewing communities dedicated to both scholarship and learning. It is essential that quality not only be taught to students, it must also be caught by students. What educational institutions do to students in the name of quality during the next decade will determine America's role in the 21st century. If students' experience with and orientation toward quality are negative, it is unlikely industry will be able to correct this deficiency by "reworking" four "wasted" years of education. Future college graduates who don't understand quality will be little more than agents of industrial entropy.

WHY USE A "SCIENTIFIC METHOD" OF DOING AND CHECKING?

As Nelson's funnel demonstrated, the value of constructing and elaborating a model is prudence and insight not perfection. Unless important factors are identified and discussed, relationships articulated and expected consequences stated clearly, subsequent measurement is likely to be haphazard and largely unproductive. Purposeful measurement and analysis are "research." They are also the second and third phases of the Shewhart (1986) cycle (viz., doing and checking). Without a theoretical model to serve as a foundation, however, such activities are likely to be characterized by hoping, groping and frustration (not unlike an adolescent's first date).

A process model also helps prevent inadvertently reversing the roles of data and theory. Specifying a model identifies which factors are most important and constrains measurement and analysis. Without a model, measurement activities are likely to gravitate toward those items which are easiest to measure. (The path of least resistance invariably leads downhill.) Unfortunately, once the administration has invested the time and money in developing measurement, accountability and assessment systems, they're unlikely to abandon them simply because they're irrelevant to the organization's customers. In fact, the administration is likely to invest even more time and energy creating institutional goals and theoretical models to justify retaining the measurement system already in place. (This is a specialty of Thinking-Judging types.) "If you can't measure what's important, measure what you can and argue its importance" is the strategy adopted.

Just having a model, however, is not enough and the search for additional information is likely to be biased. Decision makers tend to seek confirmatory evidence and also ignore "negative evidence" (no, these are not the same). As humans, each of us want to be "right." Left to our own devises, its only natural to collect anecdotes and incidents that support our own idiosyncratic, opinionated view of the world. Another reason we select information which supports our original assumptions is that it helps us avoid the anguish and energy required to reject one hypothesis and formulate a new one.

The second perceptual bias involves the tendency to focus on what occurred or what was observed rather than what didn't or wasn't. "The barking dog is the key to solving this mystery," mused the tall man with the pipe. "But Holmes, there were no reports of a dog barking!" sputtered his rotund companion. "Precisely!!!" quipped Holmes with just the hint of a smile that let Watson know the chase was afoot. Part of the reason sensitivity to negative evidence is so valuable lies in its rarity. Like many other valuable skills, learning to notice what is missing requires training, effort, practice, and profound knowledge.

Many managers assert that they've "been doing TQM all along." Most of them have "process models" although these are often implicit, ephemeral and exceedingly vague. However, managers' priorities and personal definitions of "quality" are often embedded in these models. The use of the word "quality" is not what most distinguishes TQM from other approaches which had their own three-letter monikers (e.g., MBO or ZBB). The real power and distinction of the TQM approach lies in its commitment to rigorously apply the methods of science to collecting data and drawing appropriate inferences relevant to the question of quality as seen through the eyes of customers. Most managers have little difficulty learning to "talk the quality talk". TQM, however, requires more than talk. TQM requires that managers, leaders, and administrators learn to "do science" before they claim to "walk the quality walk".

The "scientific method" refers to the techniques and procedures developed over the last few centuries to carefully observe natural phenomena and systematically interpret these observations to increase understanding. Although mastery of these methods requires years of training, familiarity and awareness of the basics is necessary for anyone who seeks to use data to answer questions. "In a word, they are the ways to avoid being misled. And when all the talk is done, that's all they are (Mook, 1982)."

WHAT MUST A QUALITY PRACTITIONER KNOW ABOUT SCIENCE?

A full discussion of the scientific method is beyond the scope of this chapter (and even this book). However, it is important to note that scientific research itself rests on an underlying theory of measurement. At its most basic level, measurement theory assumes any observation, test score, or procedural outcome is imperfect. It is useful to think of the observed score (also called the fallible score) as the sum of two general components:

> a true score, which is a perfect representation of the characteristic to be observed and error, the difference between the perfect score and the what is actually observed (Dooley, 1990).

Two concepts are particularly important: reliability and validity. The American Psychological Association's *Standards for Educational and Psychological Testing* (1985) defines reliability as the "extent to which observed scores are free from errors of measurement (p. 19)" and states that validity "refers to the appropriateness, meaningfulness and usefulness of the inferences made from measurements (p. 9)." Using data to enhance quality requires understanding both the instruments used to measure (i.e., reliability) and the way these measurements are interpreted and applied to the process of continuous improvement (validity).

Consistency is another word for reliability. Measures that have high reliability are very consistent. If an instrument is reliable then different people, measuring the same phenomenon at different times and under different conditions should arrive at nearly the same score. Measurement theory assumes no observed score is perfect; all observations are subject to some error. The possibility of error, however, is not an excuse for failing to make any process measurements at all (as some administrators contend).

Several things can be done to increase reliability. Measurement errors occur randomly; thus over many observations, they tend to cancel one another out. This is why larger samples increase our confidence that the average of observed scores is close to the true average score. Increasing standardization in measuring procedures increases reliability. Training observers also increases reliability. Starting with an instrument that has already been developed will avoid many of the errors associated with new instruments and also ease interpretation. Basically the more that is done to reduce measurement error, the greater will be the confidence in the data collected. (Measurement is a process, too!)

Although data are never perfect, some data come close to being perfectly worthless. Validity concerns whether or not the target activity is truly being measured. There are basically three ways to establish validity: criterion, content and construct. If a measure already exists which provides a valid measure, the validity of a new instrument or procedure can be established by showing that the new measurement yields the same score as the established criterion. Unfortunately, criterion instruments are themselves usually far from perfect. Therefore, variance from the criterion might indicate either a better or worse measure of the true score.

Content validity is even more subjective. Basically, it reflects the extent to which the questions asked seem reasonably related to the concept or idea they're supposed to measure. Construct validity relies on several different statistical procedures (psychometrics) designed to evaluate the mathematical properties of the data. The best approach to determining validity is to consider the question of validity from all three perspectives.

Another aspect of validity concerns "randomness". The assumption of random selection is fundamental to statistical analysis. A random sample is NOT one which has been collected haphazardly or with little attention as some students assume. Scientists try very hard to insure that their "samples" are drawn from the population in such a way that every member of that population has an equal chance of being selected. Why is this so important? Because unless the sample is "random," results cannot be extended to the rest of the population (i.e., they will not be valid). Finding five friends who like you, does not mean you're the most popular person on campus.

One final point needs to be raised before leaving the topic of measurement. Measurement can be costly. Few measures are truly unobtrusive and the search for a perfect metric or ideal procedure can lead an organization into a psychometric quagmire of escalating costs and diminishing returns. Measurement can, in fact, easily turn into inspection and the desire to increase reliability can lead to mass inspection. Although Deming earned his doctorate in statistics, his third point (cease dependence on mass inspection) clearly reduces the reliability of the information available to managers. Once they understand the process, managers need to have just enough information to "check" the system not "control" it; their real task is to improve processes not simply measure them.

The final output of the General Education Model presented earlier was "the potential intellectual contributions of graduates". This might cause some administrators to throw up their hands and decide to wait for the data. Others may use theory and experience to identify available measures likely to predict future contributions (e.g., students' knowledge, skills and attitudes) and devise centralized systems to constantly monitor them (thus justifying a huge budget and greatly elevating the level of fear throughout the system). These administrators are also likely to cite selective anecdotal evidence from the quality literature and claim that this is an appropriate application of TQM to education.

In contrast, administrators truly dedicated to quality will engage other administrators, faculty members and students in dialogues about the purpose of the university. They will insure that there is widespread understanding of quality and broad commitment to its principles and goals. They will provide training in statistical techniques to enable individuals to develop their own ability to measure process and improve quality. They will create opportunities for individuals to learn about quality from one another and remove bureaucratic and regulatory obstacles which prevent faculty and students from doing quality work. They will drive out fear and commit themselves and their institutions to continuous quality improvement.

HOW THEN CAN TQE BE IMPLEMENTED?

There are many ways educational institutions might be re-oriented toward total quality; some are likely to be more effective than others. Trying to impose a TQM philosophy from the outside through legislative or accreditation initiatives is likely to generate resistance and fear (as well as violate the basic premises of quality). Principles such as academic freedom are likely to be invoked in defense of even notoriously inept administrative bureaucracies if change is seen as being imposed from the outside.

It is unlikely quality experts who are not also educators will be afforded much initial credence nor even given the opportunity to establish credibility. Well-polished presentations, expensive audio-visual aides and slick brochures are likely to make negative impressions on many academicians. Three letter monikers, 14 points and seven deadly sins are also likely to receive short shrift. Academe has evolved traditions and rituals which render it virtually impenetrable to the uninitiated. Nodes of status and influence are surreptitiously distributed around campuses. Often latitude to control fiscal and custodial functions is granted administrators out of necessity. However, obvious changes aimed at the heart of education (i.e., classroom teaching) are likely to rouse even long-dormant academic giants into angry defiance. A frontal assault is unlikely to convert academia to the cause of quality. In fact, there may be no single "best approach".

In recognition of the diversity inherent in education, comments concerning three very different institutions will be presented. None of these institutions has actually used the term TQM until fairly recently, if at all. However, the activities undertaken and the results achieved seem relevant to education's shifting focus toward total quality. These three institutions are Harvard University, Alverno College and the US Air Force Academy.

HOW HAVE THE HARVARD ASSESSMENT SEMINARS ENHANCED QUALITY?

In 1986, Derek Bok devoted the entire Annual Report of the President of Harvard to a call for educational institutions to conduct more research on themselves and the learning process. He allocated a few thousand dollars for organizing dinners and appointed Professor Richard Light of the Graduate School of Education and Kennedy School of Government to serve as Convener for the Harvard Assessment Seminars. Planning and organizing began immediately.

A program was developed to allow small groups to work together to find answers to questions relating to the process of education. Dinner meetings were organized for presentation, critique and discussion of findings. Invitations were extended to senior colleagues from many nearby institutions as well as Harvard's own faculty and administrators. An initial grant from the Fund for the Improvement of Post Secondary Education (FIPSE) was followed by another from the Mellon Foundation. The first report, *Explorations with Students and Faculty about Teaching, Learning and Student Life* (Light, 1990), has generated interest and enthusiasm throughout academia.

Several factors contributed to the success of these seminars and their published results (Marchese, 1990). The extent to which the faculty took ownership for the project was crucial; over 100 faculty members participated in conducting the studies summarized in the first report. Because the research questions came directly from the participants, findings were awaited with eager anticipation. The one principle Light "imposed" on the seminars also contributed to success. The following comments reflect his clear recognition of the pre-eminence of process:

> ... for any project to go forward, there had to be a faculty member willing to take responsibility, ... there had to be an administrator involved who would say, 'If this works, it will make a difference'... and each project had to involve students every step of the way. We got enormous insights from students, ... We weren't looking to do studies that would wind up on a shelf, gathering dust. A key principle is that findings should in some way improve student learning (Marchese, 1990).

The desire for applicability did not diminish the desire for rigor. Light reports being "proudest" that the studies reflected "pretty good science". True "random samples" were used, instruments and protocols were tested, adjusted and retested before use, and survey return rates were often greater than 95 percent. Many of the results from the studies supported previous findings but the fact they were "home-grown" made them much more palatable to Harvard's students, faculty and administrators.

The "leadership", "new philosophy", and "constancy of purpose" provided by Harvard's president, Derek Bok, were essential. The processes of innovation, experimentation and assessment were recognized and rewarded regardless of results. The research groups themselves exemplified the dissolution of barriers between faculty, students and administrators. Slogans, exhortations and specific targets were not part of the effort. In fact, the words "total quality" aren't used anywhere in Light's (1990) report, yet the report, as well as this project, have QUALITY written all over them.

WHAT'S BEEN HAPPENING AT ALVERNO COLLEGE?

Alverno is a small liberal arts college near Milwaukee, Wisconsin, with a total enrollment of about 1500 women oriented toward professional careers. Few people outside Wisconsin would know of Alverno had it not decided to look at its role as an institution of higher education from a new perspective. In 1973, Alverno adopted the goal of developing in each student "abilities that last a lifetime". As Russ Edgerton (1984) points out, however:

Alverno has no monopoly on the idea that abilities are important. What makes the Alverno faculty unique is the extent and depth of its commitment to this proposition. They have decided that abilities are the underlying core, the heart of the enterprise. Having decided this, ... they have created a culture which sustains it (p. 4).

The eight abilities the faculty agreed to focus on as the foundation for their entire curriculum were: communication, analysis, problem solving, valuing, social interaction, environmental responsibility, responsible citizenship and aesthetic responsiveness (Alverno College Faculty, 1990). Each of these was conceptually connected to the others and to the overall goal of liberal education. Levels of competence for each ability were delineated and agreed upon. Eight competence divisions were established to integrate the activities across the six existing disciplinary divisions. Each semester, these divisions reviewed the educational process with respect to the ability goals. Measures of students' performance and perspectives as well as inputs from other faculty and outside observers were combined regularly to assess and improve the quality of students' learning experiences.

In 1977, the National Institute of Education funded an extensive study of the effects of college education entitled "Careering After College". Students at Alverno were selected to participate in this study and the results were truly impressive. Clear evidence that the "Alverno approach" was working appeared on almost every metric; increased cognitive complexity, increased responsibility for learning; greater abilities to integrate material across subjects; greater value and appreciation for liberal learning; and outstanding performance on a wide range of both internal and external measures (Mentkowski and Doherty, 1984).

The outcome-oriented curriculum has meant more work for both faculty and students but it has also imbued this work with purpose and direction. Feedback and assessment have come to be accepted as opportunities to learn and to improve. Three faculty-wide institutes are held each year and every Friday afternoon is reserved for faculty workshops and meetings (Alverno College Faculty, 1990). Faculty members reported a heightened professional awareness of their role as educators. By developing and articulating consensual educational goals, greater respect and appreciation for diversity of disciplines and teaching styles has emerged:

Indeed, we are now finding that those very diversities which used to separate us are our most valuable assets in tackling the complex teaching assignment we have set ourselves. To us as a faculty this has been the greatest benefit of the adventure that began more than fifteen years ago with a set of difficult questions (Alverno College Faculty, 1990).

Another aspect of Alverno's experience provides insight into the common problem of how to "measure the unmeasurables":

> Our expectations and (student's) goals are much more clearly stated, and the means of assessment more clearly defined. As a result, we are finding that 'self-direction' and 'self-confidence'–two obviously desirable qualities we had first assumed were unteachable and unmeasurable–are emerging quite clearly after all as by-products of developing the tangible abilities (Alverno College Faculty, 1990).

HOW MIGHT QUALITY CONCEPTS ENHANCE MILITARY INSTRUCTION?

The US Air Force Academy provides great contrasts to Alverno College's faculty, students and orientation. "Liberal learning" is a phrase seldom heard at the Academy and nearly 90 percent of the "full-time" (i.e., 24 hours-a-day and 7 days-a-week for freshmen) students are male. Most Academy products go directly to pilot training immediately upon graduation. The amount of freedom enjoyed by freshman at Alverno would be envied by even the most senior cadets at the Academy. On the other hand, the fact that cadets are paid to attend college is something that students at Alverno might covet. The apparent differences in these two institutions make certain similarities in their approaches all the more interesting.

The Air Force Academy also has focussed on educational outcomes. By specifying particular "qualities" of knowledge, character and motivation for all graduates, activities across not only academic but also military and athletic programs are being integrated. Actually, there is considerable overlap between the "skills" delineated by Alverno and the Academy's descriptions of "qualities" (e.g., "the ability to formulate problems and devise and implement solutions in diverse and ambiguous situations", "the ability to communicate and work effectively and compassionately with others", and a commitment to "lifelong personal and professional growth and development"). The similarity in approach extends beyond the goal contents, however. The Air Force Academy has also initiated a broad program of institutional assessment as a central feature of their quality transformation.

In many areas, the Air Force Academy, as well as most other institutions of higher education, are only beginning to encounter the issues Alverno struggled with over a decade ago. One area, however, where the Academy already has made progress is the assessment and improvement of the quality of classroom instruction. Several things have contributed to this success. The model presented in Figure 11.1 was initially developed as a conceptual foundation for a faculty-wide course and instructor critique. Every semester, every student in every class fills out a standard 43-question critique form. Data are compiled, analyzed and provided to every instructor on the faculty shortly after completion. Specific diagnostic profiles are provided reflecting student's perception of the relative emphasis the instructor places on students' knowledge, skills and attitudes (viz., enjoyment). Student ratings in almost every department and area have improved considerably since the program was initiated. The information about the process of education provided by this common metric has also been very useful in initiating and checking changes designed to improve courses and methods of instruction (Porter, 1988).

Another area where the Air Force Academy has been actively pursuing ways to enhance quality is in the use of student groups in academic settings to both enhance learning and develop interpersonal skills. The Interdisciplinary Education at the Academy (IDEA) Program was initiated over five years ago and continues to provide unique opportunities for students and faculty to integrate information across disciplinary boundaries. In this program students are scheduled as a class on consecutive periods to take two different courses. Instructors from one course often attend and participate in the other course in the pair. Pairings have occurred across very different disciplines (e.g., physics and psychology or astronautics and philosophy) or with more apparently complementary courses (e.g., leadership and history or political science and philosophy). One pairing which has proven to be ideal for teaching quality is the combination of statistics and leadership. Figure 11.4 reflects students' comparisons of the structure and activities in one of these classes with a traditional classroom. Quantitative measures also generally have shown extremely high levels of student performance and satisfaction.

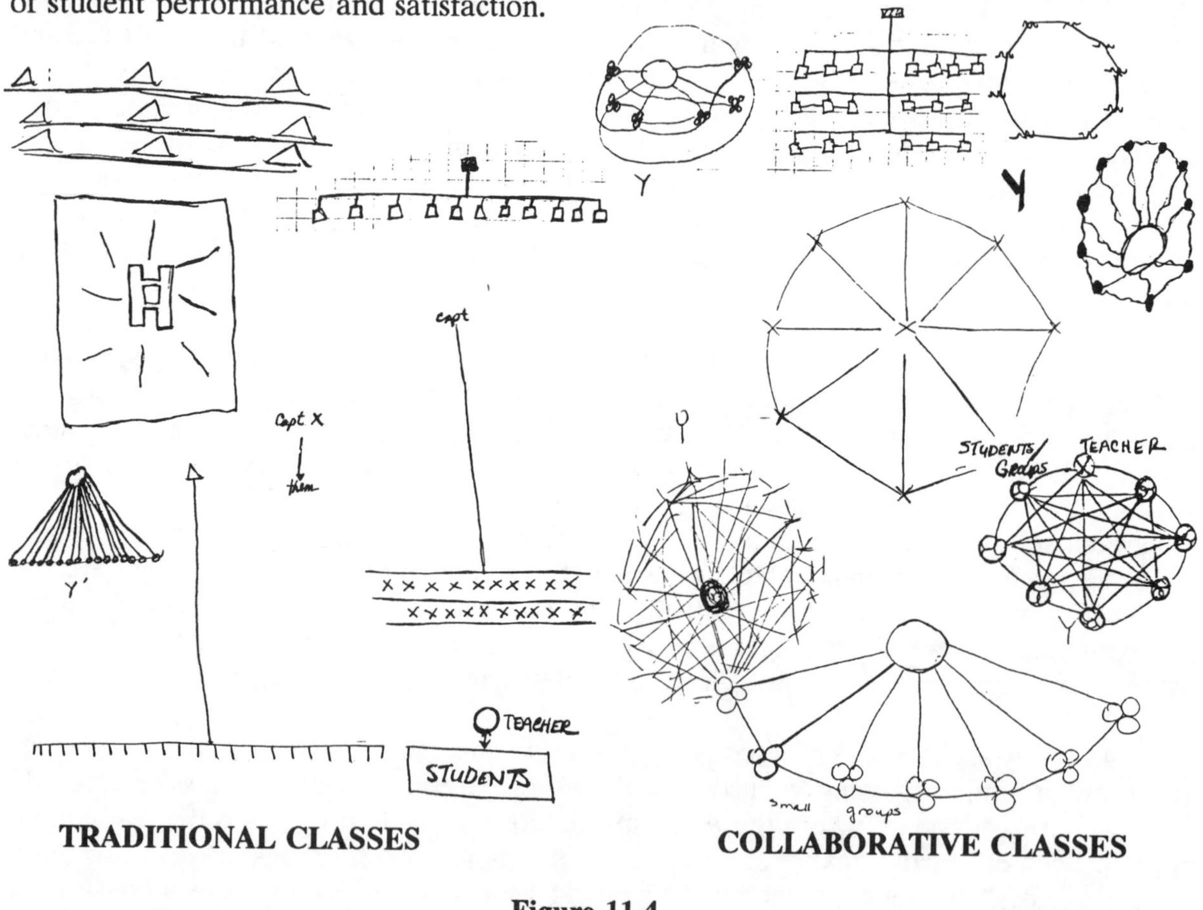

TRADITIONAL CLASSES   **COLLABORATIVE CLASSES**

Figure 11.4

Recently the Air Force Academy has also undertaken a program which resembles the Harvard Assessment Seminars. Under the auspices of the newly created Center for Teaching Excellence, interdisciplinary, biweekly lunchtime seminars on educational issues and research are offered to all faculty members. "Incorporating technology in the classroom", "the integration of women in the military", and "how to use questions to generate discussions" show the diversity of topics. Voluntary participation in the last semester involved nearly half the faculty.

SUMMARY

At its best, the relationship between total quality and education is mutually rewarding and reinforcing (i.e., symbiotic). Education differs from other industries in some ways but there is little reason to assume the general principles of the total quality approach will be any less applicable. There are important differences in training and education; both processes are important but so is understanding the difference between the two. Neither should be used as a substitute for the other.

Quality can be applied to the education process through the Shewhart Cycle. Developing a general conceptual model of education is an essential first step in planning change. Understanding each component and its relationships, interactions and effects is also important. Three issues are particularly relevant to quality: development, student groups and administration. Educational processes occur within a context of lifelong change and development. Student groups can significantly enhance the process of education. Understanding the players, processes and products of administration is the key to transforming educational institutions.

Quality processes are based on the scientific method; being an effective quality practitioner requires scientific knowledge and skill. This is perhaps the key to re-orienting educational institutions toward quality; get everyone involved in "doing" what has been talked about in classrooms and lecture halls. By doing research on the process of education the full intellectual capacity and creative energy of students, faculty and administrators can be melded together in pursuit of continuous improvement in the total quality of education. Signs of such transformations have already begun to emerge.

NOTE: The ideas and opinions expressed in this chapter are those of the author and do not necessarily reflect the view of the US Air Force Academy or any other agency of the Department of Defense.

About the author:

David Porter graduated from the Air Force Academy in 1971 with a degree in Engineering Management. After earning a Masters in Industrial Relations from UCLA the following year, he completed Undergraduate Helicopter Training with the Army and Air Force. During his Air Force career, he's been a Rescue Aircraft Commander, Aircraft Maintenance Officer, Race Relations Instructor, Chief of Quality Control and Squadron Executive Officer. After earning a D. Phil from Oxford University in Experimental Cognitive Psychology, he returned to the Academy and is currently an associate professor in the Department of Behavioral Sciences and Leadership.

REFERENCES

Alverno College Faculty, *Liberal Learning at Alverno College*, Milwaukee, WI: Alverno College, 1990.

Aguayo, R., *Dr. Deming, the American who Taught the Japanese about Quality*, New York: The Carol Publishing Group, 1990.

American Psychological Association, *Standards for Education and Psychological Testing*, Washington, DC: Author, 1985.

Boyer, E.L., *Scholarship Reconsidered; Priorities of the Professorate*, Princeton, NJ: The Carnegie Foundation for the Advancement of Teaching, 1990.

Bruffee, K.A., "The Art of Collaborative Learning", *Change*, March/April, 1987, pp. 42-47.

Crosby, P.B., *Quality Without Tears: The Art of Hassle-free Management*, New York: New American Library, 1984.

Deci, E.L., *Intrinsic Motivation*, New York: Plenum Press, 1975.

Deci, E.L., *The Psychology of Self-Determination*, Lexington, MA: Lexington Books, 1980.

Dooley, D., *Social Research Methods*, 2nd Edition, Englewood Cliffs, NJ: Prentice Hall, 1990.

Dweck, C.S. & E.L. Leggett, "A Social-Cognitive Approach to Motivation and Personality", *Psychological Review*, Vol. 95, 1988, pp. 256-273.

Erikson, E.H., *Identity, Youth and Crisis*, New York: Norton, 1968.

Glasser, W., *The Quality School: Managing Students Without Coercion*, New York: Harper and Row, 1990.

Greeno, J.G., "Perspective on Thinking", *American Psychologist*, Feb. 1989, Vol. 44-2, p. 134-141.

Johnson, D.N., and R.T. Johnson, "The Socialization and Achievement Crisis: Are Cooperative Learning Experiences the Solution?", In L. Brickman (Ed.), *Applied Social Psychology*, Annual 4, Beverly Hills, CA: Sage, 1983.

Kohn, A., "How to Succeed Without Even Vying", *Psychology Today*, Sept. 1986, pp. 22-28.

Kuhn, T.S., *The Structure of Scientific Revolutions*, Chicago, IL: University of Chicago Press, 1970.

Marchese, T., "A New Conversation About Undergraduate Teaching, *American Association of Higher Education Bulletin*, 1990.

Mentkowski, M., and A. Doherty, "Abilities that Last a Lifetime: Outcomes of the Alverno Experience, *American Association of Higher Education Bulletin*, Feb. 1984, pp. 5-14.

Mook, D.G., *Psychological Research; Strategy and Tactics*, New York: Harper & Row, 1982.

Myers, I.B., and M.H. McCaulley, *Manual: A Guide to the Development and Use of the Myers Briggs Type Indicator*, Palo Alto, CA: Consulting Psychologists Press, 1985.

Palmer, P.J., "Good Teaching: A Matter of Living the Mystery", *Change*, Jan./Feb. 1990, pp. 11-19.

Perry, W.G., "Cognitive and Ethical Growth: The Making of Meaning", In A. Chickering (Ed.), *The Modern American College*, San Francisco, CA: Jossey-Bass, 1981, pp. 76-116.

Piaget, J., *The Child's Conception of the World*, New York: Harcourt, Brace & Jovanovich, 1929.

Porter, D.B., "Course Critiques: What Students Can Tell Us About Educational Efficiency", *Proceedings of the Human Factors Society 32nd Annual Meeting*, Santa Monica, CA: Human Factors Society, 1988, pp. 473-477.

Porter, D.B., "Educating From a Group Perspective: What, Why, and How", *Proceedings of the Human Factors Society 33rd Annual Meeting*. Santa Monica, CA: Human Factors Society 1989, pp. 507-512.

Postman, N., and C. Weingartner, *Teaching as a Subversive Activity*, New York: Delacorte Press, 1969.

Reich, R.B., *Tales of a New America; the Anxious Liberal's Guide to the Future*, New York: Vintage, 1988.

Seldes, G.,(Ed.), *The Great Quotations*, Secaucus, NJ: Citadel Press, 1983.

Shaw, M.E., *Group Dynamics; the Psychology of Small Group Behavior*, New York: McGraw-Hill, 1981.

Shewhart, W.A., *Statistical Method from the Viewpoint of Quality Control*, Mineola, NY: Dover, 1986.

Shulman, L.S., "Toward a Pedagogy of Substance", *American Association of Higher Education Bulletin*, June 1989, pp. 8-13.

Skinner, B.F., *About Behaviorism*, New York: Knopf, 1974.

Walton, M., *The Deming Management Method*, New York: Putnam, 1986.

Whitehead, A.N., *The Aims of Education and Other Essays*, New York: Macmillan, 1929.

Chapter 12

TQM IN RFPs AND PROPOSALS

In acquiring goods and services for a business operation, government agency or department, the quality of the provider's organization will be directly reflected in the products and services delivered. Remember the word "total" in TQM refers to the entire system of the providing organization (e.g., its suppliers, the processes, management structures, etc.) as well as the goods and services produced by that organization. Therefore, when contracting with a supplier to fill a need in your organization, the quality of more than the delivered products and services to meet specifications should be considered. The question, then, is how to include TQM concepts in contracts to insure a total quality orientation that will provide a higher quality relationship as well as lower priced, higher quality products and services over the long run. This chapter will address this question and related areas.

GOVERNMENT'S FOCUS ON TQM IN RFPs

Most people agree that today's Request for Proposals (RFPs) need to have something in them regarding TQM. Unfortunately, few people agree on how TQM concepts should be incorporated into requests for proposals (RFPs). The government, as a customer, seems to be getting quite serious about TQM, and as the largest business entity in the U.S., it has considerable ability to influence the way business is conducted through its contracting actions. So far, the government does not seem to be content to allow a peaceful evolution of the TQM philosophy in industry or its own departments and agencies. Mr. Peter Yurcisin, Acting Deputy Assistant Secretary of Defense (TQM), has said the government is looking for ways to "increase the speed of adoption", and one of the best ways is through contract provisions. He also made his position quite clear about DoD taking its leadership role seriously and ensuring that contractors doing business with the government are focused on quality of the goods and services provided to the government through TQM methodologies (Yurcisin, 1989).

Aviation Week also noted DoD's leadership role in developing a "selection bias" toward quality oriented firms and, at the moment, is "encouraging" TQM rather than requiring it. William B. Scott asserts that the U.S. military services are "pushing TQM concepts through acquisition incentives and DoD guidelines, while simultaneously embarking on a self-assessment process aimed at getting their own houses in order (Scott, 1989)." The message to the defense industry should be clear: either change the way you do business or have it mandated in regulations and legislation. Mr. Yurcisin has already asked a Process Action Team to consider "specific language that can be used in government contract to integrate TQM into the source selection process (Yurcisin, 1989)."

The government does, however, have problems implementing TQM concepts through contractual actions. There are significant impediments in regulations and laws that prevent the application of TQM concepts in some areas such as incentives and inspections. A Process Action Team with representatives from the Office of the Secretary of Defense and other agencies was formed to recommend changes to the Federal Acquisition Regulation and the DoD supplements. The barriers and obstacles will not necessarily be easy to remove, but efforts are certainly being made (Yurcisin, 1989). For example, an article by Burstein and Sediak in *National Productivity Review*, related the success of the Forest Service in an experiment conducted in several national forests. Management removed barriers and obstacles to allow staff to get involved and take responsibility for making improvements. The result was dramatic—especially for a government agency.

> ... top management loosened up the constraints of bureaucratic red tape on employee creativity and entrepreneurship. Authority was delegated to the lowest possible level, and employees were encouraged to take risks and be innovative in responding to customer needs ... only the ordering of priorities was defined and the budget was provided in lump sum (rather than line items), maximum flexibility was given to get the job done, personnel ceilings were lifted, all savings could be retained for high priority work, experimentation and a bottom-up approach to change were encouraged—no one could 'fail.' The Forest Service had one ground rule: "If it is legal and within basic policy bounds, go for it."

> "Results were dramatic. Substantial paperwork was eliminated; morale and organizational spirit soared. Unit costs in the experimental forests were reduced 15%; of a saving pool of $175,000 in one National Forest, 20% was distributed to employees and remainder used to improve service to customers; rangers began processing all public permits in a few hours rather than a few weeks as a result of simplified paperwork; 109 employee suggestions for better ways of doing business were implemented in one experimental forest (Burstein and Sediak, 1988)."

In reality, there is more activity in TQM-related efforts in the federal government than meets the eye. By Presidential Executive Order 12552, signed by President Reagan in 1986, all departments of the federal government are to improve the efficiency, effectiveness, and quality of the products or services delivered. A goal of 20% productivity improvement is directed in appropriate functions by 1992. In early 1987 there were 700 service programs identified by 20 agencies to implement TQM concepts, affecting nearly 2 million federal workers.

The results of this effort, in some cases, have been quite dramatic. The IRS (1000% error rate reduction in FTD accounts), Naval Air Logistics Center (over $1 billion savings by 1991), and especially the Forest Service are noteworthy for the progress made in selected departments or areas. "In all three agencies, the dedication to quality of the top executives has provided the vision and leadership essential to (initiating) a TQM culture (Burstein and Sediak, 1988)."

INITIAL EFFORTS TO INCORPORATE TQM IN RFPs

The greatest concerns about incorporating TQM in RFPs are: 1) the customer will require TQM in some specific or mandated form, and 2) the fear that customers will over-specify the use of particular tools and techniques. TQM concepts need to be implemented in a manner that fits each organization's situation. Over specification might turn TQM into "just another program". Part of TQMs strength lies in the variety of tools and techniques avialable. Informed contractors should be able to choose which techniques are most appropriate. The contractor must also be allowed to modify or combine several approaches to better suit organizational capabilities and program needs. The customer must recognize that no one technique or tool is a panacea for all problems and should therefore encourage efforts to use the best of the available methodologies in a logical manner. The best results will be obtained by emphasizing customer needs and demonstrating continuous process improvement to increase the value of products and services.

Some organizations are not waiting for specific guidance and are moving forward on their own. The following are examples from recent DoD operating command RFPs where TQM was included.

Example 1

PART FOUR
QUALITY CONTROL PROGRAM

Chapter 1
General

Total Quality Management. A Total Quality Management (TQM) approach shall be implemented in this contract. Continuous improvement in system quality must be demonstrated with available resources to meet user needs and expectations while reducing overall corrective maintenance costs. TQM or some related approach shall be implemented through the disciplined application of a proven system and engineering standards and procedures to the maintenance process ...

•
•
•

Example 2

EXECUTIVE SUMMARY
REP xxxxxxxx

•
•
•

XYZ is actively pursuing the application of Total Quality Management (TQM) as explained in DOD 5000.51-G, "Total Quality Management, a Guide to Implementation". TQM is continuous process improvement involving managers and workers in an integrated effort to improve performance at every level in every function. It integrates fundamental, common-sense management techniques, existing improvement efforts and technical tools under a disciplined approach to continuous improvement of the work process. TQM must be a process which represents management commitment to true improvement from the bottom to the top of the organization. Therefore, successful contractors must actively support TQM objectives and the application of TQM principles.

•
•
•

Example 3   (An example of overspecification)

In addition to the quality requirements of the technical data package, the Contractor shall validate the quality of the product whether produced at the prime contract facility or subcontractor/ vendor facility, using Statistical Process Control (SPC) techniques as defined in American Standards Institute (AMSI) Z1.1, Z1.2 and Z1.3. Application of SPC techniques shall be considered for all characteristics identified as critical, major, and specific in the Classification of Defect Tables in the detail specification. The contractor must provide written justification for any of the characteristics where SPC is not considered justified.

A plan for the implementation of SPC shall be submitted by the Contractor for review and approval by the Government prior to the initiation of production ...

•
•
•

FOLLOW-ON EFFORTS TO INCORPORATE TQM IN RFPs

A new and interesting idea for incorporating TQM in RFPs is based on the inclusion of several questions to which the contractor must respond when submitting the proposal. The written response then becomes a statement of how the contractor intends to perform the contract. As such, this written response is subject to review during on-site visits from the customer. The following are examples of questions that might be used.

1. How has your company implemented quality improvements in previous and/or existing contracts? Summarize the results.

2. Describe the means available for all employees to effectively contribute to the company quality objectives. Summarize pervious results.

3. Describe how you intend to define processes critical to meeting customer needs and expectations.

4. Based on this RFP, what key characteristics do you find related to customer expectations and how do you intend to measure, track and control these characteristics?

5. How do you propose to implement quality improvement for critical processes? How will these improvement efforts be measured, evaluated and controlled?

6. What type of teams do you intend to form to achieve items (1) through (5)? How will they be structured and what will be their charter?

7. What other plans do you have for ensuring that customer needs and expectations will be met at lowest possible cost without increased customer risk?

High level directives indicate growing interest in having TQM concepts included in RFPs. Directives from the Assistant Secretary of Defense require TQM to be an integral part of all assessment activities within Production and Logistics as well as Research and Engineering. Further, the Under Secretary of Defense (Acquisition) has requested that TQM be included in any new program management plan.

STATEMENT OF WORK

As a precursor to an RFP, the Statement of Work (SOW) should be structured to focus on TQM concepts. The following is a sample format that may be helpful in developing the SOW to ensure that TQM is integrated into the program or contract activities (RM2000 Guidebook, 1989).

Sample Statements that may be included in Statements of Work for Service contracts:

Objective

To meet the quality and cost goals established for the contract, the contractor shall emphasize the use of TQM concepts throughout the period of this contract. Process improvements and prevention of problems using TQM tools and techniques shall be stressed to achieve higher reliability and lower cost by means of defect or problem reduction and avoidance.

Operations

The contractor shall describe an approach for implementing teamwork and robust planning and delivery of services which emphasizes planning quality into the service especially as delivery requirements evolve. Emphasis will be placed on continuous improvement towards target values, with the use of TQM tools and techniques or other such tools and techniques that accomplish the same purpose. Where applicable, target values shall be indicated in addition to the specification limits. Measurements documenting continuous improvements shall be used.

Contract Management Plan

The contractor shall develop and present a plan for the conduct and management of a fully integrated effort, building on TQM concepts, principles, methodologies, tools and techniques.

System Effectiveness

The contractor shall develop a system structure which is inherently reliable and maintainable. The contractor shall identify quantitative and qualitative reliability and maintainability characteristics, such as fault tolerance, graceful degradation of services, diagnostic approaches and accessibility, all of which will reduce process cycle times as well as operations and maintenance costs. The contractor will use, where applicable, TQM tools and techniques, or similar methodologies, to continuously improve system effectiveness and efficiency and document progress.

Quality Assurance

The contractor shall identify the critical quality characteristics for each service function or activity. These characteristics shall be derived from an analysis of processes and customer needs and expectations, preferably using TQM tools, techniques, and methodologies. This information should be compiled into an integrated quality structure from which specific process characteristics, whose variation must be controlled, are identified. The quality structure shall include service and process characteristics as well as those critical characteristics that form the critical success factors. Appropriate quality tasking shall be passed down to major subcontractors or vendors of critical items or activities. The intent is to plan and build quality into the service. Describe how this can be accomplished with minimum risk to the operation.

Service Delivery

The contractor shall ensure that the service delivery is controlled with a goal of minimizing variability of the processes that produce the critical functional characteristics of the service and that conform to target values. A feedback system shall be developed with the customer and suppliers to maintain and improve quality delivery of services. Timely delivery of services is considered a part of the quality criteria.

TQM Management Review

The contractor shall conduct a monthly Management Review or Audit to provide a critique of the contractor's Quality Management effort, following TQM concepts, to the government program office. The contractor shall conduct a Quality Review twice a year to document measured progress of Continuous Process Improvement (CPI) efforts against previously established benchmarks. Such a review will be headed by the Contract Manager or Senior Management officer of the organization's profit center.

Subcontractor

The contractor shall implement a plan for selecting subcontractors. The subcontract organizations shall have, or will implement, their own Quality Management effort modeled after the TQM philosophy, tools and techniques as a means of achieving a total quality approach to business and to customer satisfaction.

Education and Training

A plan for training all personnel (contractor and supplier) in TQM tools and techniques should be developed. The plan shall indicate the extent and level of the initial training or education activities and the extent to which this training will be offered to the subcontractor team. Continuous improvement will require continuous follow-on training and education which should be specified as to type, intensity, level, and focus.

DEPLOYMENT OF TQM THROUGH THE RFP PROCESS

The following is a suggested guide for deploying TQM concepts into the agencies and industries contracting with those agencies. Contracting, as a vehicle for TQM proliferation, is an ideal way to motivate contractor commitment. Further, this approach can help in developing the customer entity into "world-class" customer status, either between government agencies and industry or prime contractors and sub-contractors.

Very important: You, as the developer of the RFP, have to know who your customer is. The customers for the RFP are the potential providers. In the case of the government, industry is the customer for the RFP and therefore, the objective is to create a satisfied customer be delivering a top quality product (RFP) by means of a process that is continually improving. General Bernard Randolph (Ret) made this point quite clearly to the Process Action Team he chartered to improve RFP development process at Air Force Systems Command. If the Air Force expects quality proposals, it must first provide a quality RFP that is clear and specific as to the Air Force's needs and expectations.

Let's take a look at a suggested plan to be used in guiding the deployment of TQM through the government's contracting activities.

TQM DEPLOYMENT GUIDE

Deployment of TQM among aerospace and defense contractors doing business with the government is best accomplished by the government becoming a "World-Class Customer". The requirement to be a world-class customer starts with implementing TQM within the government's own departments and agencies. This plan will focus on the RFP as an instrument for deployment and make the assumption that TQM has been implemented in the government agency developing the RFP.

As a world-class customer, the government can expect the providers of goods and services to develop the quality needed and expected by the government as the customer through improving their internal processes and management practices. Consequently, the RFP will reflect those expectations. The major focus will be on results and demonstrated past performance versus unsubstantiated promises or intentions to develop TQM in the performance of the contract. Motivation to implement TQM in individual companies can be influenced by what the government emphasizes in the acquisition and procurement system. Some of the motivating factors are:

Contract Methods and Types (e.g., Source Selection)

1. TQM must be singled out as an important item in the technical and management areas where it can be used to evaluate an organization's ability to develop and deliver robust products and services that are reliable, maintainable, suitable, and sustainable.

2. Communicate TQM's importance to the contractor and its high priority as a means to productivity and quality.

3.   Signal the importance of TQM by selecting a contractor who has implemented, or perhaps is implementing, TQM as an approach to managing and improving customer satisfaction.

Incentives Used

1.   Reward successful application of TQM practices that produce results, e.g. improvement efforts to reduce cost, improve quality, and provide increasing value.

2.   Reward continuous improvement in all areas. This requires the government to be adaptable and flexible and willing to continuously improve its methods of rewarding improvements.

3.   Recognize certifiable or certified contractors and suppliers who have proven their capacity to continuously improve customer satisfaction as evidenced by increasing value of their goods and services.

Program Evaluation

1.   Assess TQM implementation progress and resulting improvements.

2.   Publicize benefits to both the government and the contractor that have accrued through using TQM methodologies and philosophy.

Application of Tools and Techniques

1.   Recognize that a variety of tools and techniques are available to achieve more reliable and less costly products and services. The necessity of incorporating quality "up front" in the design or planning stage rather than attempting to inspect it out of the product or service after the fact should be strongly encouraged through the structure and evaluation criteria.

2.   The government should resist specifying the use of specific tools or techniques unless it is of particular importance to the contract performance since there may be several tools that are applicable. Further, the contractor may modify several approaches to better suit their organizational capabilities and program needs. The government must recognize that no one technique or tool is a panacea for all problems and encourage efforts to use available methodologies in a logical manner.

3.   Avoid specifying a rigid, specific adherence to the government's TQM modality. Best results will be obtained by emphasizing robust design, capable processes, and continuous improvement both internal and external to the contractor, aimed at increasing value and creating continuously increasing customer satisfaction.

SOURCE SELECTION PROCESS

Overall Purpose

To select contractors who will apply TQM concepts and methodologies throughout the contract period and through the development cycle of products or services. The expected results are capable processes that are continuously improving the quality and subsequent value for the customer. To accomplish this, contractors and their suppliers will:

1.   Demonstrate and practice top-level commitment to TQM concepts and methodologies.

2.   Involve all personnel in TQM practices by demonstrated leadership and organization structure.

3.   Use a structured, disciplined TQM approach to problem-solving and improvement efforts.

4.   Demonstrate continuous improvement as a way of life in the day-to-day business operations.

Commerce Business Daily (CBD) Synopsis

1.   Purpose: To solicit and screen offerors.

2.   CBD Sample Statement: Potential offerors shall describe their involvement in TQM with particular emphasis on activities to continuously improve processes and create the greatest value for the government.

Source Selection Plan (SSP)

1. Purpose: The SSP is prepared for the Source Selection Authority (SSA) to assist in organizing and conducting the analysis and evaluation of the proposal and finally, the selection of a contractor. The plan should ensure that a TQM oriented source is considered a major priority. TQM orientation is best demonstrated by current TQM activities and past-performance using TQM concepts and methodologies.

2. Program or Contracting Office Responsibilities: The SSP should contain the following: "TQM type methodologies or concepts are considered important by the government in achieving continuously improving quality products and services. The use of TQM tools and techniques should be given high priority in providing quality reflected in reliable, maintainable, supportable, and producible products and services. Quality is assured by verifiable measurements."

RFP Instructions of Offerors

1. Purpose: Alert offerors of the emphasis that the government will be placing on TQM implementation and to identify any specific sections where TQM is to be addressed in the proposal.

2. General instructions: The following are examples of what might be included. Each RFP should be tailored to accommodate the specifics of the particular contract or government service need.

    a. Executive Summary: This section shall include an overview of management's TQM philosophy and the developed capacity and ability to deliver quality as a means to achieving greater customer satisfaction at decreasing costs.

    b. Technical Proposal: This section shall contain information that clearly demonstrates the offeror's approach and capability to implement TQM methodologies throughout the scope of the contract. As appropriate, discussions in this section should include items such as:

        1. How the application of TQM concepts and methodologies will contribute to the achievement of reliability, maintainability, supportability, suitability, and producibility of goals.

        2. Details of the proposed technical efforts to integrate design, manufacturing, test, and operations early in the program; for service contracts: integration of planning, design or process

work development, verification, and continuing operations. Intent: Demonstrate cross-functional structure and approach to achieving the contract purposes.

3. Application of TQM-type process control tools and techniques, such as statistical process control or histograms, to minimize variation in product or service quality.

4. How robust design or planning procedures in the early phases will identify critical product or service and process characteristics that must be measured and controlled during production or delivery of services. Include a description of the approach to measuring and controlling the process variability and factors that will be measured.

5. How personnel will be continuously educated and trained in TQM tools and techniques.

6. How value, for the customer, will be measured and maintained.

7. What processes will be used to determine and improve customer satisfaction as well as how well expectations are being met.

c. Management Proposal: This section should clearly demonstrate the offeror's senior level management commitment to TQM. Indications of corporate policy that has been developed and deployed and the degree to which it is practiced. Proven results based on key measurements should be used to demonstrate effectiveness of the policies. Demonstrate the organization's ability to produce robust designs and service plans as well as production and delivery processes. The same should apply to sub-contractors or suppliers. The material in this section should be auditable and verifiable by an independent, well-qualified TQM audit team.

3. RFP Statement of Work (see previous SOW example)

4. RFP Evaluation Factors for Award:

a. Purpose: To make clear to contractors the relative importance of TQM in meeting the needs and expectations of the government and in the selection of contractors.

b. Contract Requirements: Areas where TQM concepts or methodologies are most applicable should be well defined and structured. The priority and weighing in the evaluation process of TQM implementation or approaches in various contract requirements should be specified.

c. Source Selection Criteria: The following are only suggested criteria to illustrate the intent and possibilities in the source selection process.

– Management's policies and demonstrated actions/activities that substantiate TQM implementation, total commitment, personal involvement in continuous improvement, and a process orientation.

– A demonstrated understanding of TQM concepts and methods in current activities and contracts.

– Past experience with TQM tools and techniques and the results of their application.

– The use of Process Action Teams (or equivalent) in effecting continuous process improvements with documented policy or guidelines.

– An understanding of the most critical characteristics of the products or services requested and how they will be controlled during the term of the contract.

– Supplier or Subcontractor relationship that embody TQM concepts.

– Structure for flowing down quality requirements to major subcontractors or suppliers, especially in critical areas.

– An approach to controlling and measuring process variability to improve quality and value added.

– An on-going and continuous education and training program.

– Evaluating and Assessment factors used by the contractor (and suppliers) to recognize and promote members of the organization.

d. Site visitations and verification can be included to determine the content and intensity of TQM activities.

INCENTIVES FOR IMPLEMENTING TQM

A. Purpose: To provide incentives to contractors for expending time, money, resources and energy to implement and use TQM concepts and methods.

B. Need for Incentives: To encourage TQM type implementation in the face of a structured, rather rigid government acquisition environment, economic incentives will prove quite useful. Unlike the commercial sector, government practices may discourage extensive use of TQM methodologies where improvements increase profit levels past those allowed by regulations and the contractor's incentive is destroyed.

C. Suggested approaches for using Contract Incentives: Firm Fixed-Price typed contracts with additional set-asides could be used to encourage continuous improvements leading to savings. Cost-Plus-Award-Fee type contracts could be useful as allowed under FAR supplement guidelines. Award Fee plans could be structured to account for measured quality improvements from Continuous Process Improvements (CPI), e.g., cycle time reduction, lowered costs, improved delivery, increased tolerance to various uses, etc. Such award fee criteria could center around such things as:

- Demonstrated TQM integration throughout all levels and functions of the organization and successfully utilized to increase the quality, efficiency and effectiveness of operations.

- The contractor and suppliers create savings to the total program cost by continuous improvement techniques.

- Value engineering incentive provisions may be appropriate under certain circumstances.

CONTRACT MONITORING AND EVALUATION

Periodic reviews or audits are useful to determine levels of TQM activity and results. These reviews or audits must be done by highly capable teams fully cognizant of TQM concepts and methodologies. The emphasis would be on the processes in contrast to the usual conventional quality reviews which are focused only on products or end-results. The focus of these reviews or audits would be to determine status, find areas for mutual improvements (i.e., both government and contractor), and cross-feed success/failure information from other contractor/ government operations. Reviews or audits can be made by either the government or by the contractor (internally as well as with their subcontractors) with a specific format and reports to measure status and progress.

TQM REVIEW CHECKLIST

A.   Senior Level Commitment to TQM

    1.   Management Involvement and Leadership
    2.   Corporate Policy concerning Management and Quality
    3.   Education and Training in Problem Prevention
    4.   Strategic Planning incorporating TQM
    5.   TQM related activities, functions, and involvements

B.   Involvement of all Organizational Functions and Levels

    1.   Organization and Administration
    2.   Employee Knowledge Level
    3.   Teamwork
    4.   Supplier Involvement

C.   Application of Proven Methodologies, Tools, and Techniques

    1.   Implementation of robust design and planning practices
    2.   Customer requirements and analysis
    3.   Applications: e.g., DOE, Loss Functions, Statistical Method

D.   Evidence of Continuous Improvement

    1.   Results of Continuous Improvement Efforts
    2.   Future Plans for TQM Improvement Efforts
    3.   Education and Training in TQM
    4.   Incentives and Recognition Structure in Company

A more detailed evaluation approach to TQM involvement is included in the following section on Proposals and could prove highly functional in supplementing this broad outline check-list.

SUMMARY OF SECTION

The deployment of TQM concepts through the contracting processes is an appropriate method to motivate both the government, and particularly industry doing business with the government, to become involved in the TQM philosophy. Through the source selection procedures, incentives, and careful evaluations, TQM can be made a part of the government-industry environment.

TQM IN PROPOSALS

TQM placed in proposals should be based on demonstrated results of previous or ongoing efforts. Statements such as, "We are committed to TQM" or "Company XYZ strongly believes in and practices continuous process improvement" are meaningless without data to back them up. To show evidence of a company's ability to provide high quality products or services, on a timely basis, with lower costs and without increased customer risks is a position of strength. Contractors who have implemented TQM in previous or existing contracts are in much stronger positions. Think of how powerful your proposal would read if it contained the following:

"Company XYZ will work with the customer to develop key measures of quality, based on customer's clearly defined needs and expectations, which can be used to evaluate the continuous improvement effort. Emphasis will be on developing a clear understanding of the processes used to produce and deliver the services in order to prevent degraded service, rather than only correcting deficiencies, and continuously improve the efficiency and effectiveness of the processes. Company XYZ has implemented this strategy in a similar existing contract with the Department of the Interior where continuous process improvement efforts have reduced deficiencies by over 30%, cycle times by 23%, manpower by 12%, and increased measured customer satisfaction by 43%. Expectations are for another 5% improvement gain in the next twelve months."

The strongest proposal will be based on previous or existing TQM efforts and not on idle statements. If a contractor has not been interested in implementing TQM to any degree on previous contracts, why should one believe they can be successful on this one? Implementing TQM concepts is not without upfront costs and turmoil. If already started, the customer can consider the risk and disruptions to operations may be less than with a contractor just starting. The following will help create a stronger proposal:

1. Based on the RFP, form appropriate teams to determine key characteristics which you intend to measure, track and evaluate.

2. Discuss how implementing TQM philosophies, tools and techniques contribute to a quality effort in responding to the RFP.

3.   Indicate the percent of people trained and/or experienced in TQM philosophies, tools and techniques.

4.   Describe how quality in your company permeates every aspect of the organization versus quality efforts being a centralized activity.

5.   Discuss the make-up and purpose of the Process Action Teams (PATs) you have formed or intend to form on award of the contract.

6.   Discuss your relationship with your suppliers and how you intend to work with them in the future to be a world-class customer.

EVALUATING PROPOSALS

TQM must be incorporated into contract award decisions, but again, it is very important as to how this is done. It is our conclusion that evaluating contractor's proposals should be based on the end result (Quality) and not on the means to the end (TQM). Emphasis should be on the following:

1.   Documented and measurable evidence of top management support and leadership in such areas as:

   • policy statement
   • training of personnel
   • recognition programs
   • flattened organizational structure
   • decentralized quality improvement personnel
   • reduction of overhead
   • numbers of people involved in PATs
   • relationship with suppliers
   • evaluation based on Malcolm Baldrige criteria

2.   Using documented poor performance (or even maintaining the status quo) as a criteria to eliminate contractors from consideration.

3.   Reducing the emphasis on the "lowest bidder" and using "greatest value" based on organizational structure, environment, and demonstrated leadership values that focus on continuous improvement of quality and consequently, customer satisfaction.

4.   Past performance (i.e., data used to evaluate a track record of contractor quality and the resulting customer satisfaction as well as the proven ability to achieve improvement over the life of a past contract).

PAST PERFORMANCE CRITERIA IN RFPs

Brig General Bob Drews, Director of Contracting, HQ Air Force Systems Command, made it clear that the "Past Performance" Initiative is important to Air Force acquisitions and procurement and is being integrated into the major commands for all types of contracts to include service contracts. The message is clear; improve current performance because past performance impacts future business. The intent is to choose contractors with proven records of quality performance in any type of past activities whenever possible. At the end of 1989, there are 53 contractors in the data base with approximately 315 Contractor Performance Assessment Report (CPAR) reports available for contracting officers across the services to review and use in evaluating contractor's proposals (Drews, 1989).

Let's get more specific. The government, or a prime contractor, will expect to see tangible evidence of TQM implementation and activities. If your organization has intentions of implementing TQM concepts and methodologies, they must be structured and verifiable. The following list provides examples of areas or factors that indicate the extent of TQM involvement and some of the results:

- Reduction of overhead costs.

- Flattening of organizational structure with no decrease in quality or operational capability.

- Number of barriers to TQM implementation removed. How barriers or constraints have been, or will be, removed.

- Number of improvements that have been made in processes and resulting performance improvements (with measurements).

- Number of steps removed from processes (streamlining) and performance improvements.

- Time to do process steps/activities reduced (simplification).

- Number of problems/opportunities surfaced by people.

- Number of people involved in PATs.

- Number of people trained ... number of training hours.

- Costs associated with implementation.

- Reduction of cycle times in processes (or increase to improve quality).

- Number of inspectors eliminated with continued decrease in defects and waste.

- Productivity increases and associated measurements; for example, output/assets employed.

- Examples of TQM commitment.

  "Schedule slipped because quality was below internal standards."
  "Refused vendor/subs product because below new standards."

Dr. W. Edward Deming developed 14 points for managing that summarize his approach to quality improvements. One excellent approach to evaluating TQM involvement is to use some or all of Dr. Deming's applicable points. A proposal that reflects adherence to the following points could be seen on the road to creating a TQM environment and using TQM concepts and methodologies.

- "Require suppliers/providers to provide statistical evidence of quality" and thus, become a world class customer. Does the proposal provide evidence of using statistical methods to ensure quality products and services from sub-contractors and suppliers? Is there evidence that the contractor is a world-class customer?

- "Cease dependency on mass inspection and rely only on statistical control." Is this a documented approach in the proposal and used as applicable?

- "Train all employees and continue to train as changes occur or as anticipated." Is continuous education and training a part of the culture and highly valued in the organization?

- "Give all employees proper tools to do the job right and to do the right things." What is the level and extent of training and education in the organization? Are the people capable of using TQM tools and techniques in effective ways?

- "Structure the organization for different departments to work together to solve problems and develop opportunities." Is there a cross-functional orientation and mindset? What is the evidence?

- "Create pride in workmanship by eliminating barriers to doing the best job possible right the first time." What evidence is offered to indicate pride in workmanship and depth/breadth of employee involvement? What barriers have been removed? What evidence is there of waste reduction and a focus on doing things right the first time?

- "Clearly define top management's permanent commitment to quality that is demonstrated consciously and continuously." What policies, mission statements, goals and objectives are stated? What is the depth and breadth of knowledge of these statements within the organization? What evidence is offered of top management's actions and involvement in quality improvements?

MEASUREMENT

We keep referring to "documented evidence" and "proof" of TQM activities and involvement. This usually refers to meaningful measurements that provide hard-core tangible evidence which is verifiable and reproducible. Below are a few points about traditional measurement systems which are not usually adequate in the TQM environment.

1. Rarely assesses customer satisfaction. Usually measures amount of resources expended because they are the easiest to quantify.

2. Isolates single factors which can distort the performance picture, for example, the number of programs developed, which doesn't indicate how successful or useful the programs were to the customer.

3. Measures done from outside the work group are usually inaccurate–those inside the group know best.

4. Performance comparisons of individuals in the work group do not reflect the interdependence of the group.

5. Numerical systems are easy to manage but can be misleading. Standards for the number of drawings per month can have little bearing on how well the customer is being served.

Now let's take a look at characteristics of more desirable measurements that would be more often found in a TQM organization.

1. Stress effectiveness over efficiency if there is a conflict.

2. Stress outcome of service more than amount of output.

3. Stress quality of products/services in ways that reflect the value added.

4. Stress responsiveness to the customer and meeting needs and expectations.

Mr. Salemme, in his book "Measuring White Collar Work", suggests the following questions can be used to assess the value of the measurements being used or to develop good measures within your organization.

- Are we providing correct services to customers?
- Are we providing those services in the best possible way?
- Are we fulfilling our mission?

Measurements framed around these questions or developed to answer these questions are very useful and informative (Salemme, 1988).

Some examples of different types of measurements used by HQ Air Force Logistics Command in their Total Quality Contracting Briefing are as follows (HQ AFLC):

EFFECTIVENESS	EFFICIENCY
Error Rate	Cost per Transaction
Accuracy	Time per Activity
Actual to Plan	Turnaround Time
Demand Satisfaction	Asset Utilization
Cancel/Deter	Output per Unit
Response Time	Inventory
Etc.	Etc.
Meeting Requirements = Customer Satisfaction	With Minimum Resources = Productivity

Like Dr. Deming is fond of saying: "In God we trust, but all others, bring data." It's fine to say in a proposal that "We are doing ...", or "We emphasize ...", but bringing data that documents the assertion is much more powerful. This gives the proposal validity and credibility. Mr. J. Wires, Vice President at Boeing Commercial Airplanes, while talking about accepting undocumented statements in proposals from possible suppliers, said: "Taking action based on heresay is just poor judgement (Salemme, 1988)".

This decade will very likely be referred to as the quality revolution. Those companies who faithfully and persistently implement TQM will not only be awarded contracts, but will also see vast improvements in their competitiveness which will lead to continued success and increased profitability. The blame for our waning competitiveness need not be placed on overseas companies. The out-dated philosophies, tools, and techniques within your company may well be the cause of the lack of competitiveness that will lead to extinction. To win contracts on a continuous basis requires implementing the most powerful weapon available: Your people, armed with TQM methodologies, tools and techniques, supported by management that creates environments, structures, and values that empower their people to be individually and collectively successful.

EVALUATION OF TQM IMPLEMENTATION
AND PRACTICES IN GOVERNMENT AGENCIES

The following was used by the Federal Government to evaluate the progress of its various agencies in implementing TQM concepts. The measurement scale was a very simple "Extensive-Some-Little" evaluation of the department's involvement (Burstein, p. 122).

- Top management commitment to quality productivity shown in practical management actions.

- Customer orientation permeates agency.

- Teamwork at all levels seen as key to improving service delivery.

- Quality management training provided at all levels.

- Accountability for quality and productivity improvement tied to performance evaluation.

- Measures and standards set for quality service delivery.

- Efforts underway to eliminate barriers to productivity and quality.

- Constant stimulation to improve quality and productivity.

SAMPLE EVALUATION CRITERIA FOR PROPOSALS
OR CONTRACT PERFORMANCE

This section will provide a comprehensive set of evaluation criteria that may be used in a number of different ways. Most obvious is in customer evaluation of offerors proposals and further, of contractor's performance under a contract that included a TQM orientation. The contractor would find this criteria most useful, however, in doing a self-evaluation to assess the status and progress of TQM implementation efforts. The uses are many and limited only by your creativity.

It should also be noted that this criteria applies equally well to government organizations. Evaluation of a government organization by self-assessment or evaluation of component organizations by upper level staff would be well served using this criteria.

The use of the criteria in any form would serve two purposes for either government or contractor environments: 1) Assess status, and 2) Create focus by members towards TQM concepts and methodology. The second point is perhaps the most potent and useful as management's intention is to foster adoption of the TQM values and principles using as many different methods as possible. All the Malcolm Baldrige Award winners have noted the efforts to win the award created a tremendous focus on quality improvements and that was the real benefit from focusing on the award.

Another great value of this criteria is its use in "benchmarking" the organization. From the chapter on the Tools and Techniques, you will remember that benchmarking is useful in assessing where the organization is at the current moment to create focused plans for the future and to measure progress. How else would you determine and measure movement towards quality improvements without knowing, and periodically assessing, your current position? In addition to "absolute" benchmarking, "relative" benchmarking would prove quite useful in comparing one organization against another to assess differences and similarities. Each organization gains from learning more about itself relative to others.

CHAPTER SUMMARY

TQM concepts and/or continuous process improvement should be included in RFPs. Those who write RFPs should avoid over specification of TQM tools, techniques, and methodologies. Emphasis should be on getting contractors to be specific in proposals as to how they intend to achieve better quality, increased response times, and lower costs without increasing customer risks. Contractors need to be encouraged to provide evidence of how they have or will implement TQM, and discouraged from making only "window dressing" statements in their proposals. Writers of RFPs should also recognize that the RFP should clearly present the customer's needs and expectations. A contractor will achieve "world class" status much faster with the assistance of "world class" customers.

Proposals should include clear evidence that can be audited. The TQM concepts are being implemented or, at the very least, firmly committed to implementation. Evaluating proposals should focus on the organization's capability to produce an end result of quality using TQM concepts as a means to that end. Past performance using TQM methodologies that produced superior products and services is perhaps the strongest evidence of an organizations potential to deliver continuously improving quality as experienced by the customer. Measurements of quality and value is difficult at first but needs to evolve from traditional approaches centered on efficiency to measures of effectiveness relating to customer satisfaction and the organization systems as well as efficiency of the processes. The evaluation format should prove useful as a framework to custom design an evaluation instrument for your various needs.

REFERENCES

ASD (P&L) (IPQ) briefings concerning "Institutionalizing TQM in the Defense Acquisition Process".

Burstein, C., and Sediak, K., "The Federal Productivity Improvement Effort: Current Status and Future Agenda", *National Productivity Review*, V7N2, Spring, 1988, p. 122.

Drews, Bob, Brig Gen (sel), Presentation at Andrews AFB, MD, December 3, 1989.

HQ AFLC Briefing on "TQM in Contracting".

"Malcolm Baldrige Application Guidelines", NIST, Gaithersburg, MD 20899.

RM2000 Guidebook (Draft Copy) HQ USAF/LE-RD, 1989.

Salemme, T.A., "Measuring White Collar Work", *Team*, BCA, December 1988.

Scott, William B., "TQM Expected to Boost Productivity, Ensure Survival of U.S. Industry", *Aviation Week and Space Technology*, December 4, 1989, p. 64.

Yurcisin, Peter, "The Way to Quality", *Contract Management*, November 1989, p. 6.

APPENDIX A

MALCOLM BALDRIGE NATIONAL
QUALITY AWARD EXAMINATION
Categories, Items and Point Values
Examination categories/items and maximum allotted points

Leadership	**100**
Senior executive leadership	30
Quality values	20
Management for quality	30
Public responsibility	20
Information and Analysis	**60**
Scope and management of quality data and information	35
Analysis of quality data and information	25
Strategic Quality Planning	**90**
Strategic quality planning process	40
Quality leadership indicators in planning	25
Quality priorities	25
Human Resource Utilization	**150**
Human resource management	30
Employee involvement	40
Quality education and training	40
Employee recognition and performance measurement	20
Employee well-being and morale	20
Quality Assurance of Products and Services	**150**
Design and introduction of quality products and services	30
Process and quality control	25

Continuous improvement of processes, products, and services	25
Quality assessment	15
Documentation	10
Quality assurance, quality assessment and quality improvement of support services and business processes	25
Quality assurance, quality assessment and quality improvement of suppliers	20
Quality Results	**150**
Quality of products and services	50
Comparison of quality results	35
Business process, operational and support service quality improvement	35
Supplier quality improvement	30
Customer Satisfaction	**300**
Knowledge of customer requirements and expectations	50
Customer relationship management	30
Customer service standards	20
Commitment to customers	20
Complaint resolution for QI	30
Customer satisfaction determination	50
Customer satisfaction results	50
Customer satisfaction comparison	50
TOTAL POINTS	**1000**

APPENDIX B

INTERNATIONAL ORGANIZATION FOR STANDARDIZATION: ISO 9000

Quality System Requirements

Management responsibility
Quality system
Contract review
Design control
Document control
Purchasing
Purchaser-supplied product
Product identification and traceability
Process control
Inspection and testing
Inspection, measuring, and equipment
Inspection and testing
Control of non-conforming product
Corrective action
Handling, storage, packaging, and delivery
Quality records
Internal quality audits
Training
Servicing
Statistical techniques

Source: ISO 9001, a quality systems subsection of ISO 9000. It is considered a good overview of the content of ISO 9000.

Source: Quality Digest, April 1991

APPENDIX C

TEXT LEARNING OUTCOMES

- To be able to define TQM, and to be able to list the essential elements of Total Quality.

- To be able to compare and contrast the old and new definitions of quality.

- To gain a familiarity with the total quality philosophy of Deming.

- To understand the concept of the cost of quality, and to be able to state examples of the cost of quality.

- To understand the importance of teamwork and the key elements of successful process action teams.

- To know the key steps in the process improvement process.

- To know how to use the basic tools and techniques of Total Quality.

- To understand the elements of a process and how to construct a process flow diagram.

- To understand the concept of non-value added activities and be able to simplify processes.

- To understand basic statistical concepts and their application to design and problem solving.

- To understand the application of TQM to education, software, and to RFP's and proposals.

GLOSSARY

ACTIVE LISTENING – A communication techniques which involves repeating back/re-phrasing what you thought the speaker just said. Sometimes referred to as the Rogerian technique, named after psychologist, Carl Rogers.

ACTIVITY BASED COSTING (ABC) – A costing method that concentrates on any event or activity that is a cost driver, or causal factor in the incurrence of cost for an organization. Improved traceability of overhead costs, particularly for organizations with many products of varying degrees of volume and complexity, will result in more accurate unit cost data for management decisions.

APPRAISAL COSTS – Costs associated with inspecting products or services to insure they satisfy the customer.

ASSIGNABLE (SPECIAL) CAUSE OF VARIATION – Causes of variation that are random, i.e., not statistically predictable given the capability of a process. One of the purposes of statistical process control is to identify and eliminate special causes of variation.

ATTRIBUTE DATA – Non numeric data with two categories (e.g., pass/fail, works/doesn't work, defective/non-defective, etc.).

AVERAGE (MEAN) – A measure of the center of the distribution of data. Calculated by adding the sample values and dividing by the number of elements in the sample.

BRAINSTORMING – An idea generating technique characterized by free–wheeling, no evaluation of ideas, quantity over quality.

CAPABILITY – See Process Capability

CAUSE AND EFFECT ANALYSIS – An analysis to identify the potential causes of a process problem. Typically done using an Ishikawa (fish bone) diagram.

CHECK SHEET – A data collection tool. Used to record measures on a process or product.

COLLABORATION – Working together to achieve a common goal.

COMMON CAUSE OF VARIATION – Sources of variation that are random, i.e., are statistically probable, given the capability of a process. These are causes of variation that can be reduced by increasing the capability of the process.

CONSENSUS – Webster defines as an opinion held by all or most. Consensus requires that all team members ideas have been listened to and understood, and the ideas agreed to by the most members represents the consensus.

CONTROL CHART – A graphical presentation of data over time which contains limits of the natural state of variation. Used to assess whether a process is in control and to monitor processes to insure they stay in control.

CONTROL LIMITS – Limits which provide boundaries of natural variation of the data.

COST OF QUALITY – How much it costs to produce quality products and services. Consists of appraisal costs, prevention costs and failure costs. The concept that ties process control and process optimization into a total process improvement effort.

CROSS FUNCTIONAL TEAM – A group of individuals working together for a common purpose. Team members represent different functions in an organization.

CULTURE – The prevailing pattern of values, attitudes, norms, beliefs, and behaviors in an organization.

CUSTOMER – The recipient of process outputs. Customers can be internal to the organization or external.

DATA – Measured (variable data) or counted (attribute data) facts or sets of facts.

DEFECT – A product or service which does not satisfy the customer.

FACILITATOR – An individual that manages team process, i.e., involves themselves to insure high quality team interaction and problem solving.

FAILURE COSTS – Costs required to achieve quality products and services (generally associated with defective items) such as rework, repair and scrap.

FLOWCHART – A graphical representation of a process.

FORCE FIELD ANALYSIS – A systematic method for understanding competing forces that increase or decrease the likelihood of successfully implementing change. It provides a framework for developing change strategies aimed at increasing driving forces and decreasing restraining forces.

FREQUENCY DISTRIBUTION – The count of the number of occurrences of individual values over a given range (discrete variables), or the count of cases lying between predetermined limits over the range of values a variable may assume (continuous variable).

GAINSHARING – A reward system which shares profits across all organization members.

GYMNASTIC SCORING TECHNIQUE – A customer focus technique that is similar to the rating system used at gymnast meets. How well you are meeting your customers' requirements and the importance of the requirements can be evaluated using this tool.

HISTOGRAM – A graphical display of data which depicts frequency of occurrence for specific intervals (depicts the distribution of the data). Sometimes called a bar chart.

HYPOTHESIS – An assertion made about the value of some parameter of a population.

INPUTS – Those items which are supplied to be transformed by processes into outputs. Can consist of people, materials, energy, environment, equipment, and/or procedures.

ISHIKAWA FISHBONE DIAGRAM – A problem solving tool which facilitates brainstorming to identify potential causes of process problems.

KLOC – Thousand lines of code

LCL – Lower control limit (e.g., $y - 3\sigma$), the limits above which a process remains if it is in control.

MEAN – See "Average"

NOMINAL GROUP TECHNIQUE – A technique to quickly and critically examine, evaluate and narrow down, and obtain consensus on a group of brainstormed ideas.

OUTPUT – The end result of a process. Could be a product, information, or a service.

PARADIGM – The knowledge or structure which underlies a science or discipline .

PARETO CHART – A histogram or bar chart which shows the frequency of occurrence of process problems, rank ordered with the most frequent ones listed first.

POPULATION – The entire set or collection of data of interest (usually a nearly infinite number).

PREVENTION COSTS – Costs associated with actions taken to control and improve processes to prevent the occurrence of defects, scrap, rework and/or repair.

PROBLEM STATEMENT – The starting point for a cause and effect analysis. Must be stated to describe a problem and not a potential solution (e.g., "lack of training" would not be a good problem statement because it implies the solution).

PROCESS – A series of actions which repeatedly come together to transform supplier inputs into value added outputs for a customer.

PROCESS CAPABILITY – A comparison of the ability of a process to meet the specification with the control limits of the process.

PROCESS CONTROL – Managing processes to insure the average and standard deviation of the measured quality characteristic are stable over time.

PROCESS IMPROVEMENT – Managing processes to increase customer satisfaction (frequently by reducing variation).

PROCESS OWNER – A designated individual who has authority to manage and continuously improve the process. It should be someone involved in the process, not outside of it.

QUALITY – Customer satisfaction. Also reduction of variation.

QUALITY ASSURANCE – The function of insuring quality products and services.

QUALITY CONTROL – Attempting to insure quality through sampling, measuring, and sorting good from bad.

QUALITY FUNCTION DEPLOYMENT (QFD) – A disciplined method for multi-disciplined teams to develop a full set of requirements and to fully integrate those requirements into a design.

RANGE – The difference between the maximum and the minimum values of a sample of data.

REQUIREMENTS BREAKDOWN STRUCTURE – A tool similar to a work breakdown structure which enables you to display the component pieces of a requirement in a hierarchical way.

REWORK – The act of doing something over because it was not done right the first time.

ROGERIAN FEEDBACK – See Active Listening.

ROOT CAUSE – The true underlying cause for process problems.

RUN – A point or a consecutive number of points that are above or below the central line in a run chart. Can be evidence of the occurrence of special causes of variation.

RUN CHART – A display of data in the order in which they occur in time.

SAMPLE – A finite number of items chosen to represent a population in order to make valid statistical inferences.

SHEWHART CYCLE – A continuous improvement process consisting of 4 steps: Plan, Do, Check, and Act (also referred to as the PDCA cycle). First developed by Dr. Walter Shewhart, but popularized in the 1950's by Dr. W.E. Deming.

SPECIAL CAUSE OF VARIATION – Variation in a process which does not occur as part of the natural variation resident in the process, but arises because of special circumstances such as tool wear, operator hang-over, etc. Also called "assignable causes."

SPECIFICATION LIMITS – Limits over which a quality characteristic can occur and still have a product/process functionality to meet customers' needs.

STANDARD DEVIATION – A parameter which describes the spread of the process output, designated by the Greek letter sigma, σ. The standard deviation is the positive square root of the variance.

STATISTICAL PROCESS CONTROL (SPC) – A term which in its broadest sense encompasses all statistical tools for quality improvement.

STRATIFICATION – Separating samples into groups that have distinctly different characteristics.

SUPPLIER – The person(s) responsible for the inputs to a process.

TAGUCHI LOSS FUNCTION – A method used to quantify loss and thus dollarize the current state of quality.

TAMPERING – A phrase popularized by Dr. W.E. Deming which involves taking action on a process without determining whether variation is caused by common or special causes.

TEAM – A group of individuals working together for a common purpose. Recommended size is between 6 and 10.

TRANSFORMATION – A term popularized by Dr. W.E. Deming describing a change of state, a metamorphosis of management, industry, education and government. It requires profound knowledge to achieve and should not be confused with cosmetic improvement programs.

UCL – Upper control limit (e.g., $y + 3\sigma$), the limits below which a process remains if it is in control.

USER – The entity for which a product or service is designed.

VARIABLE (CONTINUOUS) DATA – Data characterized by values (numeric as opposed to attribute data).

VARIANCE – A measure of how much the data varies from the average.

VARIATION – deviation of data from the target value or average.

VISION – A description of where the organization would like to go. It should include a declaration of what the organization needs to care about most in order to achieve its most desirable future.

WORLD CLASS CUSTOMER – A customer whose behavior represents the best in the world for assisting suppliers to achieve quality.

INDEX